PENG!

ACTION SPORTS ADVENTURES!

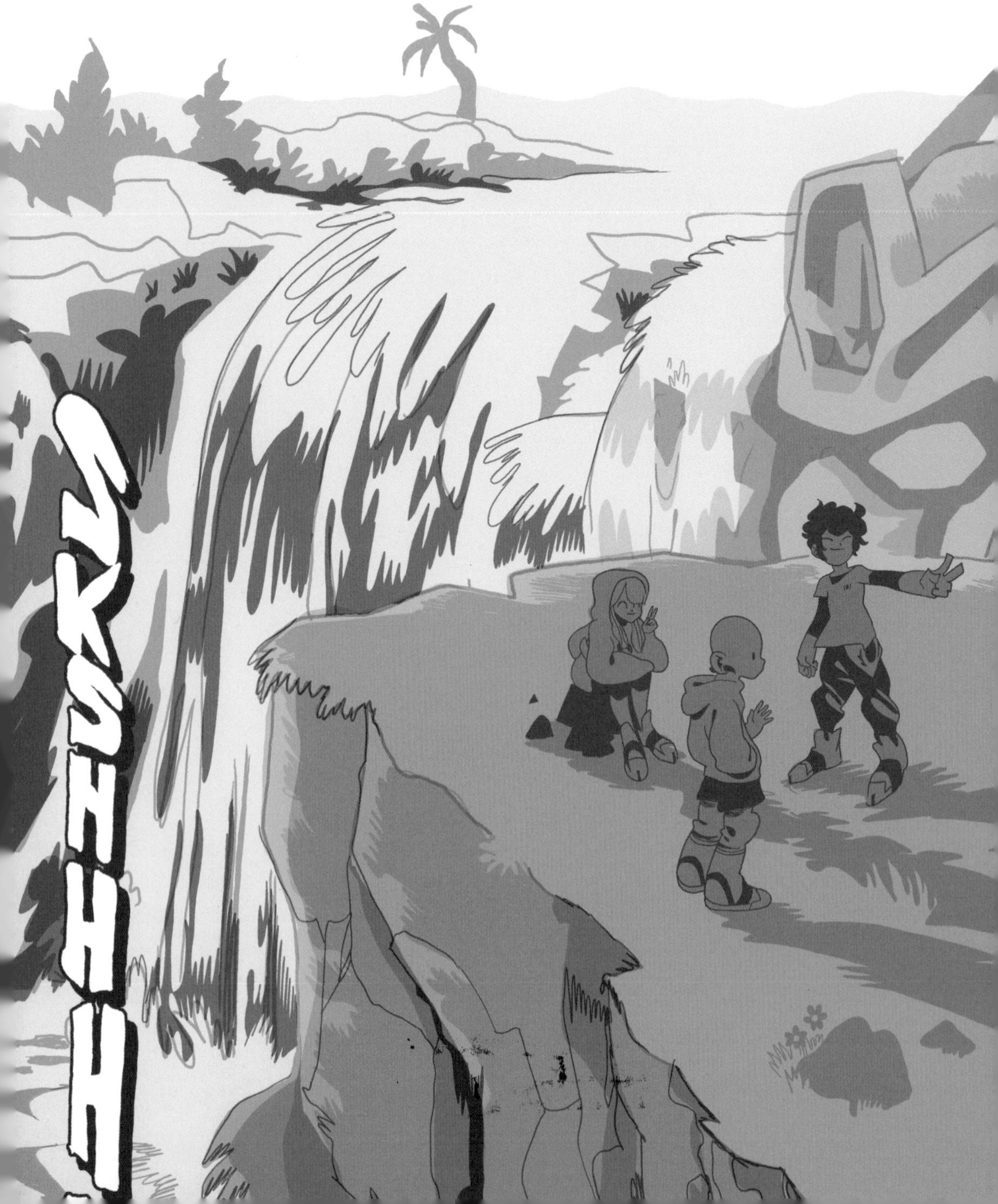

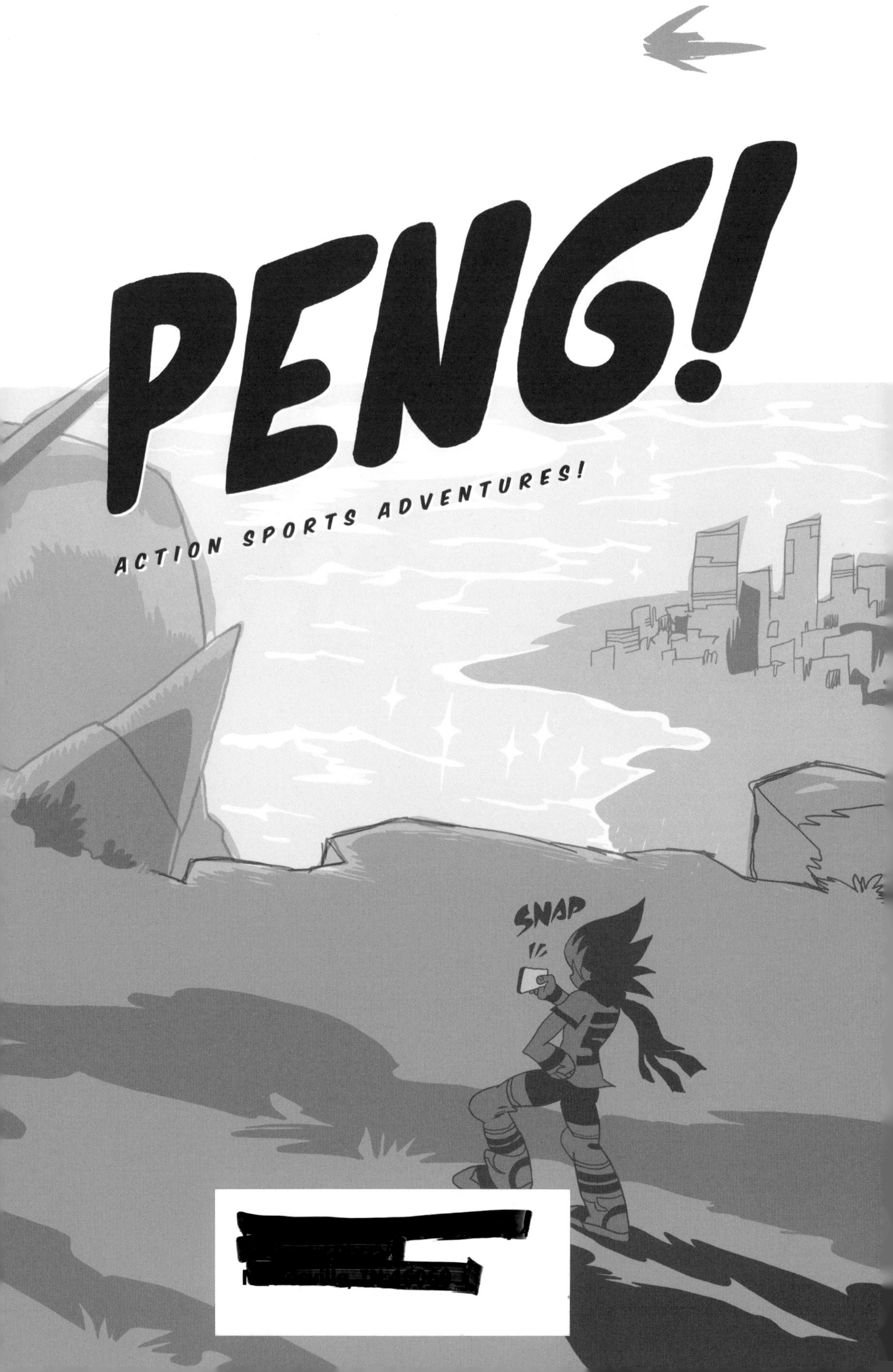
PENG!
ACTION SPORTS ADVENTURES!
SNAP

[redacted]

PUBLISHED BY ONI-LION FORGE PUBLISHING GROUP, LLC

JAMES LUCAS JONES, PRESIDENT & PUBLISHER
SARAH GAYDOS, EDITOR IN CHIEF
CHARLIE CHU, E.V.P. OF CREATIVE & BUSINESS DEVELOPMENT
BRAD ROOKS, DIRECTOR OF OPERATIONS
AMBER O'NEILL, SPECIAL PROJECTS MANAGER
HARRIS FISH, EVENTS MANAGER
MARGOT WOOD, DIRECTOR OF MARKETING & SALES
JEREMY ATKINS, DIRECTOR OF BRAND COMMUNICATIONS
DEVIN FUNCHES, SALES & MARKETING MANAGER
KATIE SAINZ, MARKETING MANAGER
TARA LEHMANN, MARKETING & PUBLICITY ASSOCIATE
TROY LOOK, DIRECTOR OF DESIGN & PRODUCTION
KATE Z. STONE, SENIOR GRAPHIC DESIGNER
SONJA SYNAK, GRAPHIC DESIGNER
HILARY THOMPSON, GRAPHIC DESIGNER
SARAH ROCKWELL, JUNIOR GRAPHIC DESIGNER
ANGIE KNOWLES, DIGITAL PREPRESS LEAD
VINCENT KUKUA, DIGITAL PREPRESS TECHNICIAN
SHAWNA GORE, SENIOR EDITOR
ROBIN HERRERA, SENIOR EDITOR
AMANDA MEADOWS, SENIOR EDITOR
JASMINE AMIRI, SENIOR EDITOR
GRACE BORNHOFT, EDITOR
ZACK SOTO, EDITOR
STEVE ELLIS, VICE PRESIDENT OF GAMES
BEN EISNER, GAME DEVELOPER
MICHELLE NGUYEN, EXECUTIVE ASSISTANT
JUNG LEE, LOGISTICS COORDINATOR

JOE NOZEMACK, PUBLISHER EMERITUS

DESIGNED BY ANGIE KNOWLES
EDITED BY ZACK SOTO

ONIPRESS.COM
FACEBOOK.COM/ONIPRESS
TWITTER.COM/ONIPRESS
INSTAGRAM.COM/ONIPRESS

LIONFORGE.COM
FACEBOOK.COM/LIONFORGE
TWITTER.COM/LIONFORGE
INSTAGRAM.COM/LIONFORGE

@REYYYSTATION
REYYY.COM

FIRST EDITION: JULY 2020

ISBN 978-1-62010-757-7
EISBN 978-1-62010-762-1

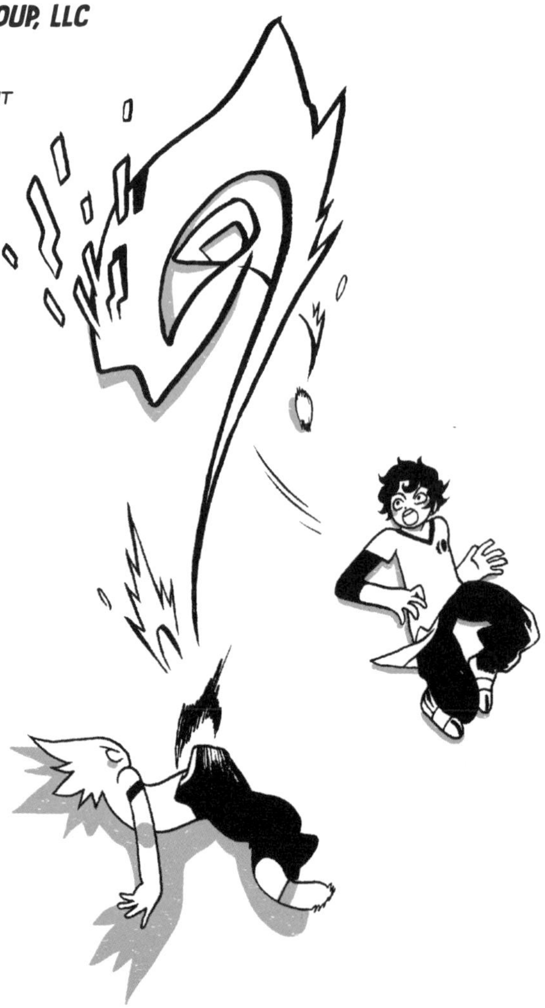

PRINTED IN SOUTH KOREA THROUGH FOUR COLOUR PRINT GROUP, LOUISVILLE, KY.

LIBRARY OF CONGRESS CONTROL NUMBER: 2019955381

1 2 3 4 5 6 7 8 9 10

AN ONI PRESS PUBLICATION

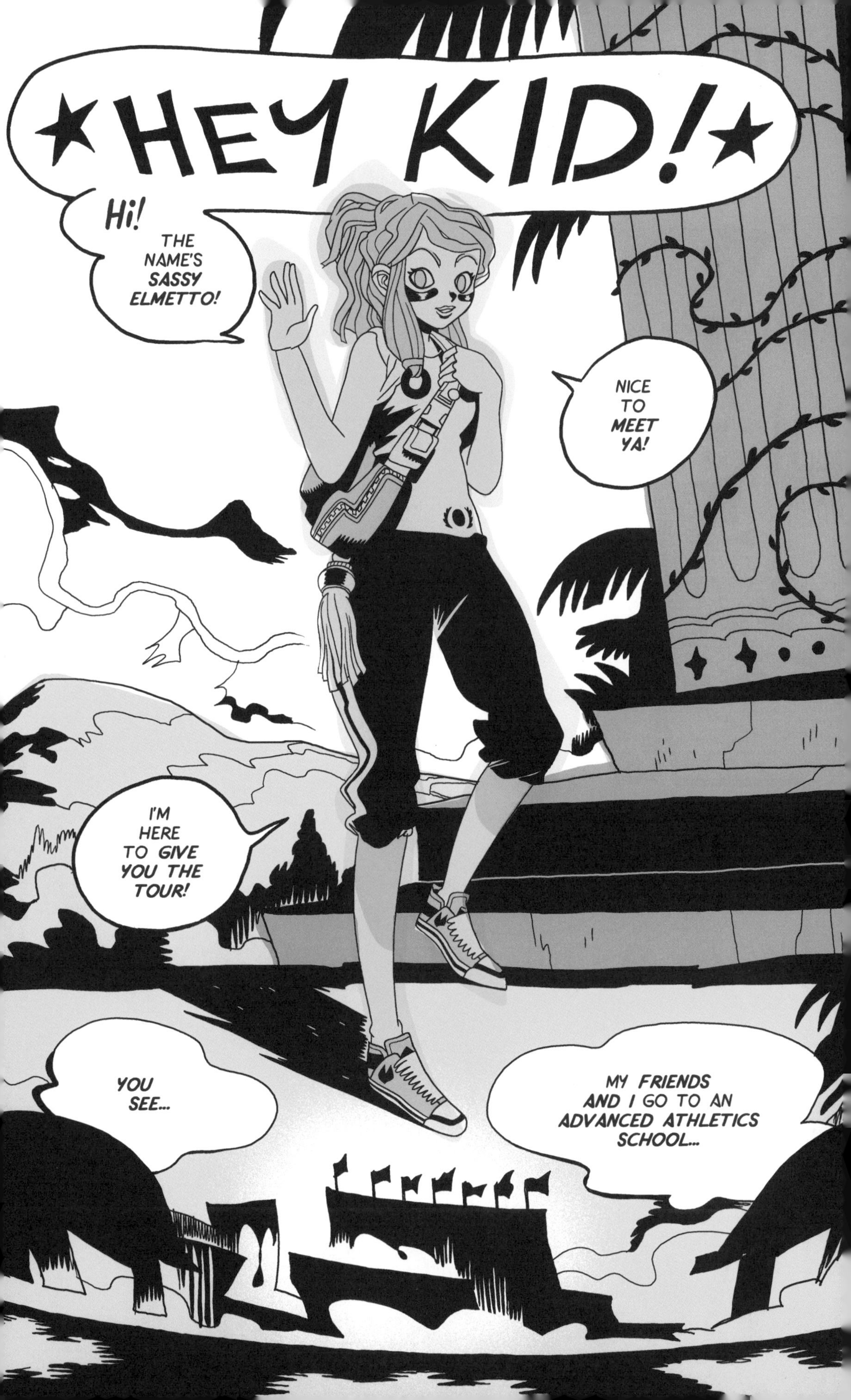
★HEY KID!★
Hi! THE NAME'S SASSY ELMETTO!
NICE TO MEET YA!
I'M HERE TO GIVE YOU THE TOUR!
YOU SEE...
MY FRIENDS AND I GO TO AN ADVANCED ATHLETICS SCHOOL...

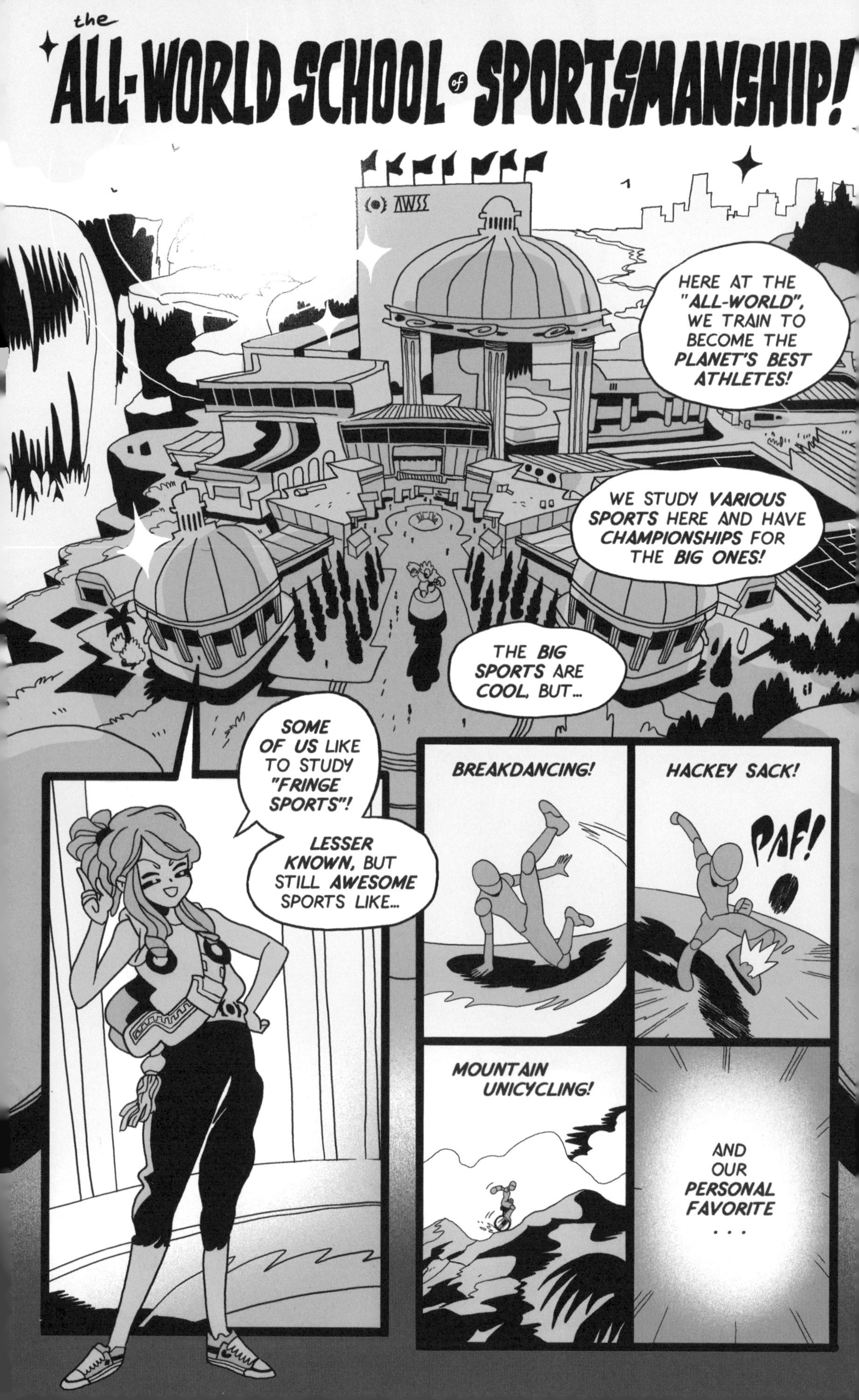
the ALL-WORLD SCHOOL of SPORTSMANSHIP!
AWSS
HERE AT THE "ALL-WORLD", WE TRAIN TO BECOME THE PLANET'S BEST ATHLETES!
WE STUDY VARIOUS SPORTS HERE AND HAVE CHAMPIONSHIPS FOR THE BIG ONES!
THE BIG SPORTS ARE COOL, BUT...
SOME OF US LIKE TO STUDY "FRINGE SPORTS"!
LESSER KNOWN, BUT STILL AWESOME SPORTS LIKE...
BREAKDANCING!
HACKEY SACK!
PAF!
MOUNTAIN UNICYCLING!
AND OUR PERSONAL FAVORITE . . .

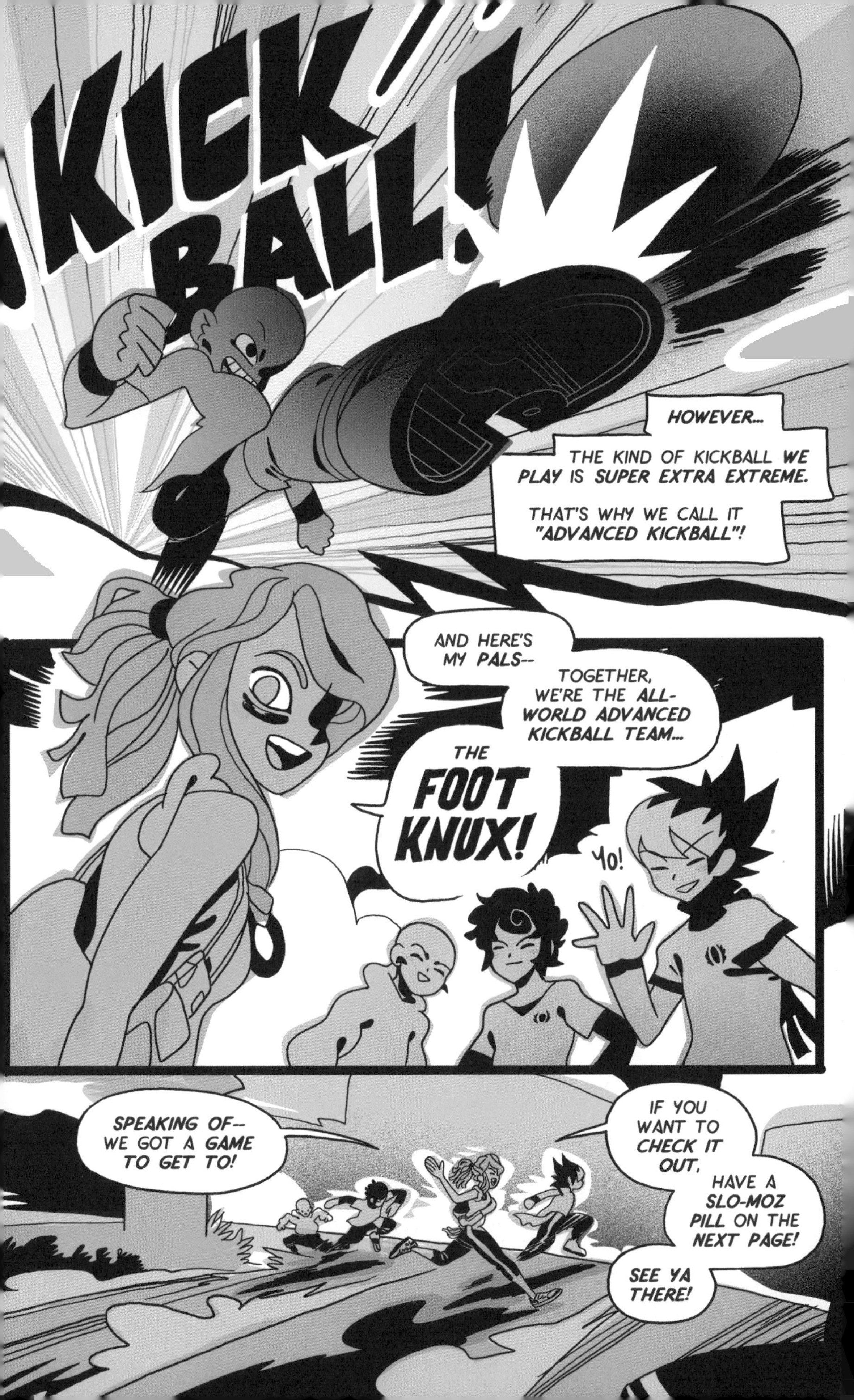
KICK BALL!
HOWEVER...
THE KIND OF KICKBALL WE PLAY IS SUPER EXTRA EXTREME.
THAT'S WHY WE CALL IT "ADVANCED KICKBALL"!
AND HERE'S MY PALS--
TOGETHER, WE'RE THE ALL-WORLD ADVANCED KICKBALL TEAM...
THE FOOT KNUX!
YO!
SPEAKING OF-- WE GOT A GAME TO GET TO!
IF YOU WANT TO CHECK IT OUT,
HAVE A SLO-MOZ PILL ON THE NEXT PAGE!
SEE YA THERE!

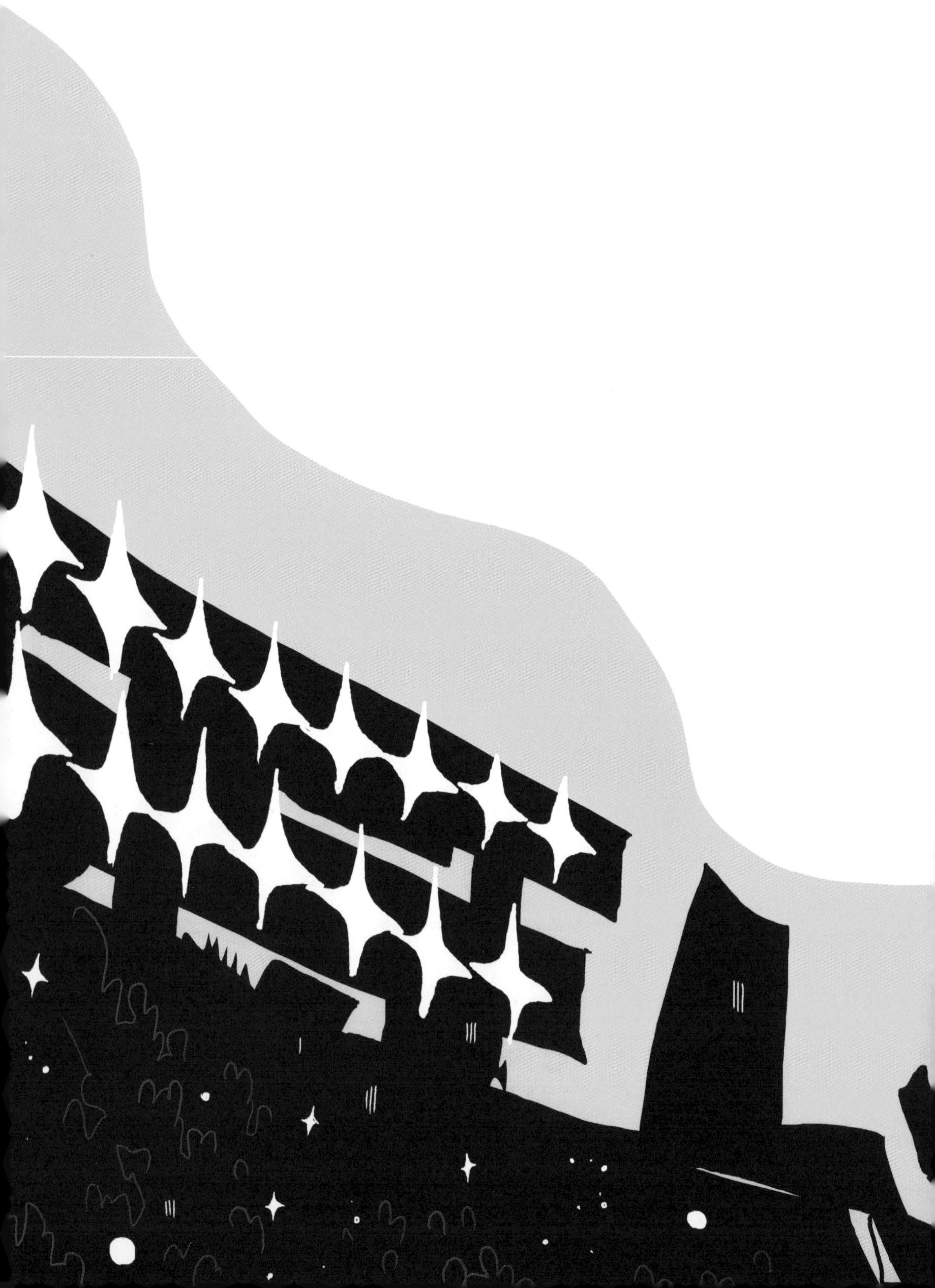

FOR YOUR VIEWING PLEASURE

THE ADVANCED KICKBALL ASSOCIATION HAS PROVIDED A LIGHT PRE- GAME SNACK-PACK + SLO-MOZ BRAND PROCESS-ALTERING PILL. PLEASE INDULGE TO BETTER PREPARE FOR THE ENTERTAINMENT TO FOLLOW.

SNACK-PACKS DISTRIBUTED BY *ADVANCED KICKBALL* CERTIFIED MEDICAL TEAM.

DO NOT CONSUME SLO-MOZ PILLS FROM 3RD PARTY VENDORS.

SLO-MOZ PILLS UNSUITABLE FOR CHILDREN UNDER 5.

CHEESE AND CRACKERS SUITABLE FOR ALL-AGES.

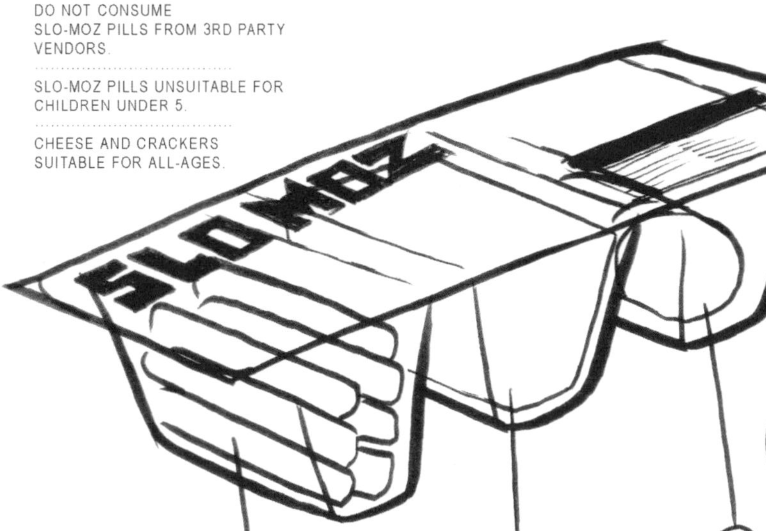
PEEL HERE
SLO MOZ

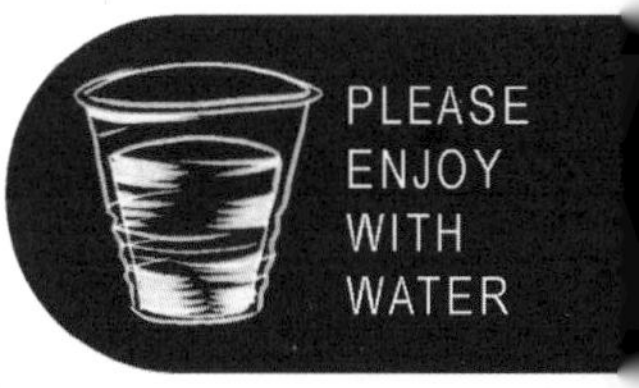
PLEASE ENJOY WITH WATER

.③ **SLO-MOZ PILL**
CRUCIAL FOR MAXIMUM *ADVANCED KICKBALL* ENJOYMENT. PLEASE CONSUME AFTER CHEESE AND CRACKERS. (DO NOT EAT ON EMPTY STOMACH)

.② **100% REAL CHEESE**
MADE TO SPREAD ON STIX. TEASE YOUR TONGUE WITH THIS ORANGEY DAIRY DELIGHT.

.① **LO-FAT DIPPIN' STIX**
SMALL, CRUNCHY, FLUFFY AND FLAKY, THE PERFECT CRISPY CONFECTION TO TAME YOUR PALETTE

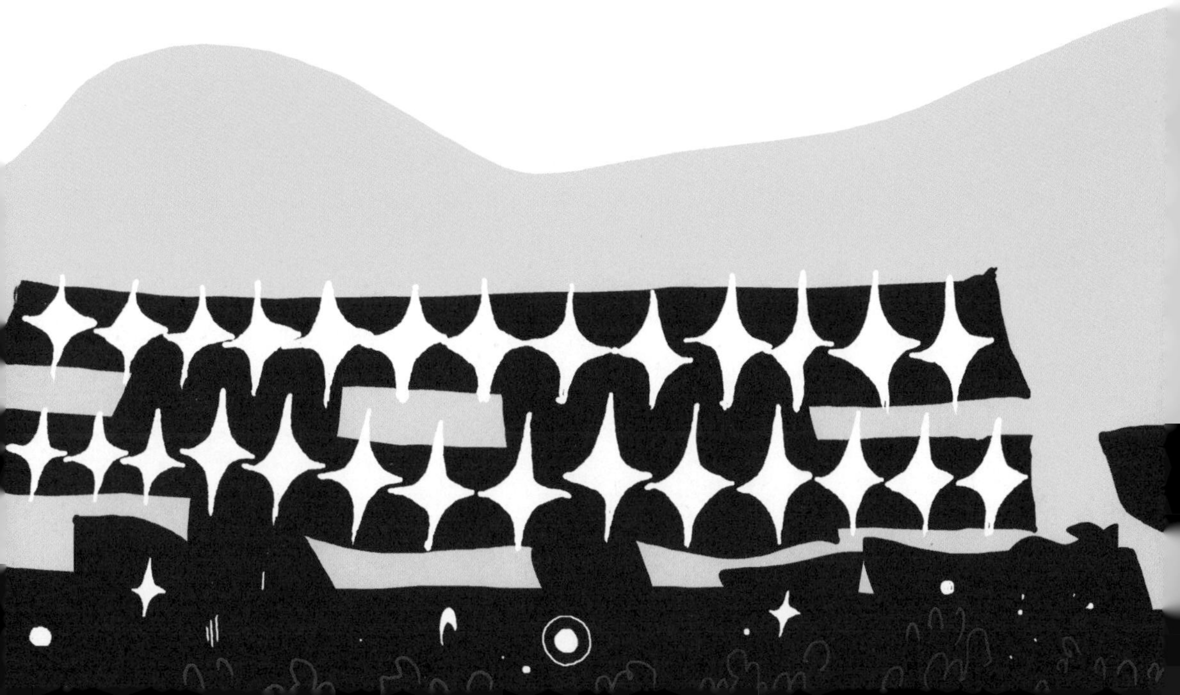

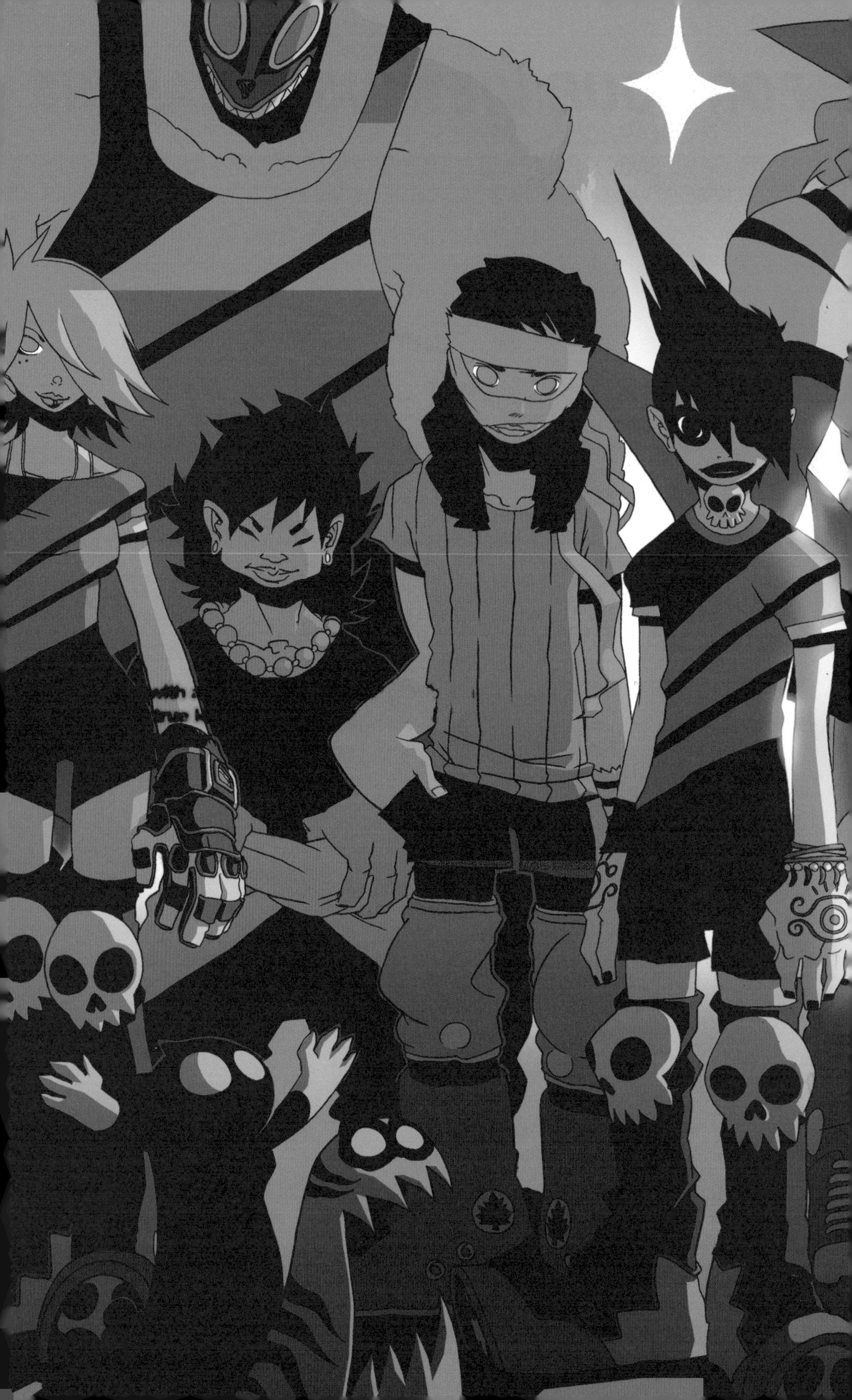

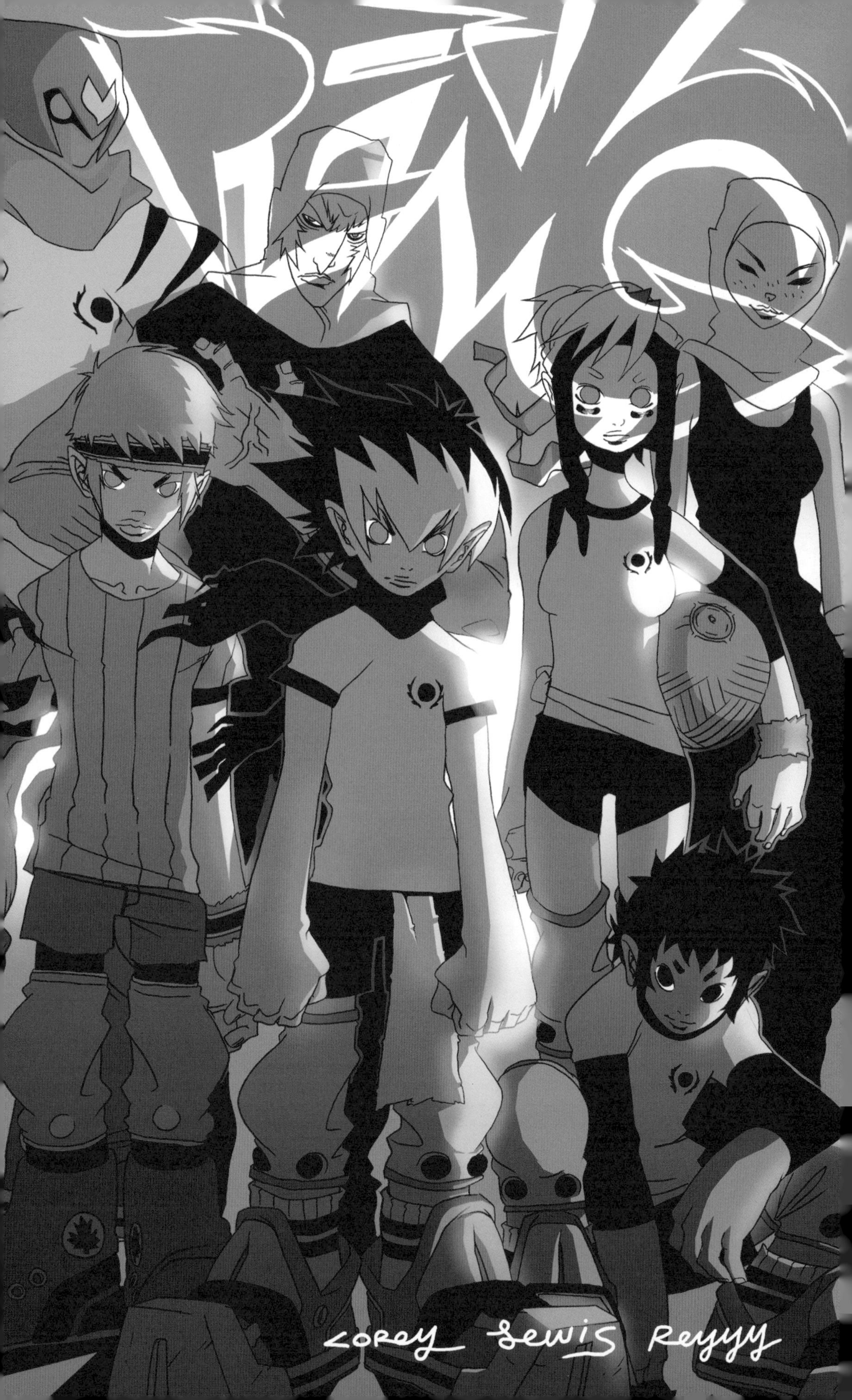
Corey Lewis Reyyy

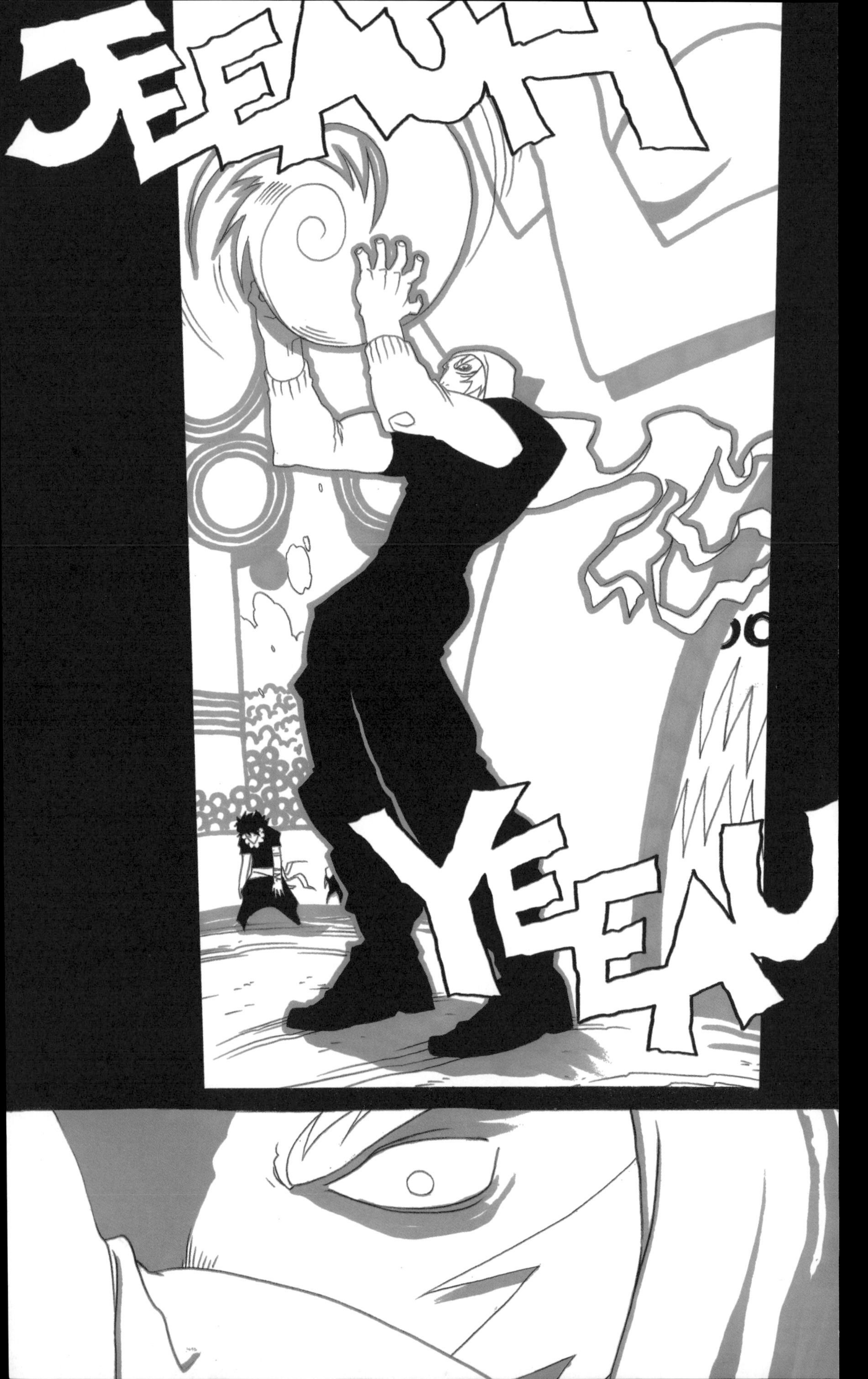
JEEAUH
YEEAU

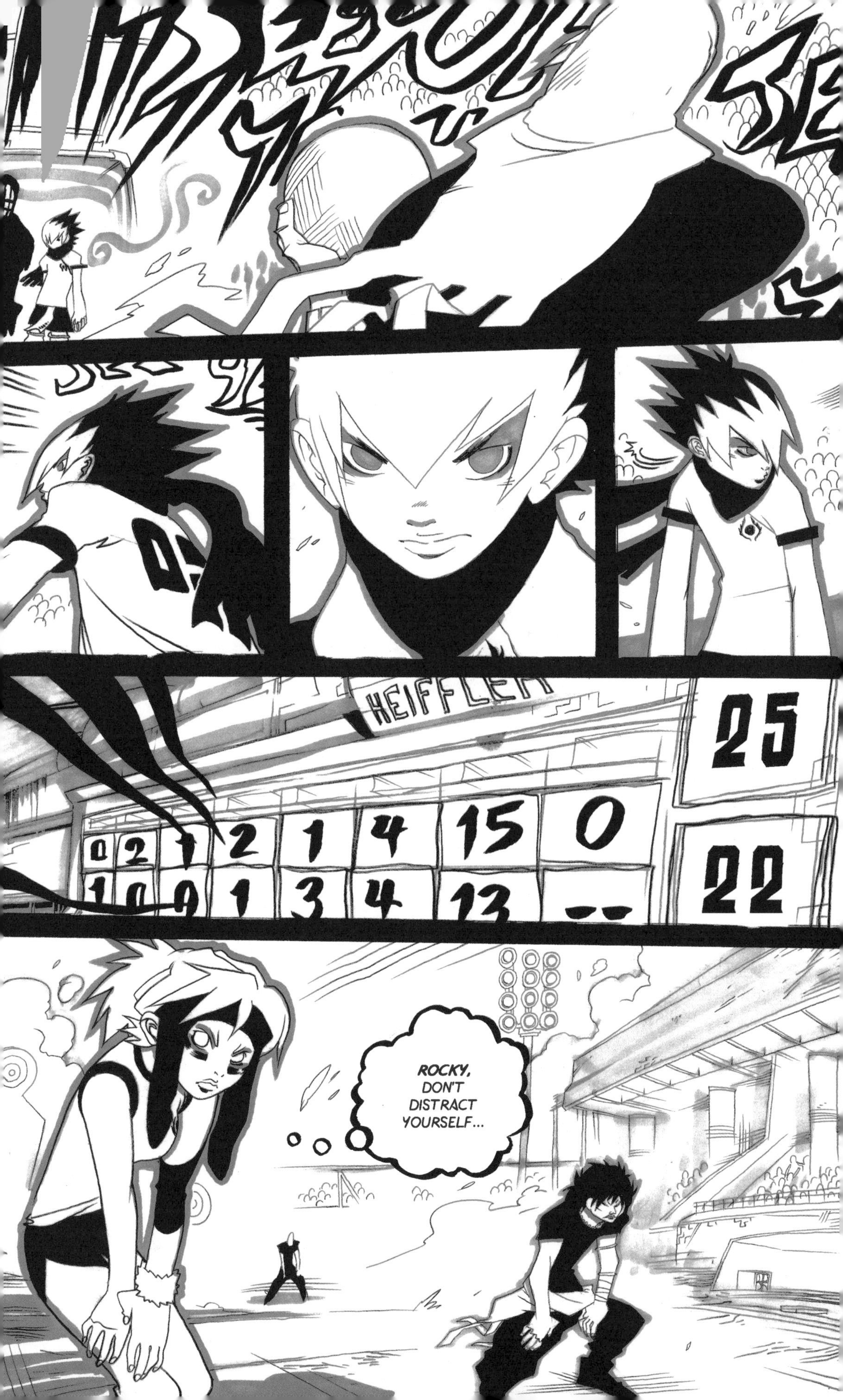
25
22
ROCKY, DON'T DISTRACT YOURSELF...

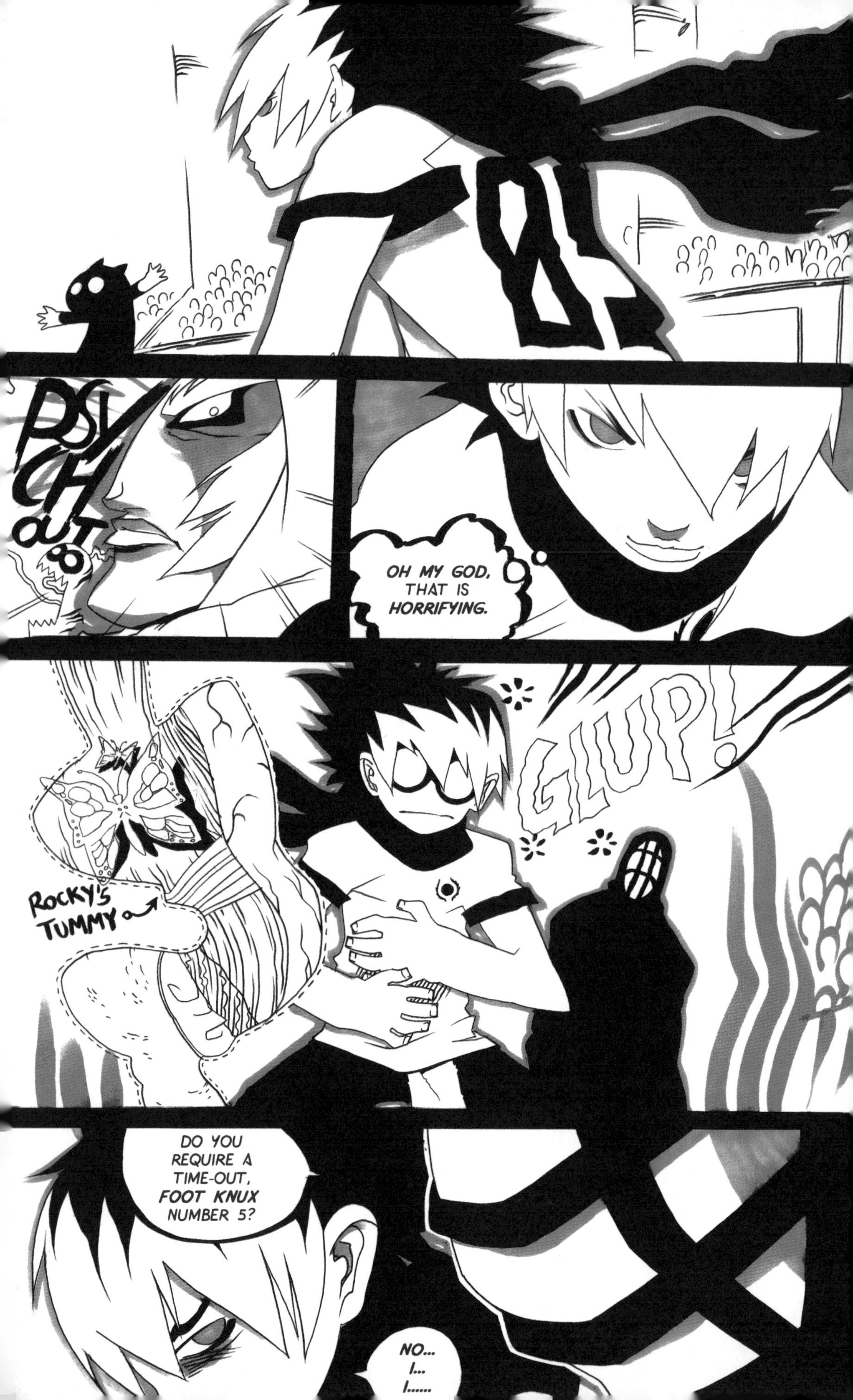
PSYCH OUT
OH MY GOD, THAT IS HORRIFYING.
ROCKY'S TUMMY
GLUP!
DO YOU REQUIRE A TIME-OUT, FOOT KNUX NUMBER 5?
NO... I... I......

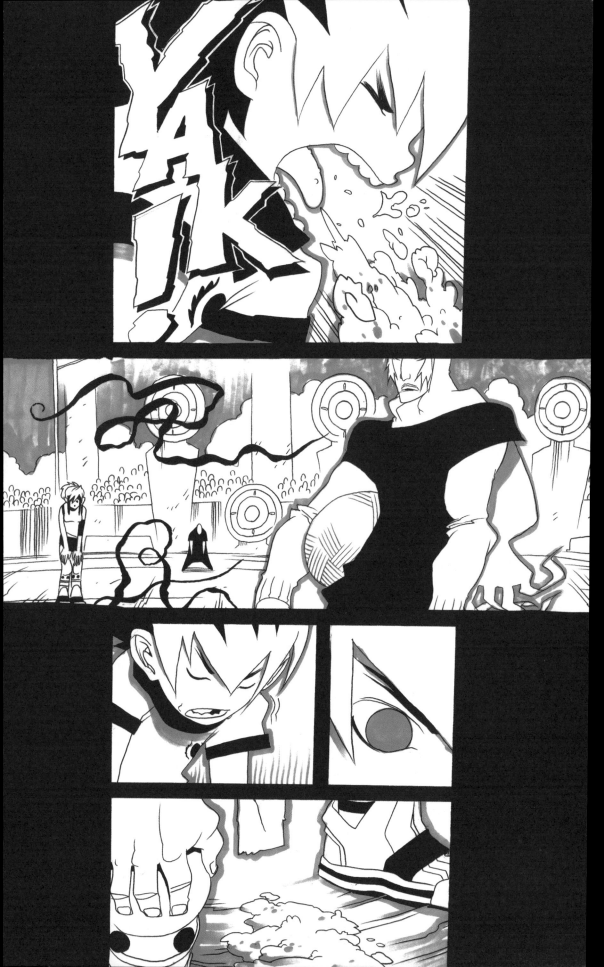

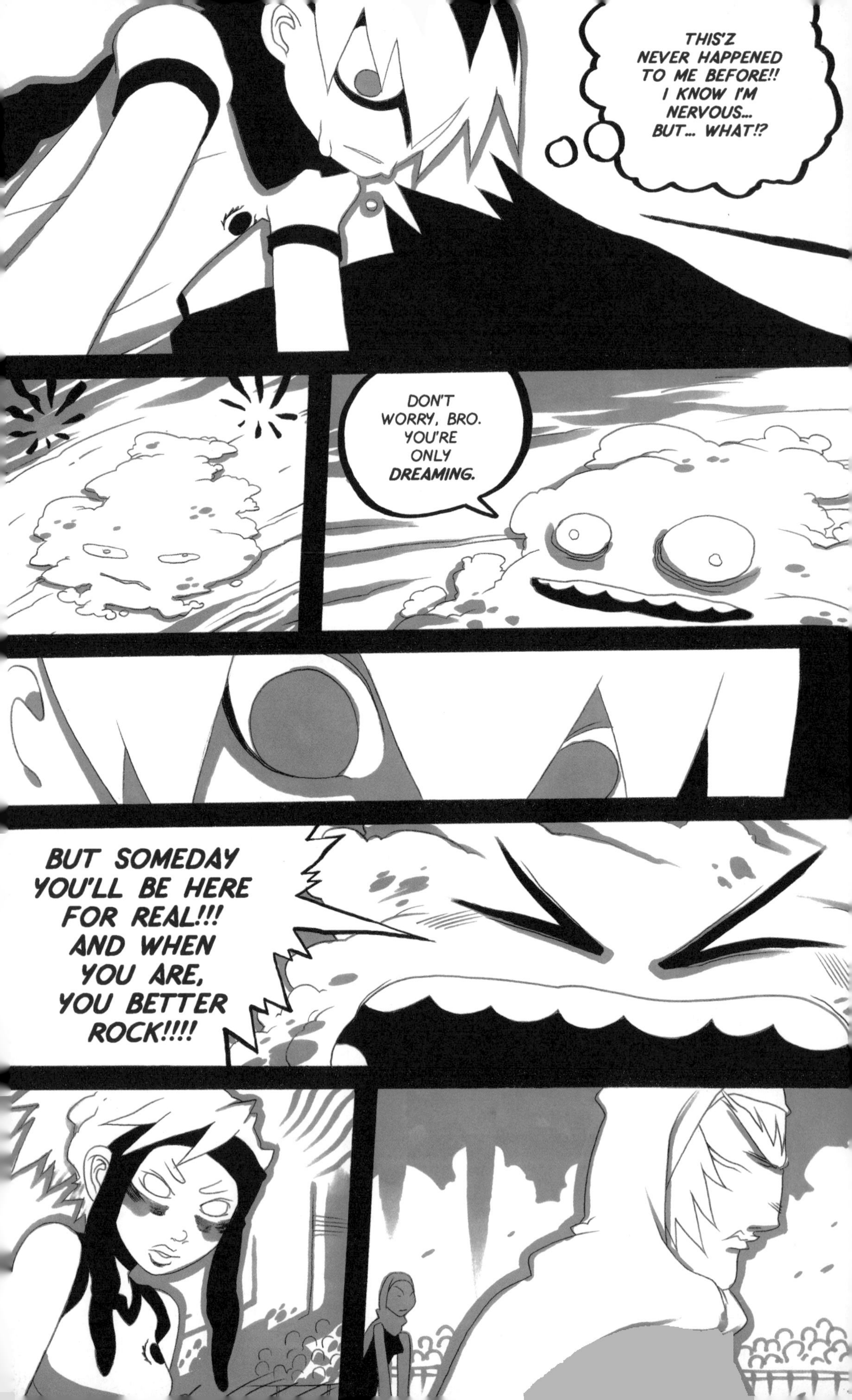
THIS'Z NEVER HAPPENED TO ME BEFORE!! I KNOW I'M NERVOUS... BUT... WHAT!?
DON'T WORRY, BRO. YOU'RE ONLY *DREAMING.*
BUT SOMEDAY YOU'LL BE HERE FOR REAL!!! AND WHEN YOU ARE, YOU BETTER ROCK!!!!

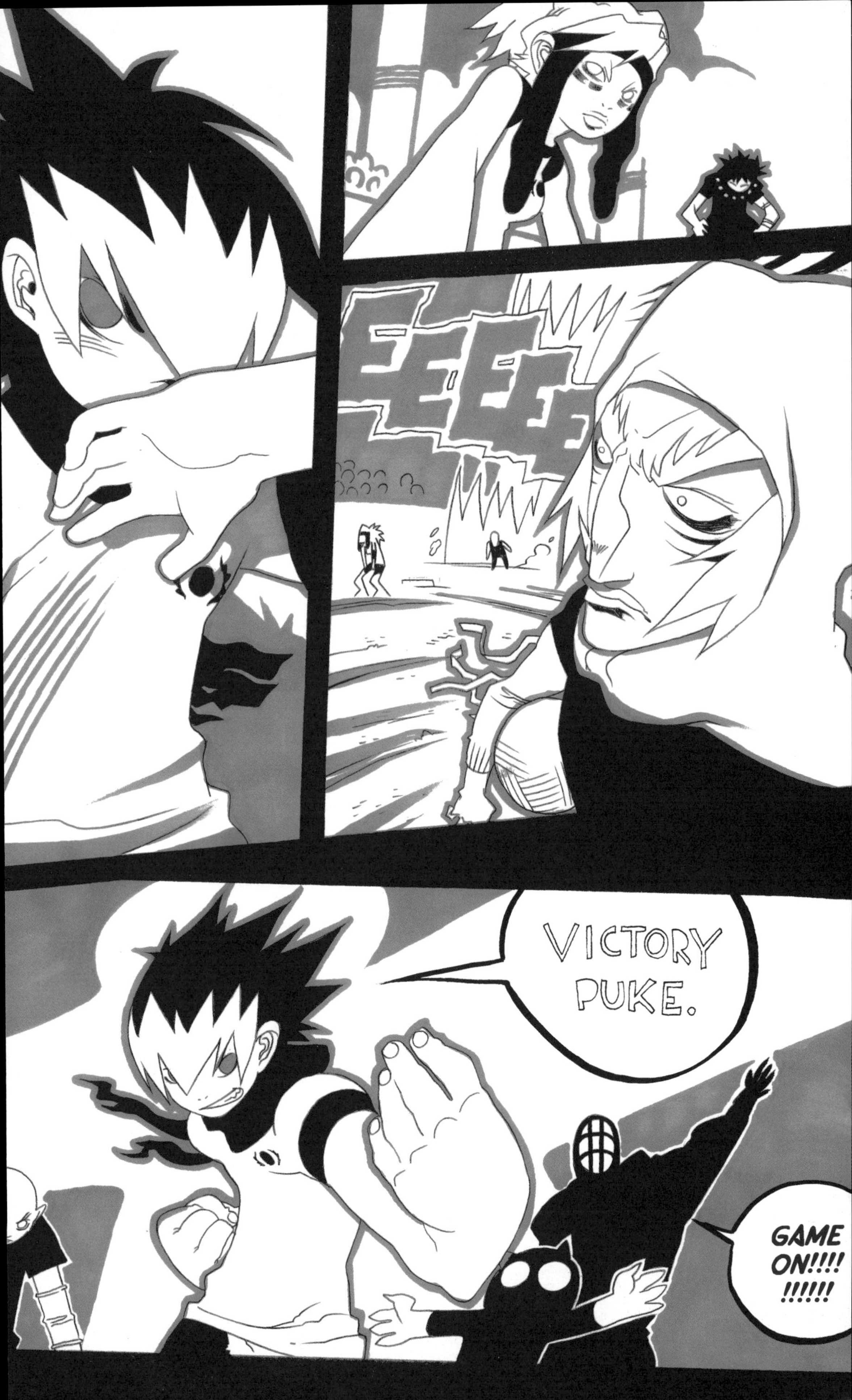
EEEE
VICTORY PUKE.
GAME ON!!!! !!!!!!

THE SCOOP-SHIFTERS
Entry-level ambassadors of blitz play

THE FOOT KNUX
This season's rookie favorite

THE RED-GO'S
Old-school team with big feet

THE DEVIL-HUMPS
Typical and generic

THE ANOLOGGERS
Formed by various musical artists

THE NOUGAT FILLS
Tasty and delightful

THE FIERCE PUNCHES
Better at kickball video games

THE VAGABONDS
They have eyes like a demon

THE KICK-SPINNERS
Competetive youth spirits

THE AURORA SKEDDOS
Protectors of kickball purity

THE CANNON ARMS
Intense pitching roster

THE BROKEN SPELLS
Adept to illusionary techniques

THE ARROWHEADS
Shoot straight and forward

THE DOLPHEETS
The best Canadian team ever

THE BREAKBEATS
Urban and hip

THE FLOOD WARNINGS
Skilled in technical abilities

FOOT KNUX

RED-GO'S

ANOLOGGERS

VAGABONDS

AURORA SKEDDOS

CANNON ARMS

DOLPHEETS

FLOOD WARNINGS

THE FOOT KNUX

THE ANOLOGGERS

THE AURORA SKEDDOS

THE DOLPHEETS

THE FINAL FOUR TEAMS
WILL NOW FACE

YOUR FINAL FOUR TEAMS

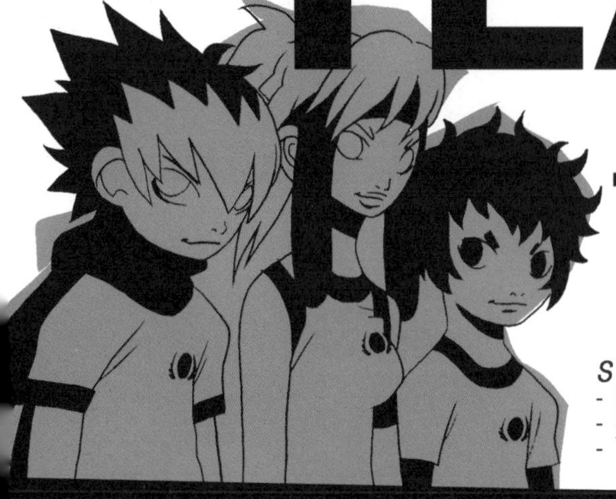

THE FOOT KNUX

A pro-active freshmen team who surprised all kickballing elite with their sheer tenacity and burning golden spirit.

STAR PLAYERS
- Rocky Hallelujah
- Sassy Elmetto
- Ven Morcada

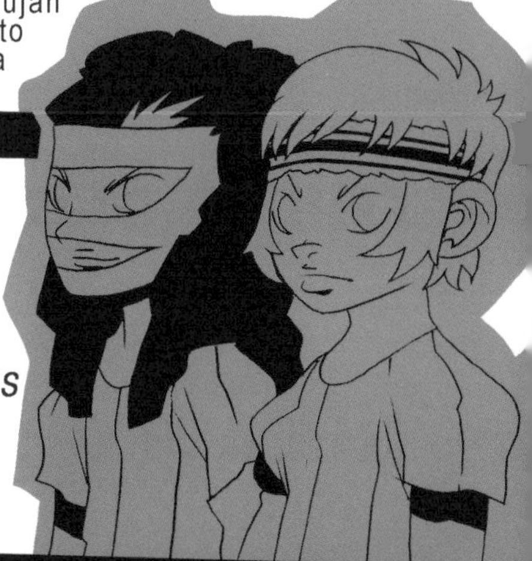

THE DOLPHEETS

A seasoned younger team. Looking to steal some of the Foot Knux's fire by beating them in the final-four. Canadian.

STAR PLAYERS
- Gloro Welch
- Abe Bolson

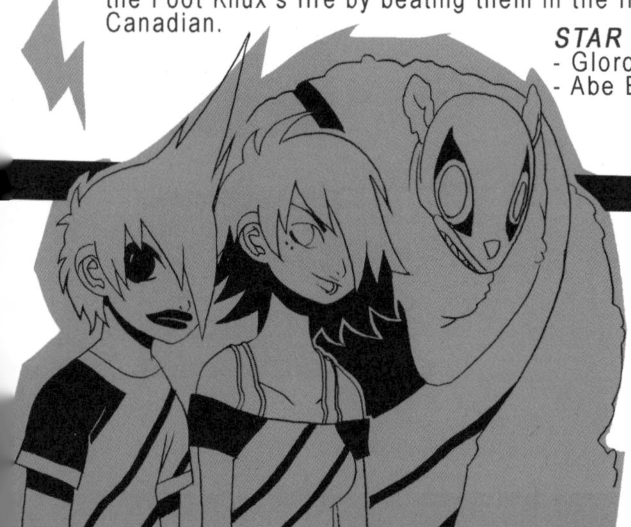

THE ANOLOGGERS

Members of a rock band known as "Apollonia No," adventuring in Advanced Kickball for the first time, winning a surprise slot in the final-four.

STAR PLAYERS
- Aves Ives
- Helen of Boys
- Luchadorio

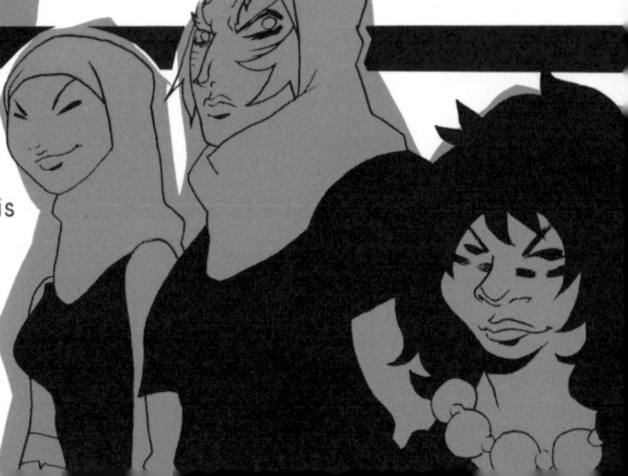

THE AURORA SKEDDOS

Long-time Advanced Kickball warriors, winners of many previous Adv.K seasons. Their goal this season: to keep the harmony of Adv.Kickball pure by destroying any unworthy competitors.

STAR PLAYERS
- Smarmy Ellie
- Jeeyuh Yeeauh
- Gleff Shujo

ADVANCED KICKBALL

- Team-vs-Team matches
- 9-Inning game
- 3 outs per inning
- "Home Runs" attained by hitting targets in outfield
- 5-player team lineup:
  2 Short-basers,
  2 Out-fielders,
  1 Catcher,
  1 Pitcher
- Special-move pitches, special-move kicks allowed and encouraged
- Pitcher does not roll ball, instead throws above home plate
- Once ball is kicked, an out can be scored either by catching ball, or hitting runner with ball.

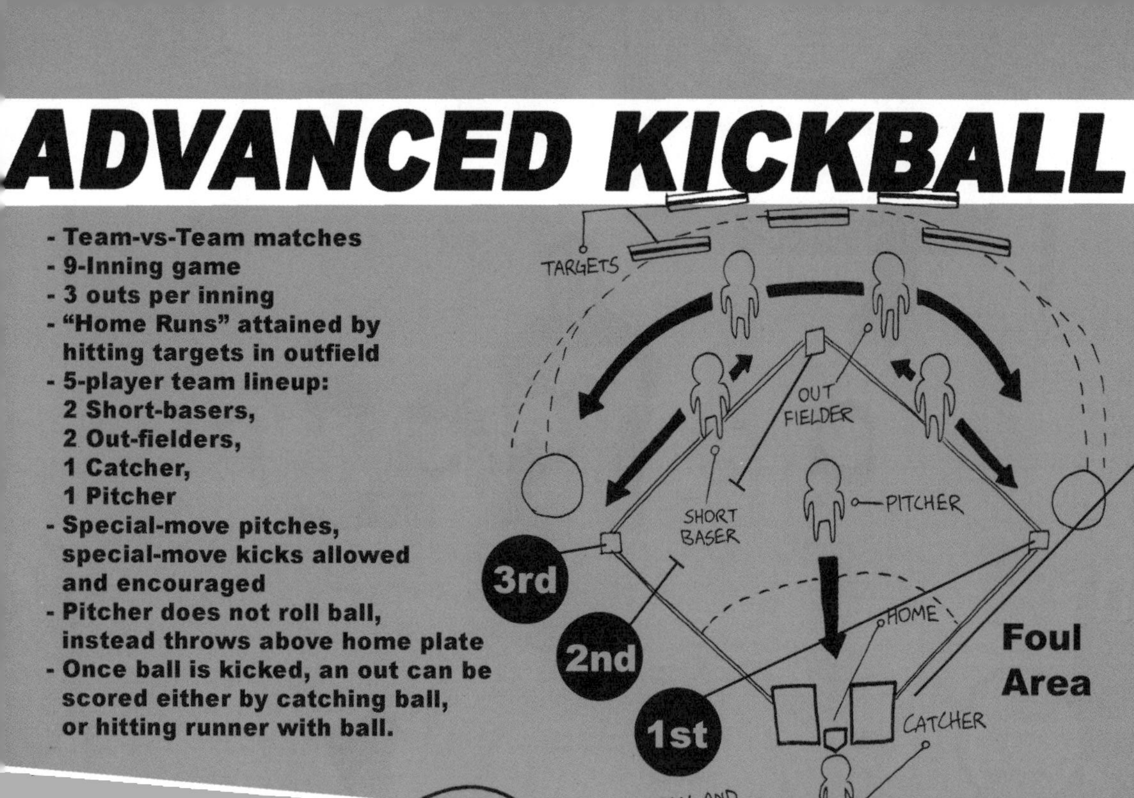

TARGETS
OUT FIELDER
SHORT BASER
PITCHER
3rd
2nd
1st
HOME
Foul Area
CATCHER

KICKBALLER ANATOMY

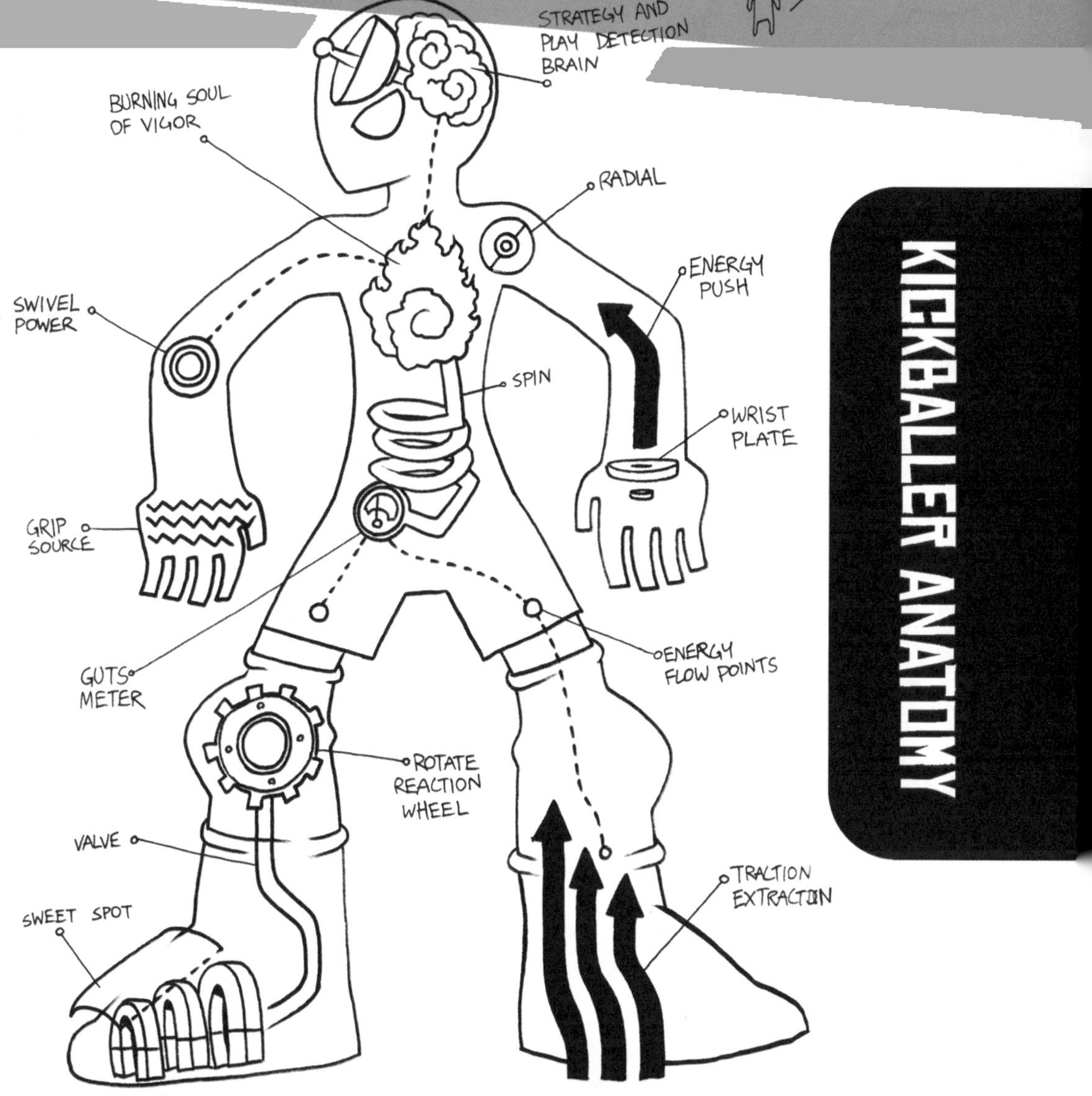

STRATEGY AND PLAY DETECTION BRAIN
BURNING SOUL OF VIGOR
RADIAL
ENERGY PUSH
SWIVEL POWER
SPIN
WRIST PLATE
GRIP SOURCE
GUTS METER
ENERGY FLOW POINTS
ROTATE REACTION WHEEL
VALVE
TRACTION EXTRACTION
SWEET SPOT

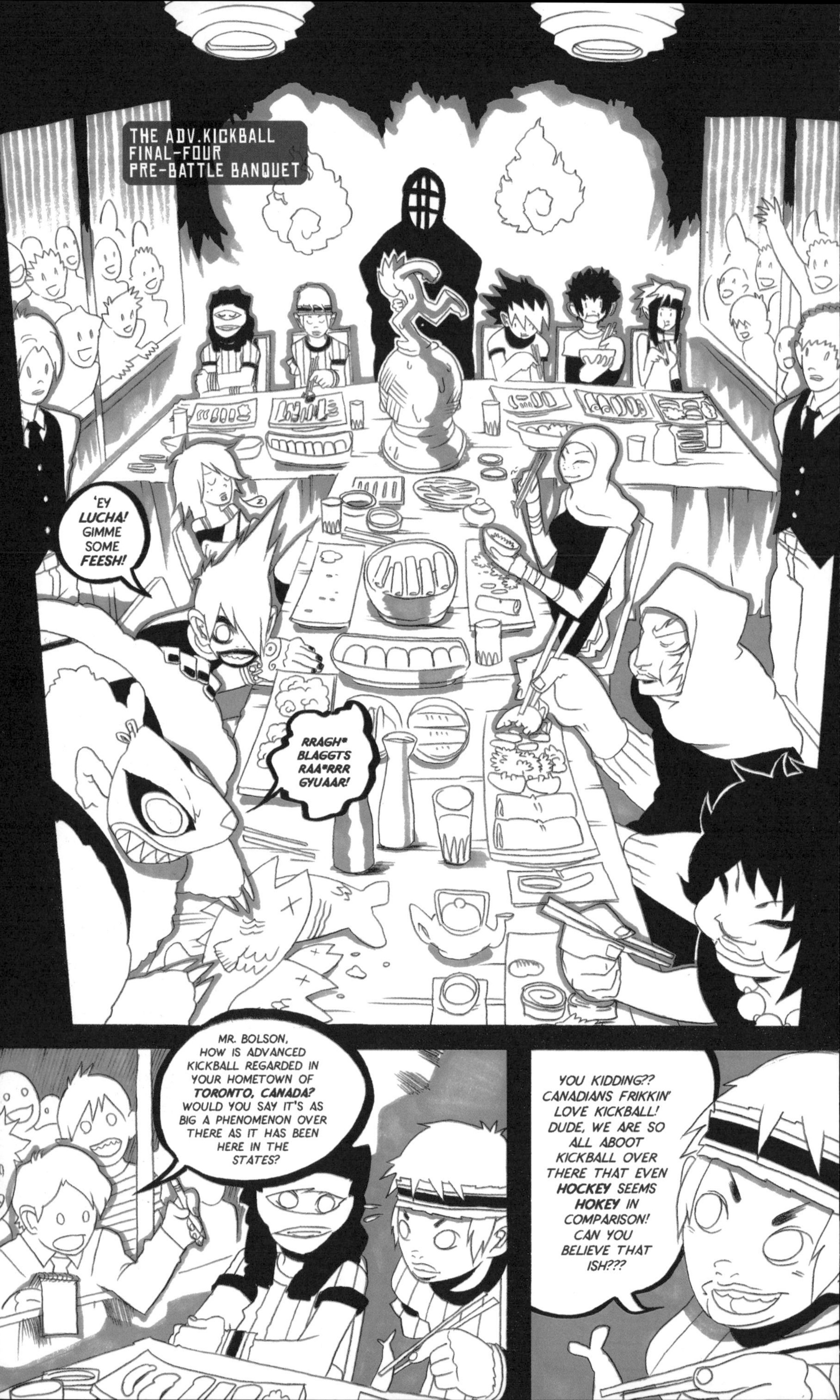
THE ADV.KICKBALL FINAL-FOUR PRE-BATTLE BANQUET
'EY LUCHA! GIMME SOME FEESH!
RRAGH* BLAGGTS RAA*RRR GYUAAR!
MR. BOLSON, HOW IS ADVANCED KICKBALL REGARDED IN YOUR HOMETOWN OF TORONTO, CANADA? WOULD YOU SAY IT'S AS BIG A PHENOMENON OVER THERE AS IT HAS BEEN HERE IN THE STATES?
YOU KIDDING?? CANADIANS FRIKKIN' LOVE KICKBALL! DUDE, WE ARE SO ALL ABOUT KICKBALL OVER THERE THAT EVEN HOCKEY SEEMS HOKEY IN COMPARISON! CAN YOU BELIEVE THAT ISH???

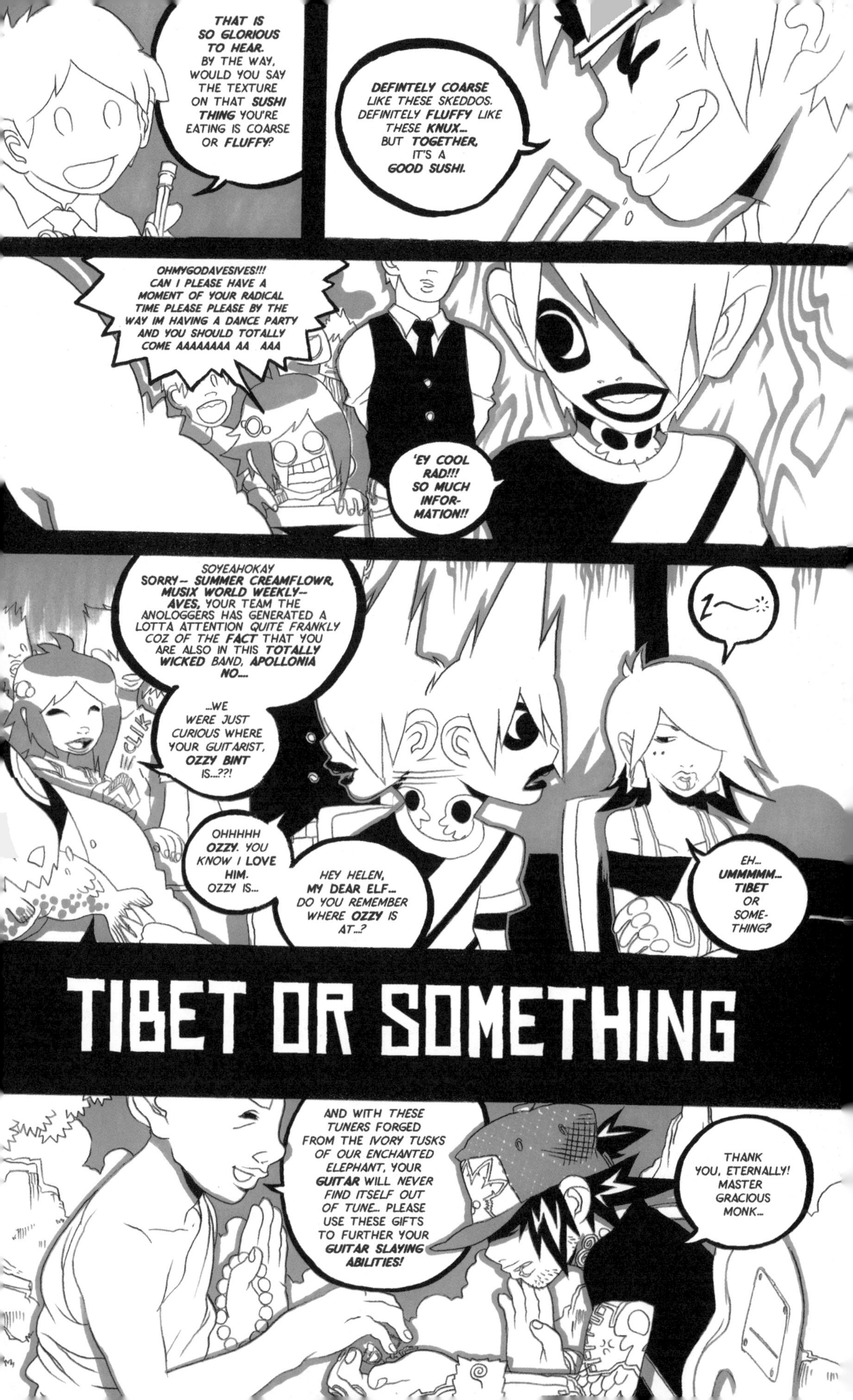
THAT IS SO GLORIOUS TO HEAR. BY THE WAY, WOULD YOU SAY THE TEXTURE ON THAT SUSHI THING YOU'RE EATING IS COARSE OR FLUFFY?
DEFINTELY COARSE LIKE THESE SKEDDOS. DEFINITELY FLUFFY LIKE THESE KNUX... BUT TOGETHER, IT'S A GOOD SUSHI.
OHMYGODAVESIVES!!! CAN I PLEASE HAVE A MOMENT OF YOUR RADICAL TIME PLEASE PLEASE BY THE WAY IM HAVING A DANCE PARTY AND YOU SHOULD TOTALLY COME AAAAAAAA AA AAA
'EY COOL RAD!!! SO MUCH INFOR-MATION!!
SOYEAHOKAY SORRY-- SUMMER CREAMFLOWR, MUSIX WORLD WEEKLY-- AVES, YOUR TEAM THE ANOLOGGERS HAS GENERATED A LOTTA ATTENTION QUITE FRANKLY COZ OF THE FACT THAT YOU ARE ALSO IN THIS TOTALLY WICKED BAND, APOLLONIA NO....
...WE WERE JUST CURIOUS WHERE YOUR GUITARIST, OZZY BINT IS...??!
CLIK
OHHHHH OZZY. YOU KNOW I LOVE HIM. OZZY IS...
HEY HELEN, MY DEAR ELF... DO YOU REMEMBER WHERE OZZY IS AT...?
EH... UMMMMM... TIBET OR SOME-THING?
TIBET OR SOMETHING
AND WITH THESE TUNERS FORGED FROM THE IVORY TUSKS OF OUR ENCHANTED ELEPHANT, YOUR GUITAR WILL NEVER FIND ITSELF OUT OF TUNE... PLEASE USE THESE GIFTS TO FURTHER YOUR GUITAR SLAYING ABILITIES!
THANK YOU, ETERNALLY! MASTER GRACIOUS MONK...

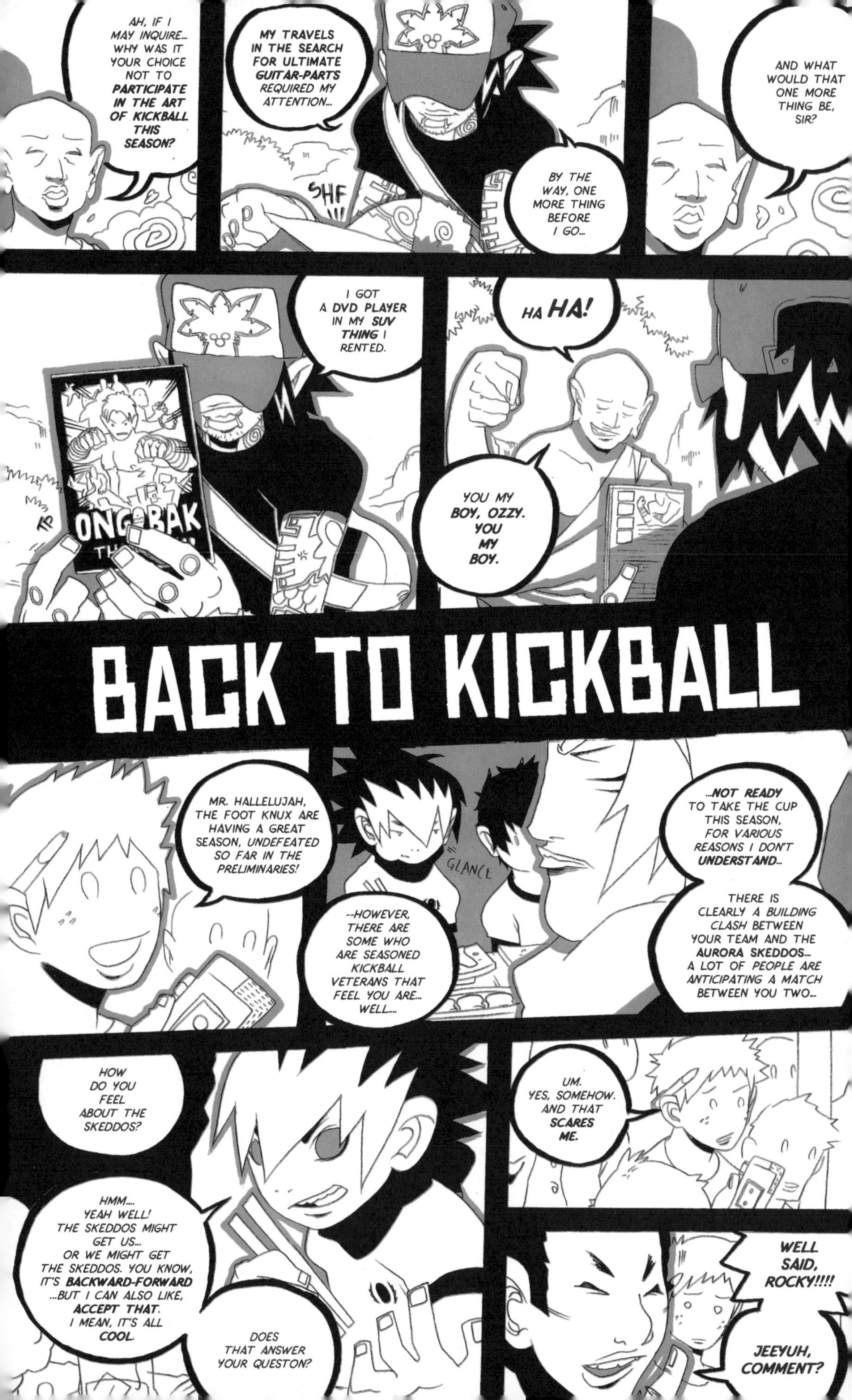
AH, IF I MAY INQUIRE... WHY WAS IT YOUR CHOICE NOT TO PARTICIPATE IN THE ART OF KICKBALL THIS SEASON?
MY TRAVELS IN THE SEARCH FOR ULTIMATE GUITAR-PARTS REQUIRED MY ATTENTION...
SHF
BY THE WAY, ONE MORE THING BEFORE I GO...
AND WHAT WOULD THAT ONE MORE THING BE, SIR?
I GOT A DVD PLAYER IN MY SUV THING I RENTED.
ONG BAK
HA HA!
YOU MY BOY, OZZY. YOU MY BOY.
BACK TO KICKBALL
MR. HALLELUJAH, THE FOOT KNUX ARE HAVING A GREAT SEASON, UNDEFEATED SO FAR IN THE PRELIMINARIES!
GLANCE
--HOWEVER, THERE ARE SOME WHO ARE SEASONED KICKBALL VETERANS THAT FEEL YOU ARE... WELL....
...NOT READY TO TAKE THE CUP THIS SEASON, FOR VARIOUS REASONS I DON'T UNDERSTAND...
THERE IS CLEARLY A BUILDING CLASH BETWEEN YOUR TEAM AND THE AURORA SKEDDOS... A LOT OF PEOPLE ARE ANTICIPATING A MATCH BETWEEN YOU TWO...
HOW DO YOU FEEL ABOUT THE SKEDDOS?
HMM.... YEAH WELL! THE SKEDDOS MIGHT GET US... OR WE MIGHT GET THE SKEDDOS. YOU KNOW, IT'S BACKWARD-FORWARD ...BUT I CAN ALSO LIKE, ACCEPT THAT. I MEAN, IT'S ALL COOL.
DOES THAT ANSWER YOUR QUESTON?
UM. YES, SOMEHOW. AND THAT SCARES ME.
WELL SAID, ROCKY!!!!
JEEYUH, COMMENT?

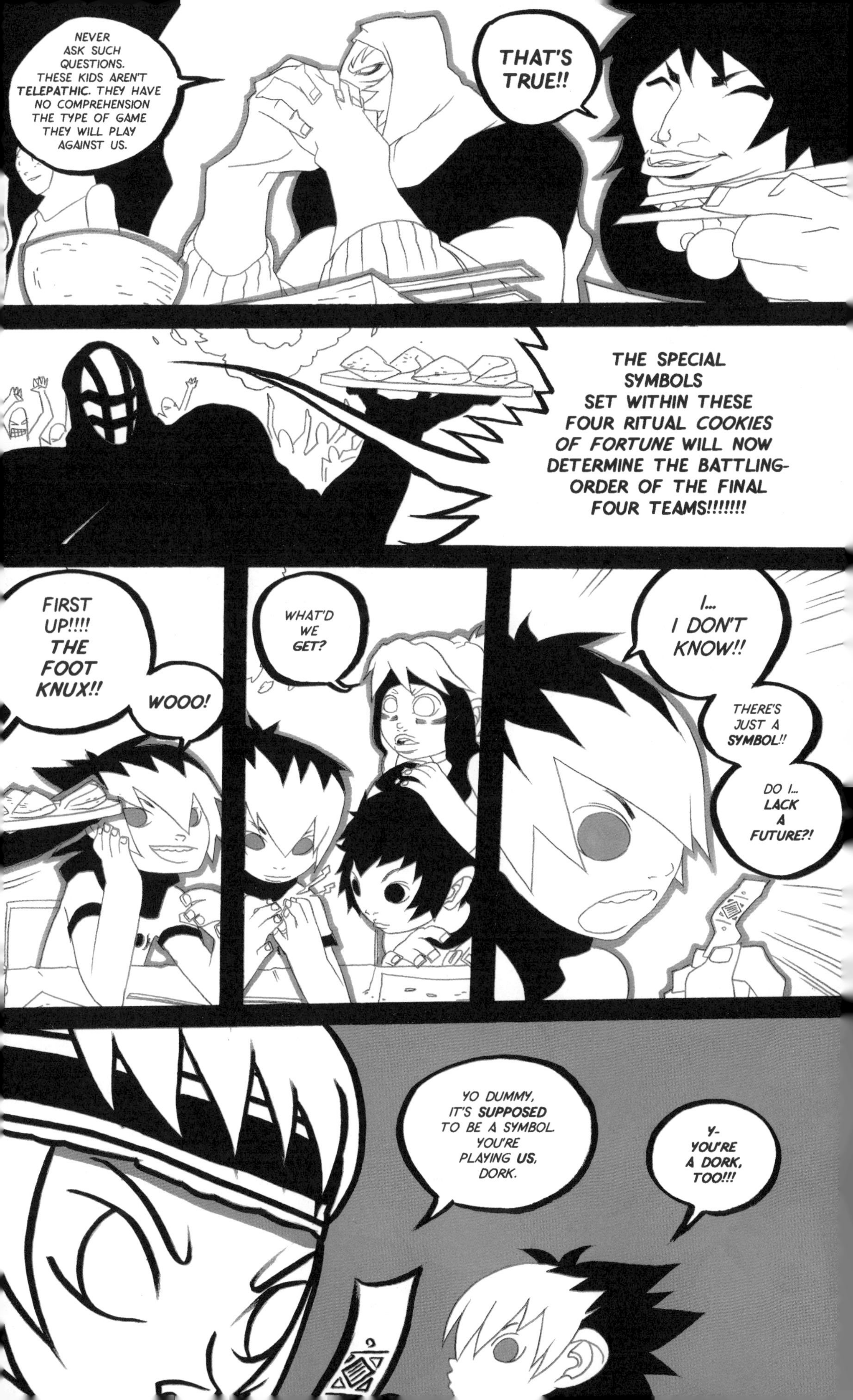
NEVER ASK SUCH QUESTIONS. THESE KIDS AREN'T TELEPATHIC. THEY HAVE NO COMPREHENSION THE TYPE OF GAME THEY WILL PLAY AGAINST US.
THAT'S TRUE!!
THE SPECIAL SYMBOLS SET WITHIN THESE FOUR RITUAL COOKIES OF FORTUNE WILL NOW DETERMINE THE BATTLING-ORDER OF THE FINAL FOUR TEAMS!!!!!!!
FIRST UP!!!! THE FOOT KNUX!!
WOOO!
WHAT'D WE GET?
I... I DON'T KNOW!!
THERE'S JUST A SYMBOL!!
DO I... LACK A FUTURE?!
YO DUMMY, IT'S SUPPOSED TO BE A SYMBOL. YOU'RE PLAYING US, DORK.
Y- YOU'RE A DORK, TOO!!!

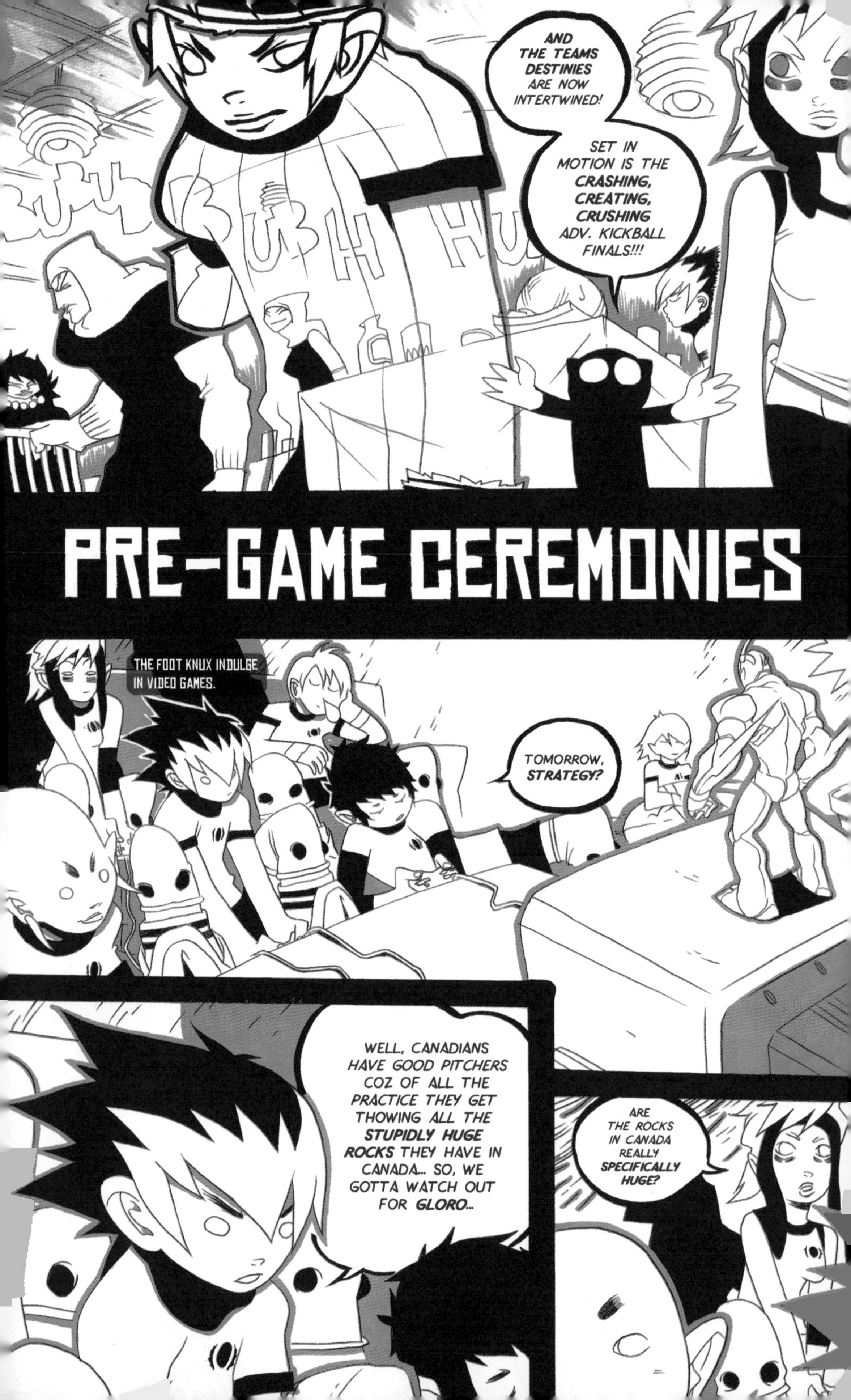
AND THE TEAMS DESTINIES ARE NOW INTERTWINED!
SET IN MOTION IS THE CRASHING, CREATING, CRUSHING ADV. KICKBALL FINALS!!!
PRE-GAME CEREMONIES
THE FOOT KNUX INDULGE IN VIDEO GAMES.
TOMORROW, STRATEGY?
WELL, CANADIANS HAVE GOOD PITCHERS COZ OF ALL THE PRACTICE THEY GET THOWING ALL THE STUPIDLY HUGE ROCKS THEY HAVE IN CANADA... SO, WE GOTTA WATCH OUT FOR GLORO...
ARE THE ROCKS IN CANADA REALLY SPECIFICALLY HUGE?

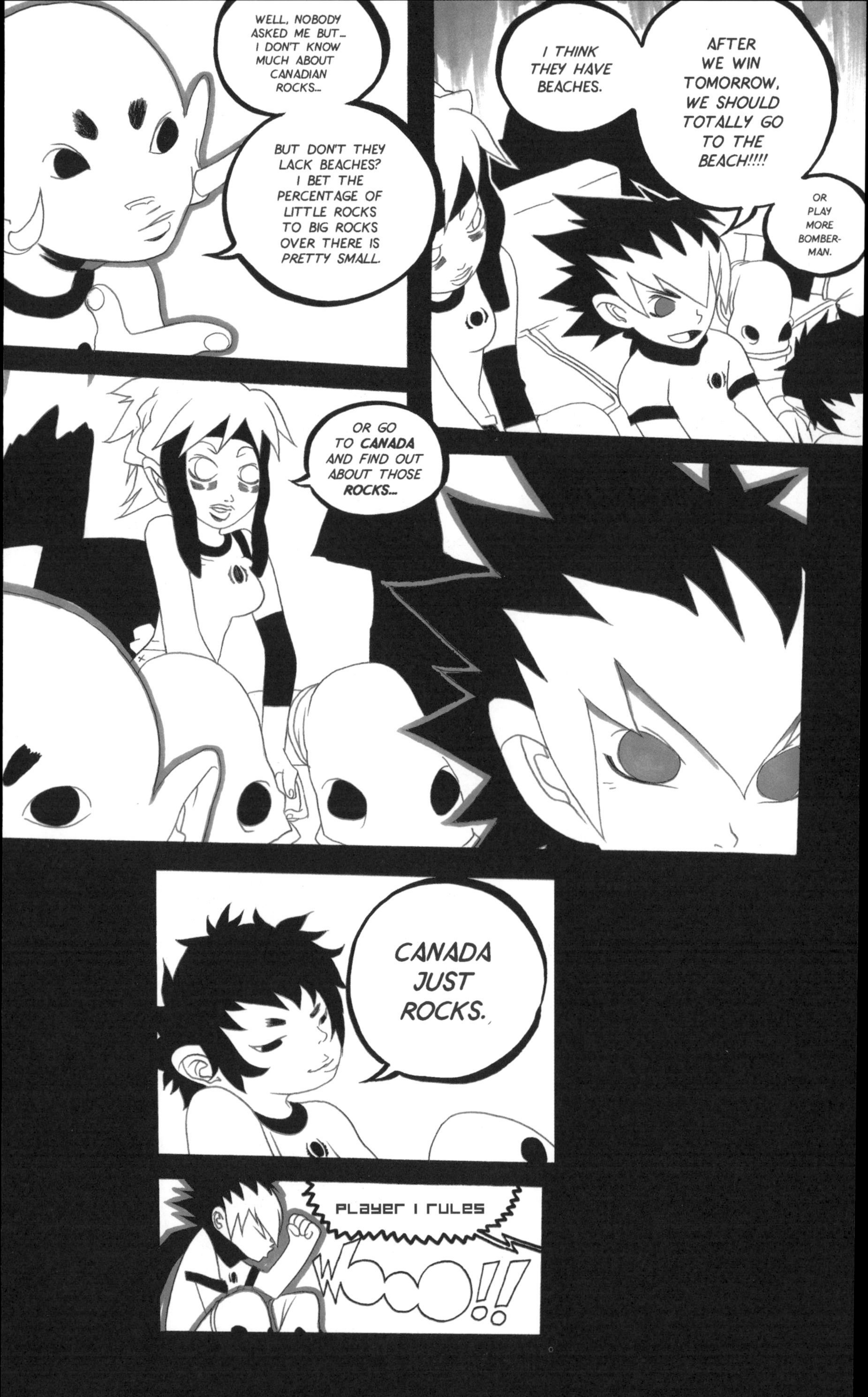
WELL, NOBODY ASKED ME BUT... I DON'T KNOW MUCH ABOUT CANADIAN ROCKS...
BUT DON'T THEY LACK BEACHES? I BET THE PERCENTAGE OF LITTLE ROCKS TO BIG ROCKS OVER THERE IS PRETTY SMALL.
I THINK THEY HAVE BEACHES.
AFTER WE WIN TOMORROW, WE SHOULD TOTALLY GO TO THE BEACH!!!!
OR PLAY MORE BOMBER-MAN.
OR GO TO CANADA AND FIND OUT ABOUT THOSE ROCKS...
CANADA JUST ROCKS.
PLAYER 1 RULES
WOOOO!!

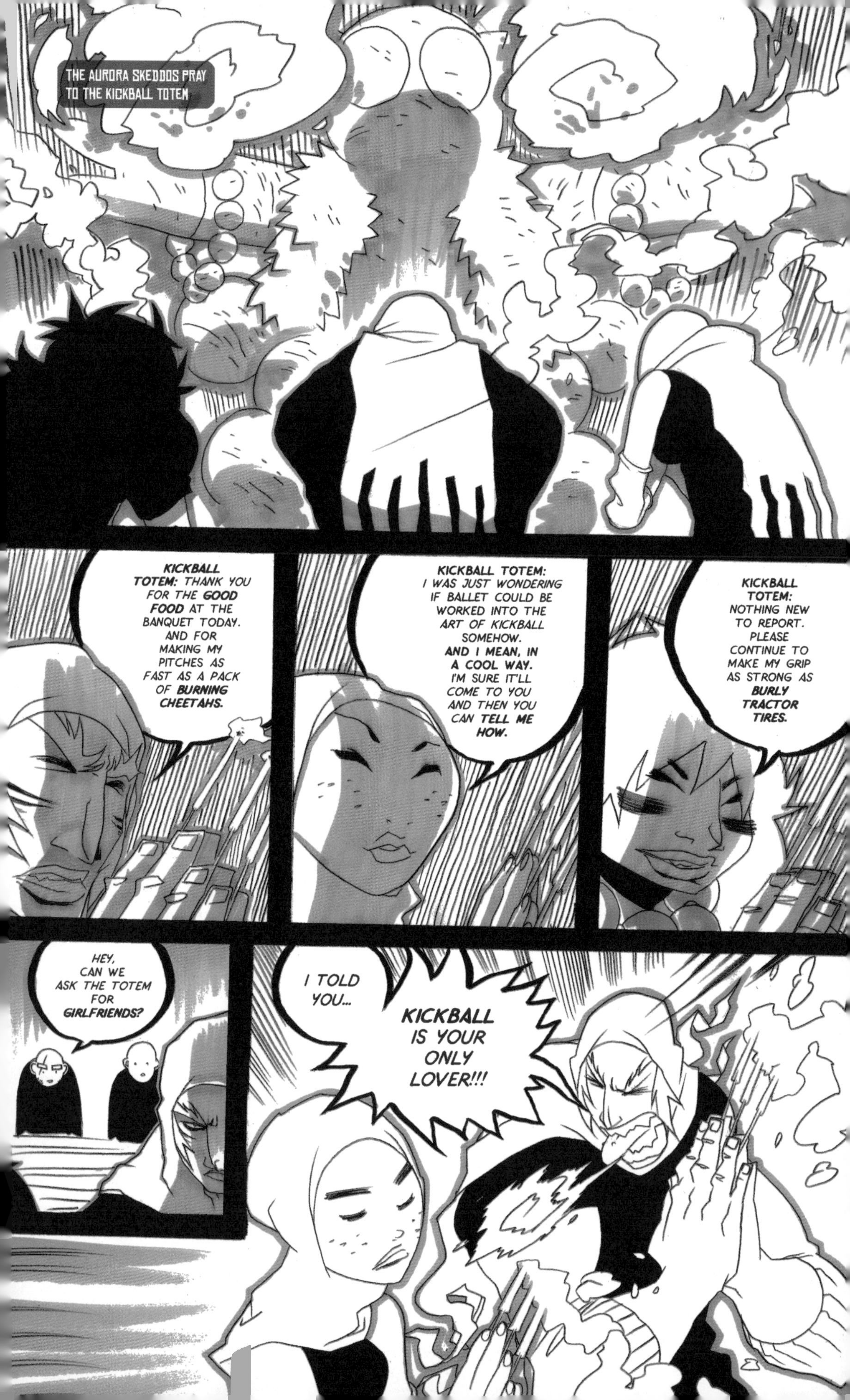
THE AURORA SKEDDOS PRAY TO THE KICKBALL TOTEM
KICKBALL TOTEM: THANK YOU FOR THE GOOD FOOD AT THE BANQUET TODAY. AND FOR MAKING MY PITCHES AS FAST AS A PACK OF BURNING CHEETAHS.
KICKBALL TOTEM: I WAS JUST WONDERING IF BALLET COULD BE WORKED INTO THE ART OF KICKBALL SOMEHOW. AND I MEAN, IN A COOL WAY. I'M SURE IT'LL COME TO YOU AND THEN YOU CAN TELL ME HOW.
KICKBALL TOTEM: NOTHING NEW TO REPORT. PLEASE CONTINUE TO MAKE MY GRIP AS STRONG AS BURLY TRACTOR TIRES.
HEY, CAN WE ASK THE TOTEM FOR GIRLFRIENDS?
I TOLD YOU...
KICKBALL IS YOUR ONLY LOVER!!!

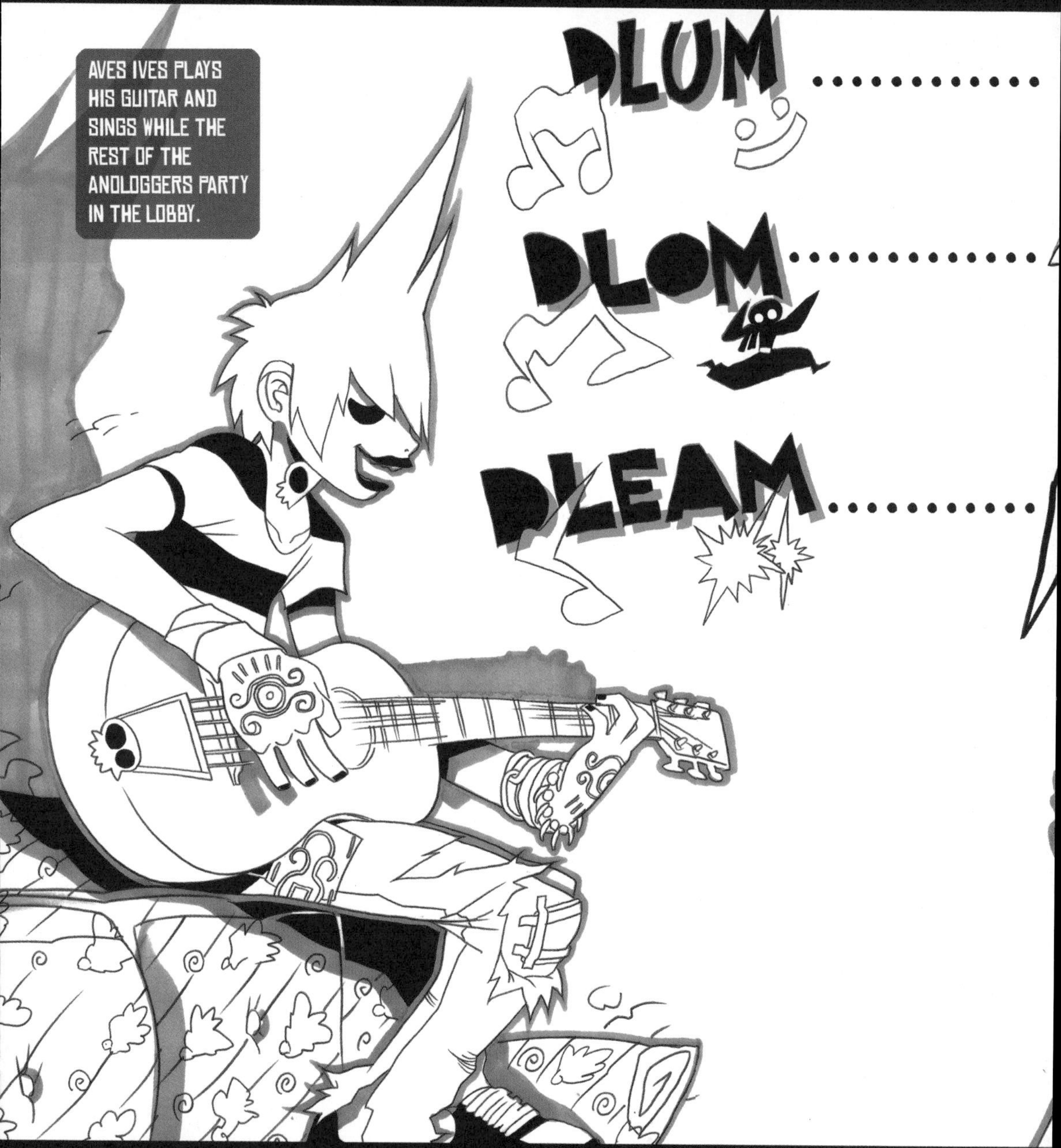
AVES IVES PLAYS HIS GUITAR AND SINGS WHILE THE REST OF THE ANOLOGGERS PARTY IN THE LOBBY.
DLUM
DLOM
DLEAM

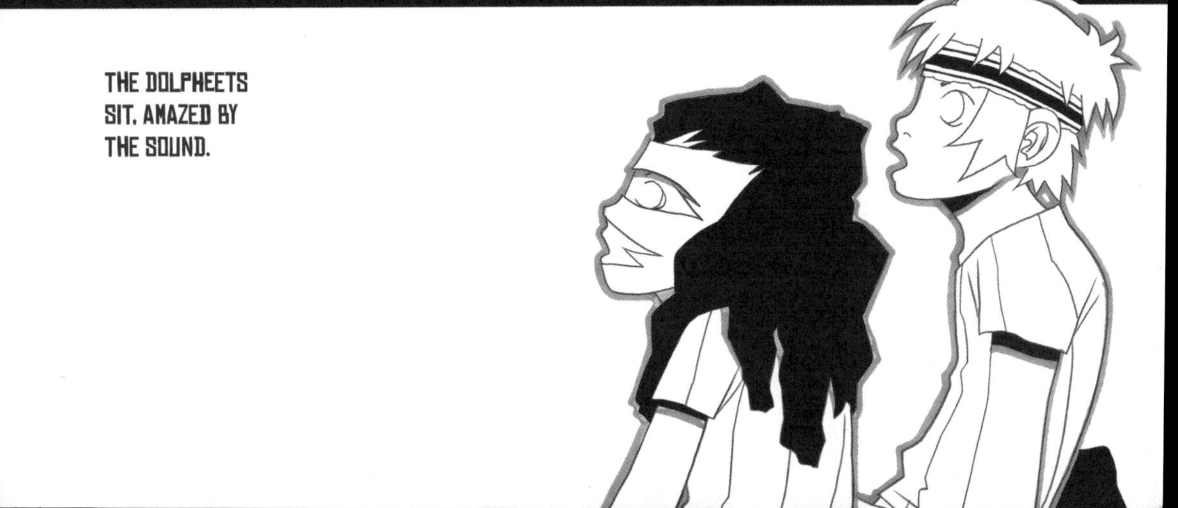
THE DOLPHEETS SIT, AMAZED BY THE SOUND.

GAME
DAY:

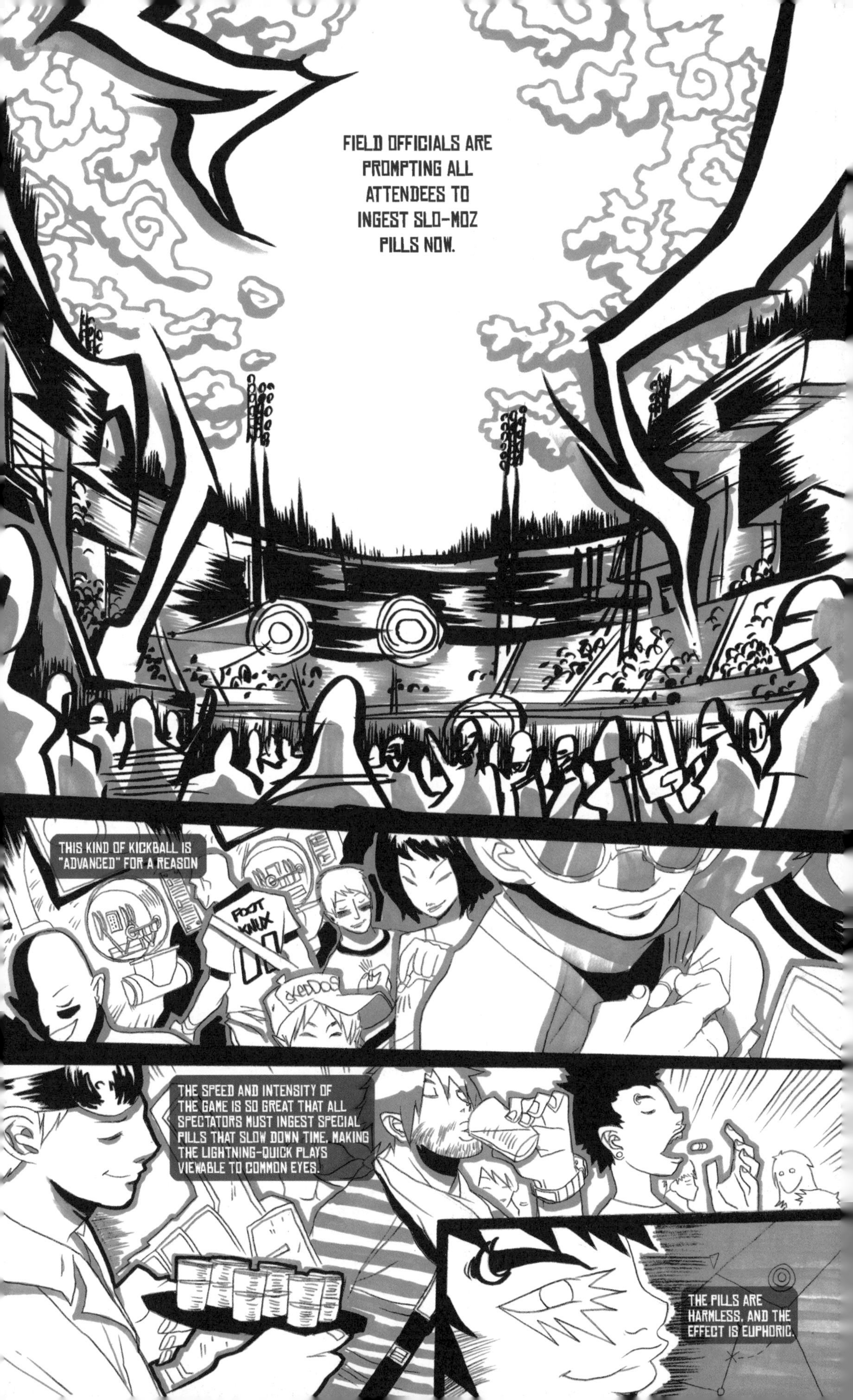
FIELD OFFICIALS ARE PROMPTING ALL ATTENDEES TO INGEST SLO-MOZ PILLS NOW.
THIS KIND OF KICKBALL IS "ADVANCED" FOR A REASON
FOOT KNUX
SKEDDOS
THE SPEED AND INTENSITY OF THE GAME IS SO GREAT THAT ALL SPECTATORS MUST INGEST SPECIAL PILLS THAT SLOW DOWN TIME, MAKING THE LIGHTNING-QUICK PLAYS VIEWABLE TO COMMON EYES.
THE PILLS ARE HARMLESS, AND THE EFFECT IS EUPHORIC.

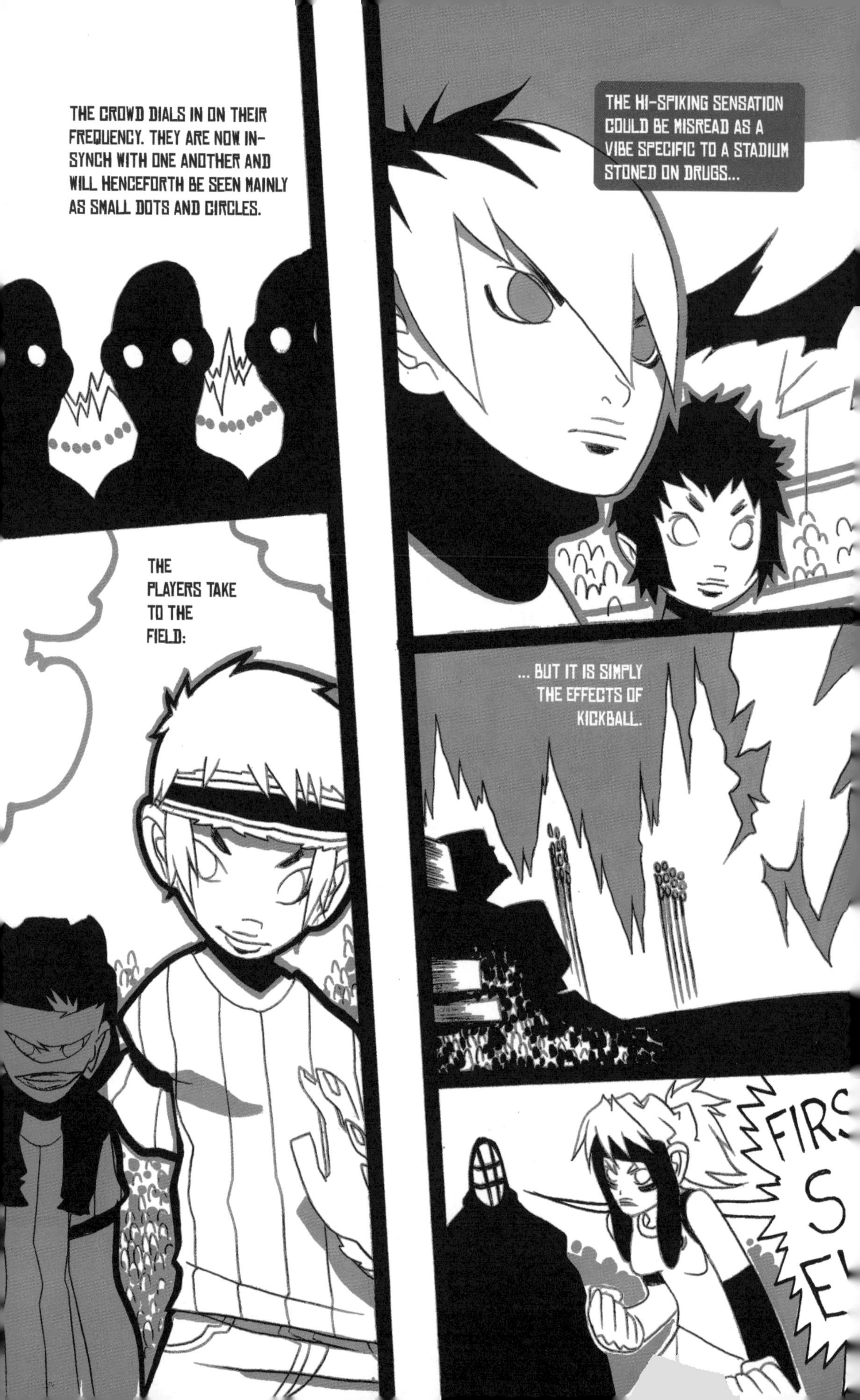
THE CROWD DIALS IN ON THEIR FREQUENCY. THEY ARE NOW IN-SYNCH WITH ONE ANOTHER AND WILL HENCEFORTH BE SEEN MAINLY AS SMALL DOTS AND CIRCLES.
THE PLAYERS TAKE TO THE FIELD:
THE HI-SPIKING SENSATION COULD BE MISREAD AS A VIBE SPECIFIC TO A STADIUM STONED ON DRUGS...
... BUT IT IS SIMPLY THE EFFECTS OF KICKBALL.

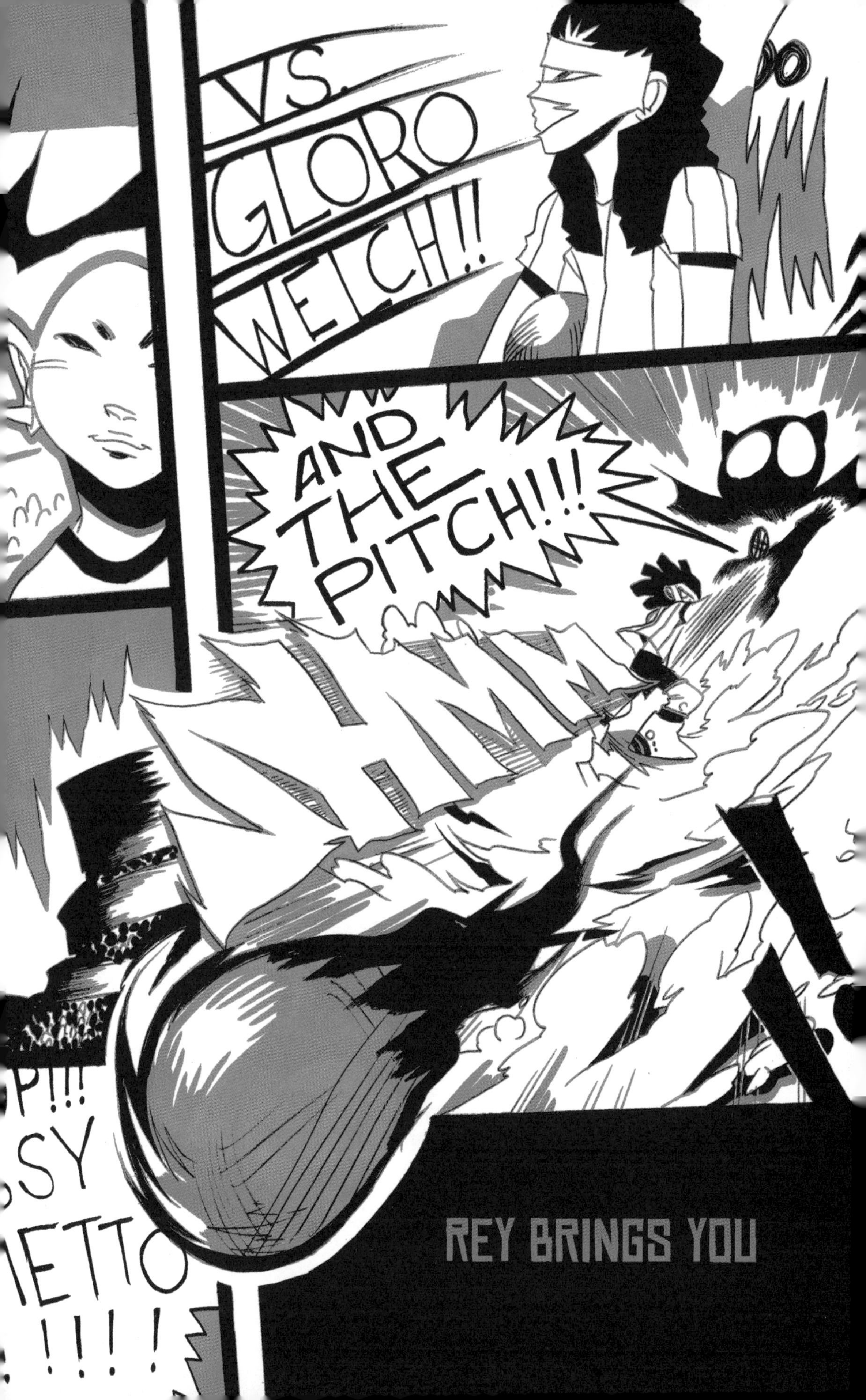
VS.
GLORO
WELCH!!
AND THE PITCH!!!
REY BRINGS YOU

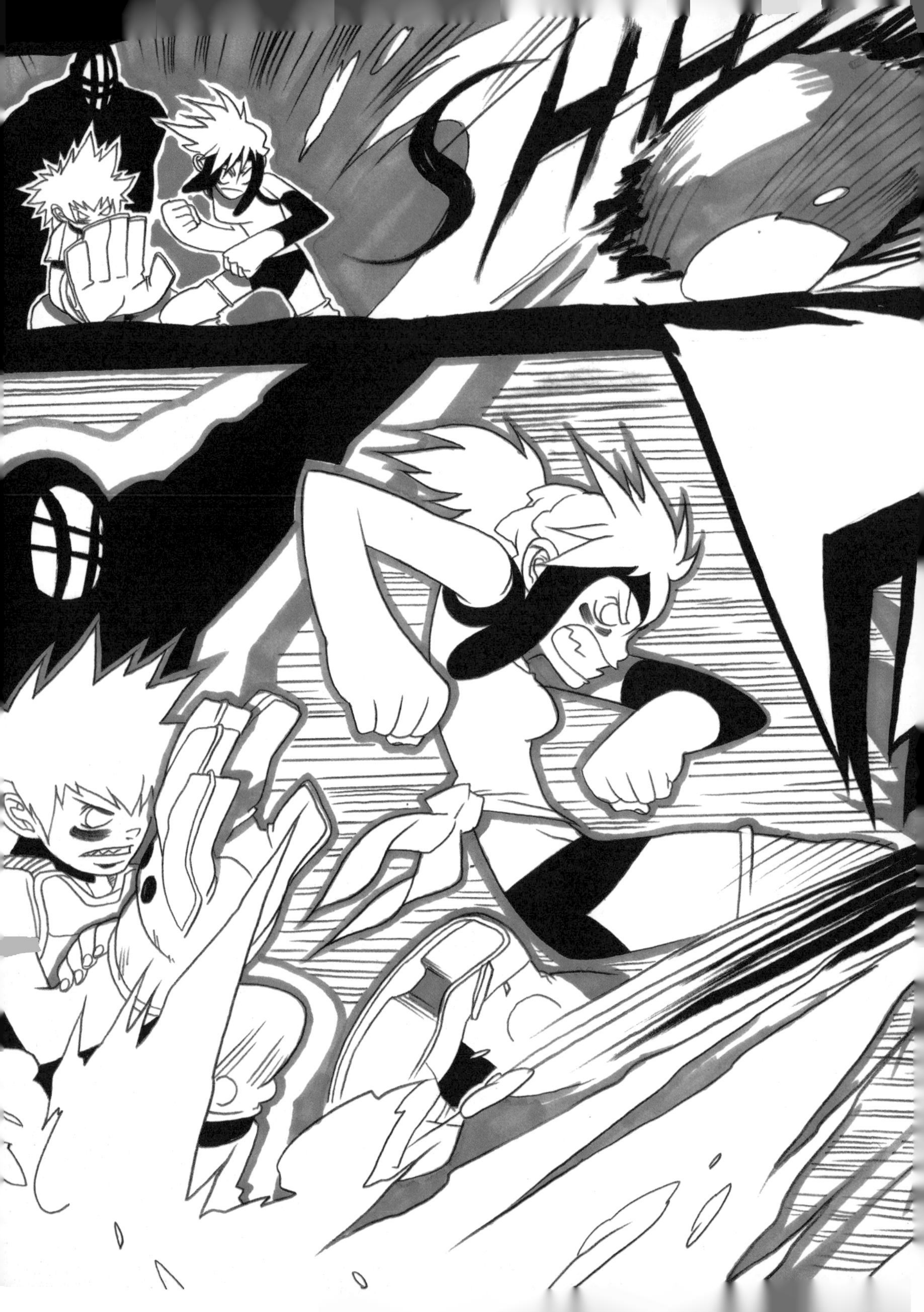

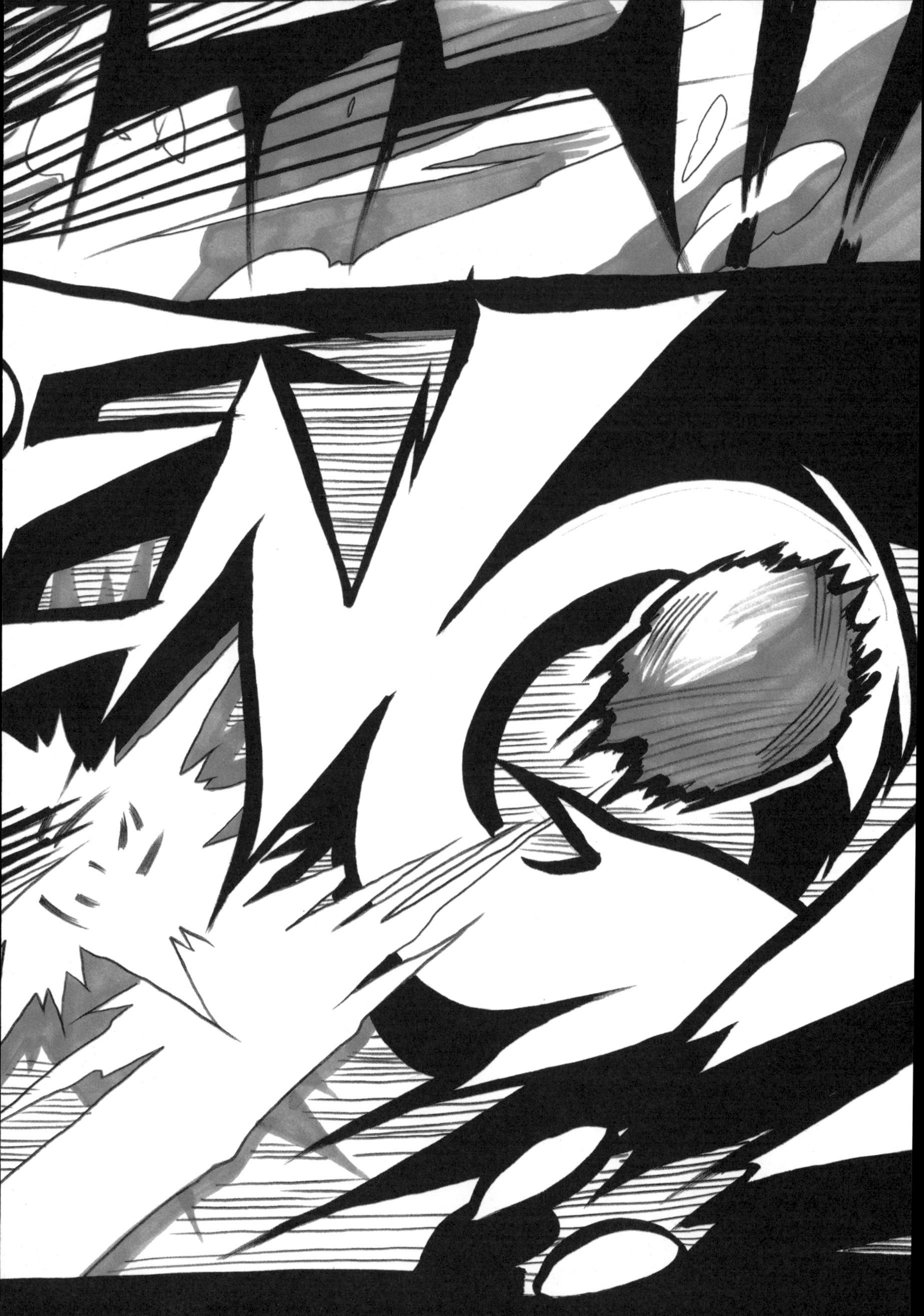

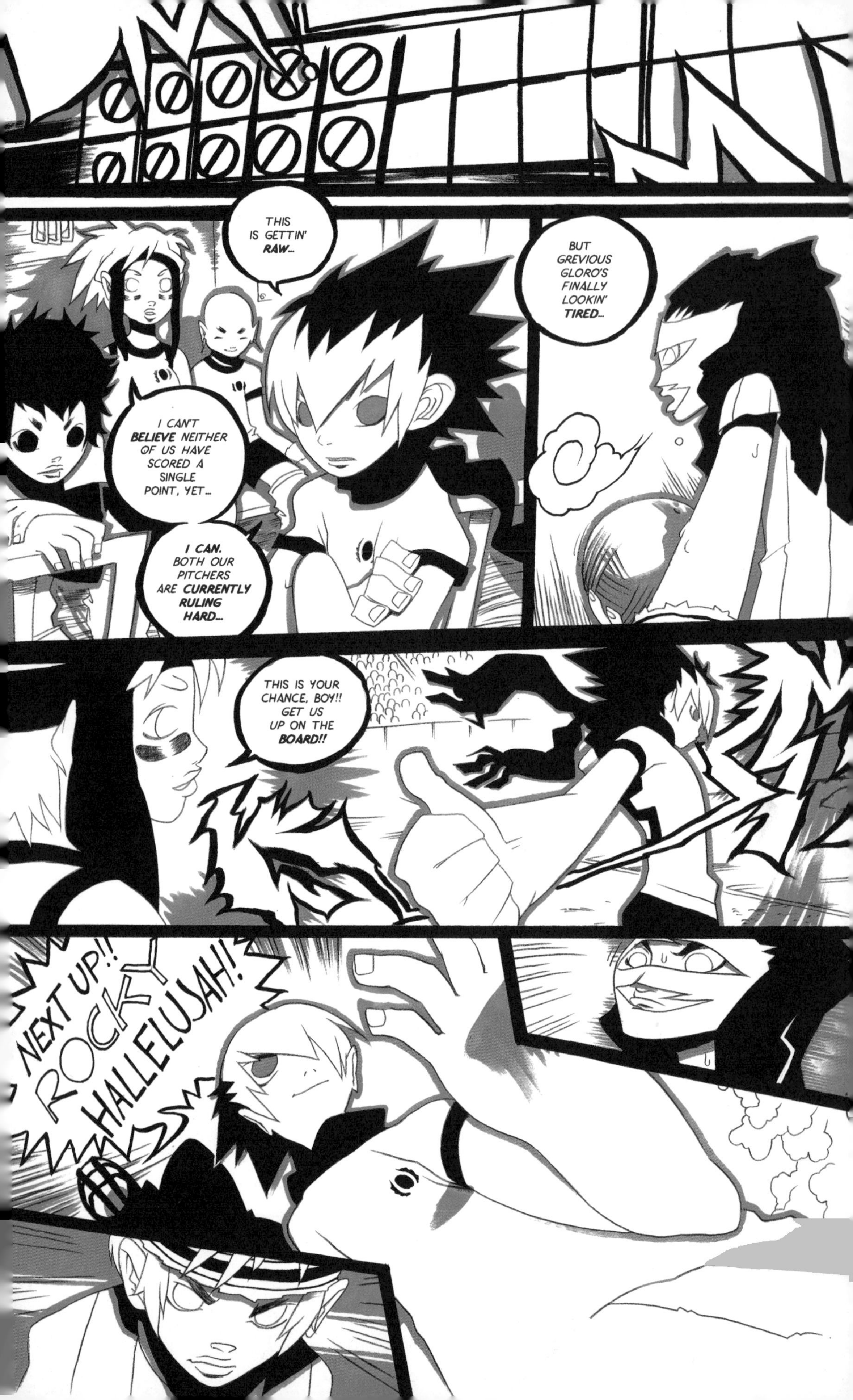
THIS IS GETTIN' RAW...
I CAN'T BELIEVE NEITHER OF US HAVE SCORED A SINGLE POINT, YET...
I CAN. BOTH OUR PITCHERS ARE CURRENTLY RULING HARD...
BUT GREVIOUS GLORO'S FINALLY LOOKIN' TIRED...
THIS IS YOUR CHANCE, BOY!! GET US UP ON THE BOARD!!
NEXT UP!! ROCKY HALLELUJAH!!

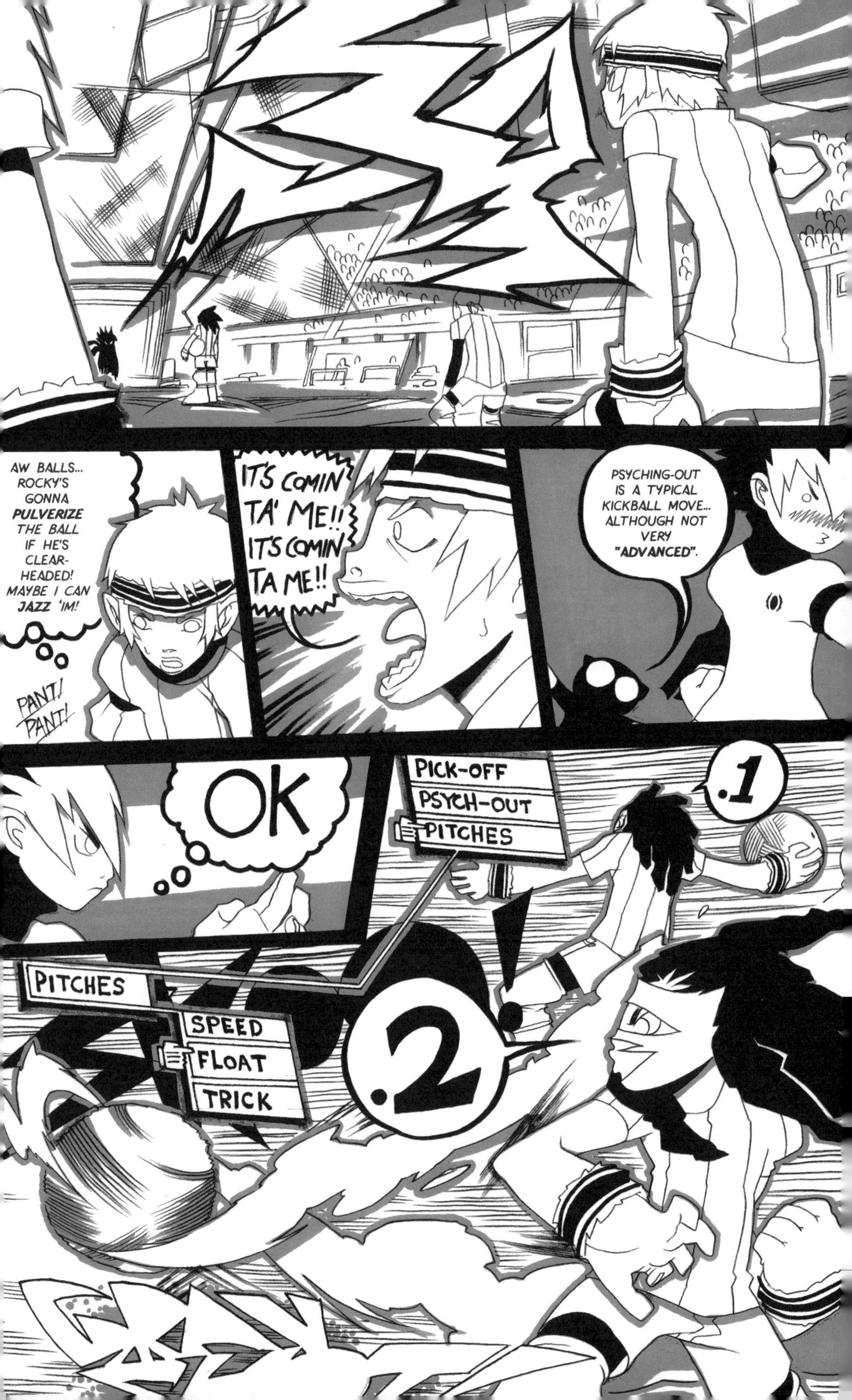
AW BALLS... ROCKY'S GONNA PULVERIZE THE BALL IF HE'S CLEAR-HEADED! MAYBE I CAN JAZZ 'IM!
PANT! PANT!
IT'S COMIN TA' ME!! IT'S COMIN TA ME!!
PSYCHING-OUT IS A TYPICAL KICKBALL MOVE... ALTHOUGH NOT VERY "ADVANCED".
OK
PICK-OFF
PSYCH-OUT
PITCHES
.1
PITCHES
SPEED
FLOAT
TRICK
.2
!

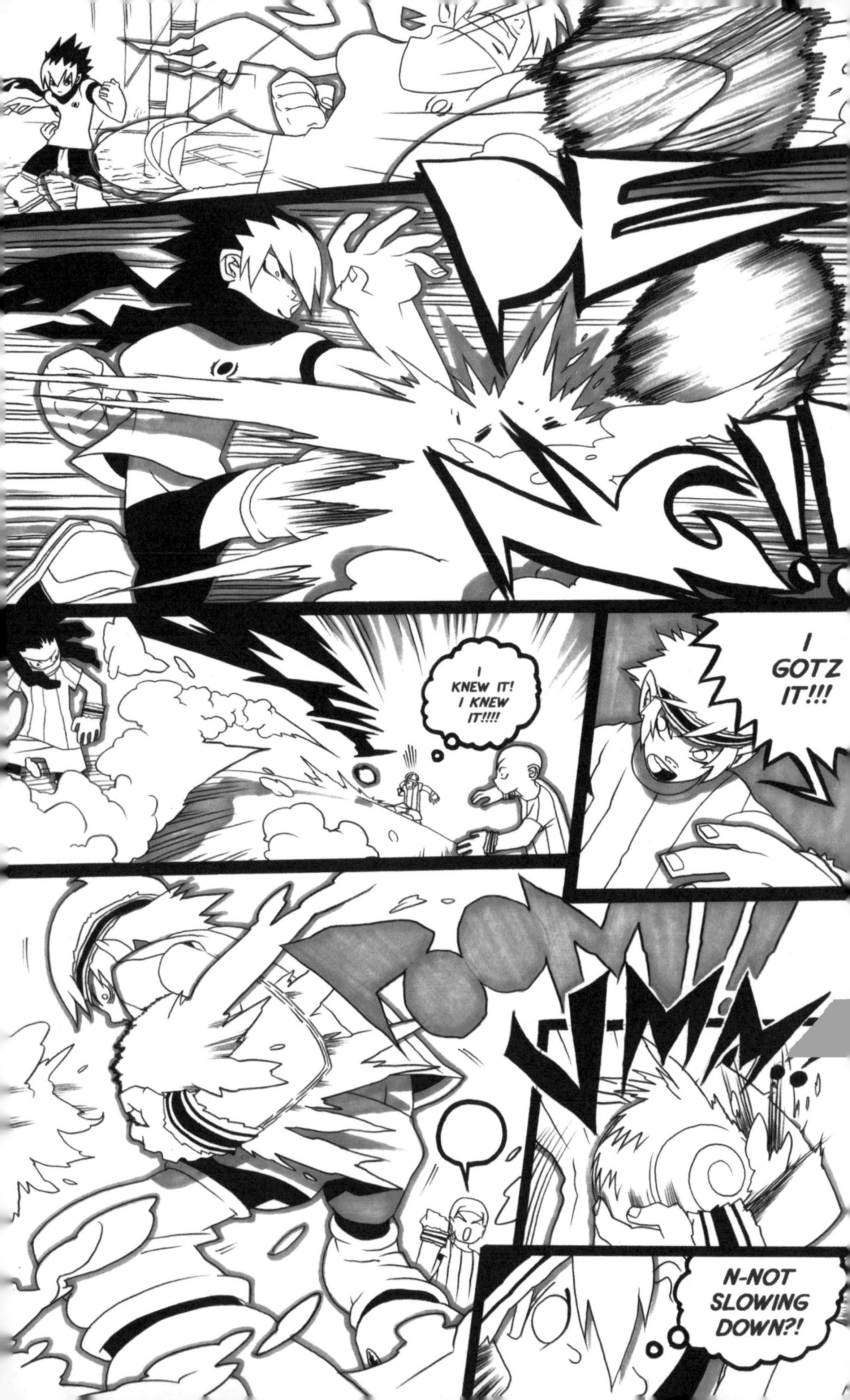
I KNEW IT! I KNEW IT!!!!
I GOTZ IT!!!
N-NOT SLOWING DOWN?!

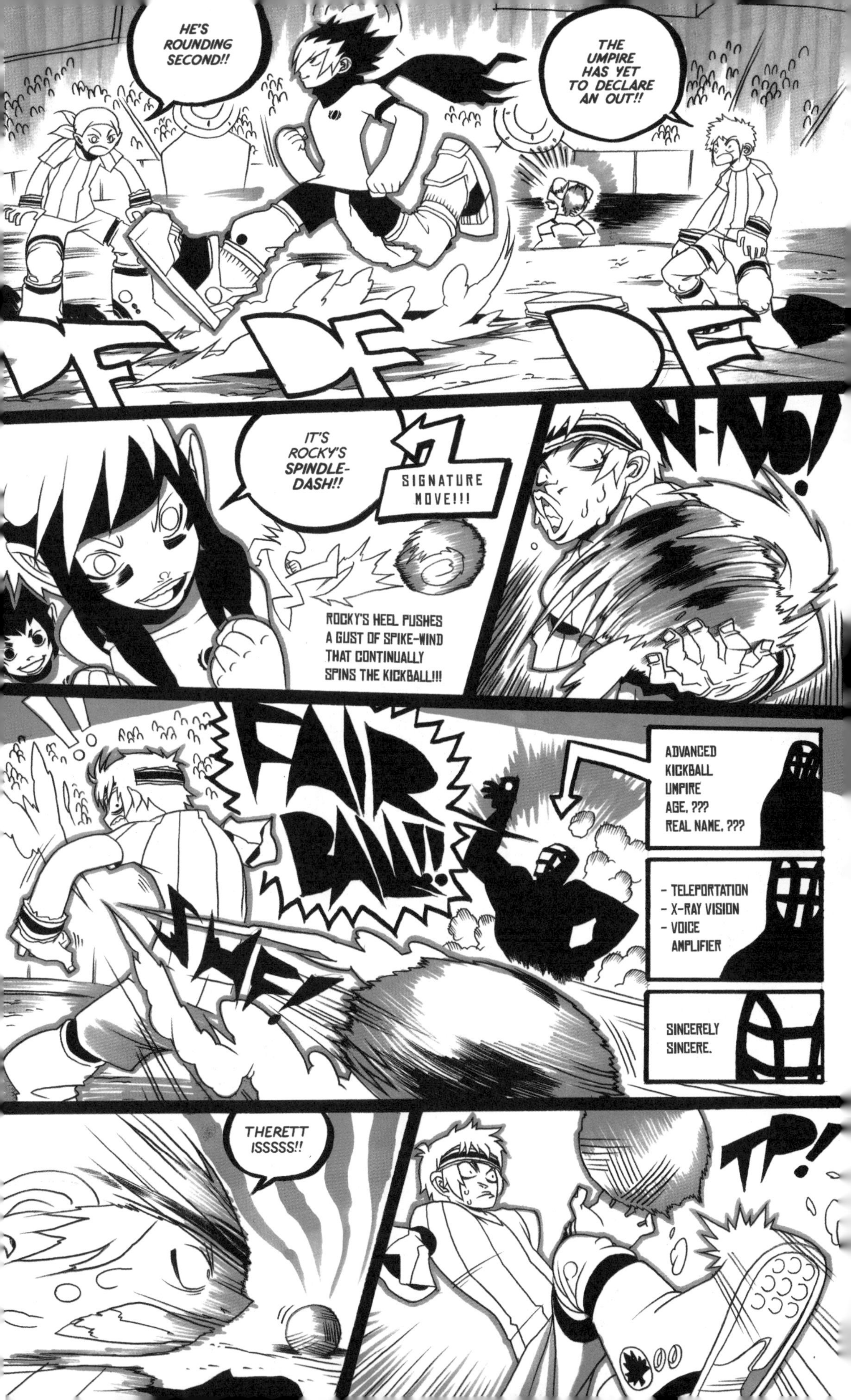
HE'S ROUNDING SECOND!!
THE UMPIRE HAS YET TO DECLARE AN OUT!!
IT'S ROCKY'S SPINDLE-DASH!!
SIGNATURE MOVE!!!
ROCKY'S HEEL PUSHES A GUST OF SPIKE-WIND THAT CONTINUALLY SPINS THE KICKBALL!!!
FAIR BALL!!
ADVANCED KICKBALL UMPIRE
AGE. ???
REAL NAME. ???
- TELEPORTATION
- X-RAY VISION
- VOICE AMPLIFIER
SINCERELY SINCERE.
THERETT ISSSSS!!

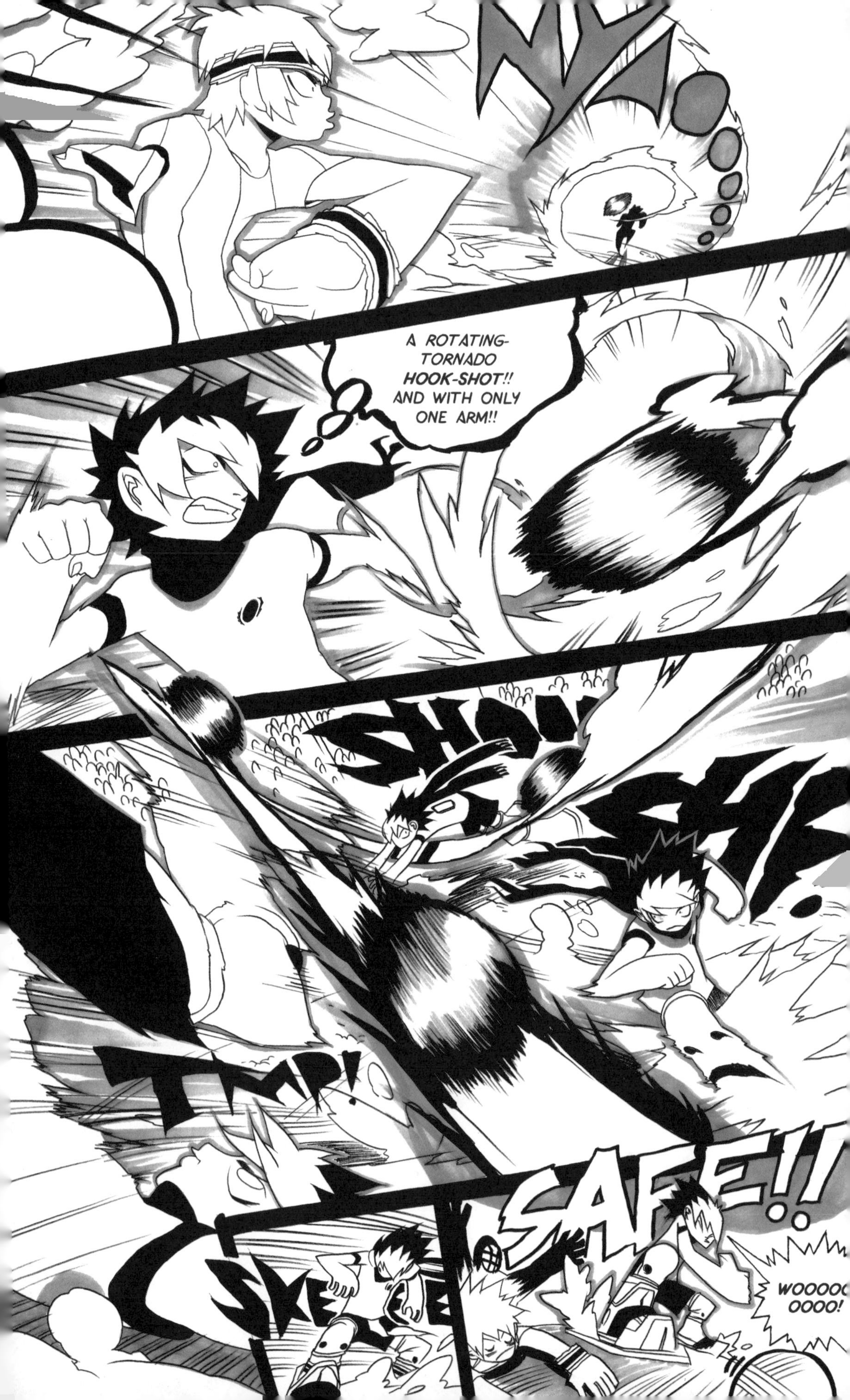
A ROTATING-TORNADO HOOK-SHOT!! AND WITH ONLY ONE ARM!!
TMP!
SAFE!!
WOOOO
OOOO!

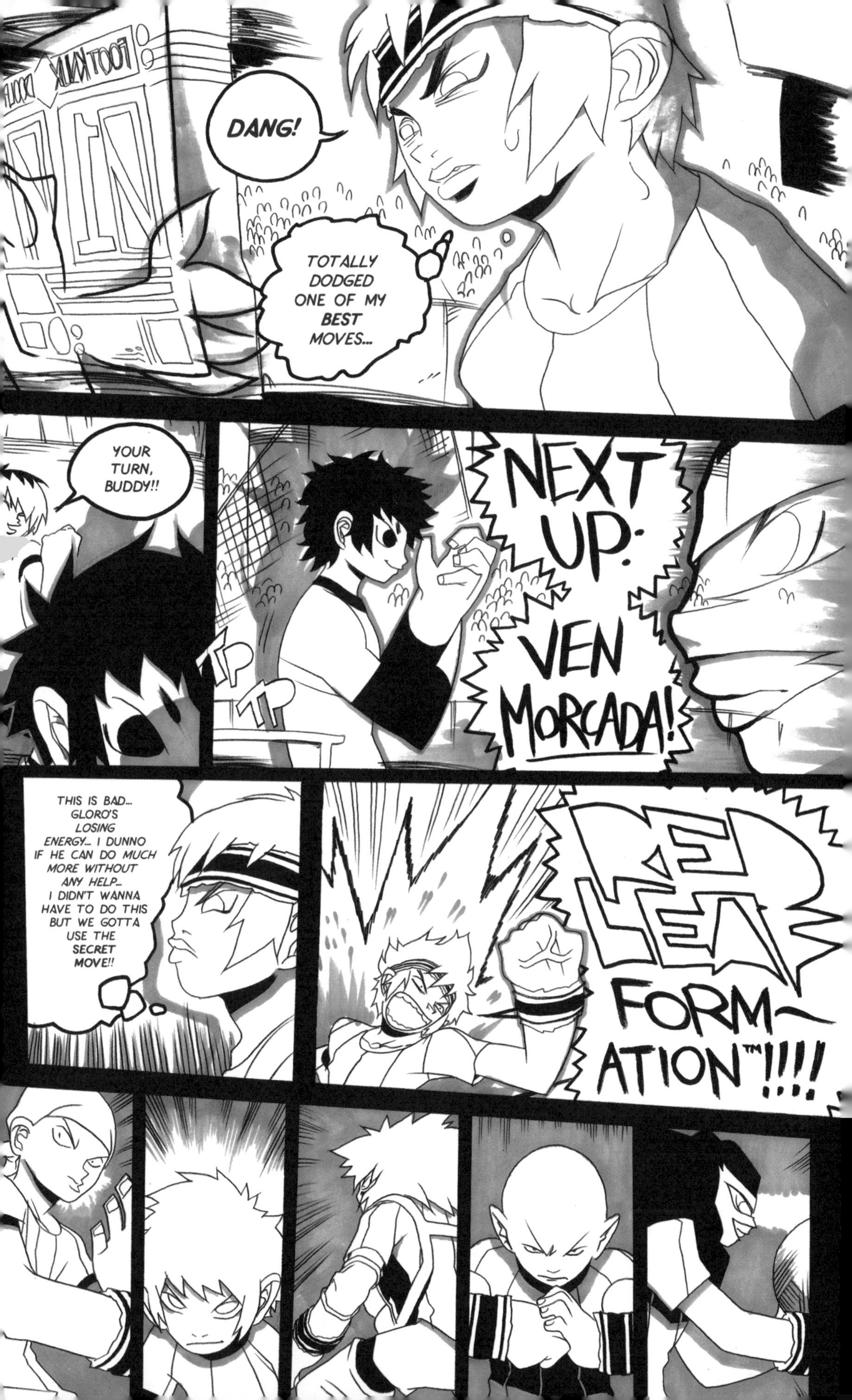
DANG!
TOTALLY DODGED ONE OF MY BEST MOVES...
YOUR TURN, BUDDY!!
NEXT UP: VEN MORCADA!
THIS IS BAD... GLORO'S LOSING ENERGY... I DUNNO IF HE CAN DO MUCH MORE WITHOUT ANY HELP... I DIDN'T WANNA HAVE TO DO THIS BUT WE GOTTA USE THE SECRET MOVE!!
RED LEAF FORM~ATION™!!!!

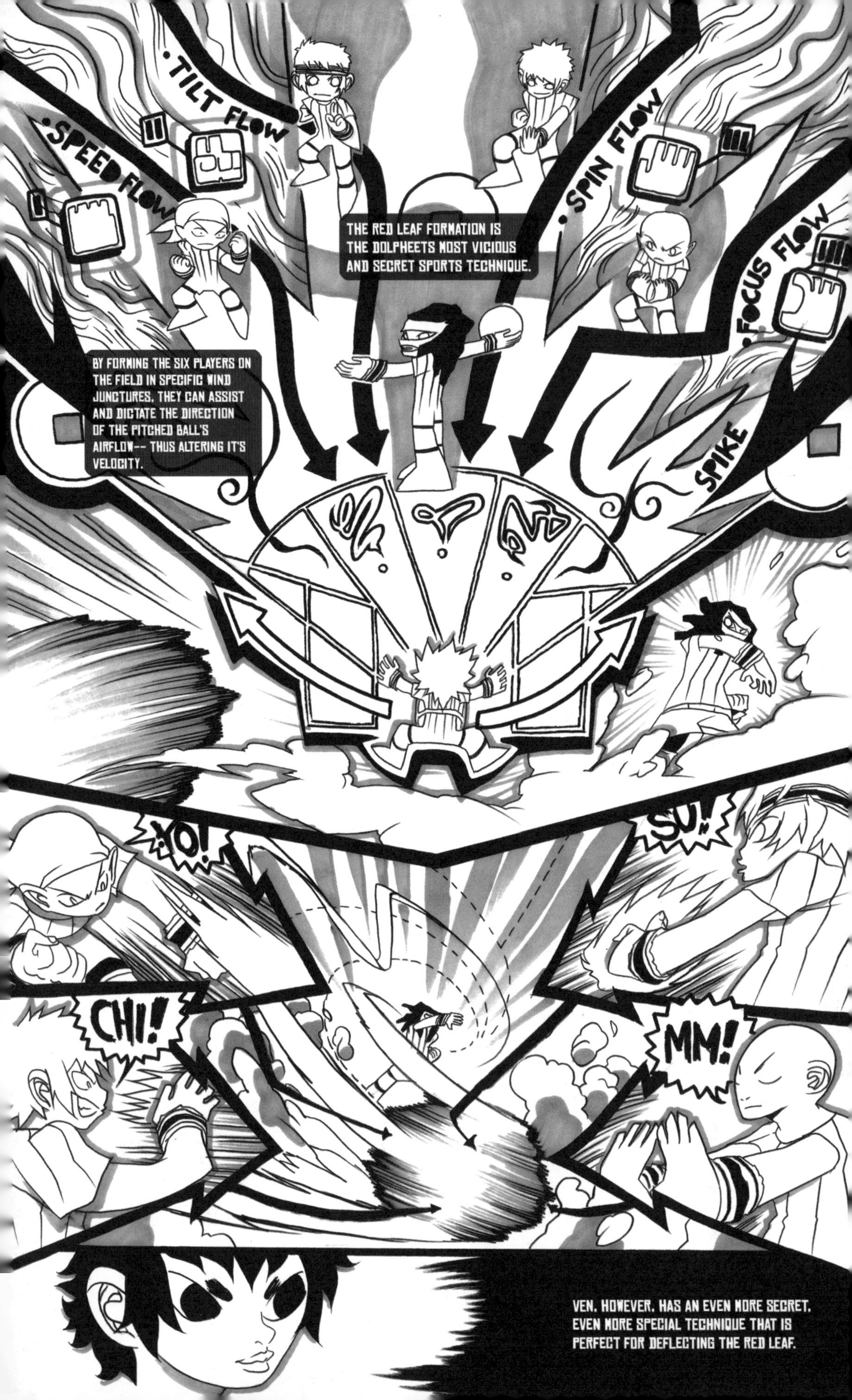
TILT FLOW
SPEED FLOW
SPIN FLOW
FOCUS FLOW
THE RED LEAF FORMATION IS THE DOLPHEETS MOST VICIOUS AND SECRET SPORTS TECHNIQUE.
BY FORMING THE SIX PLAYERS ON THE FIELD IN SPECIFIC WIND JUNCTURES, THEY CAN ASSIST AND DICTATE THE DIRECTION OF THE PITCHED BALL'S AIRFLOW-- THUS ALTERING IT'S VELOCITY.
SPIKE
YO!
SU!
CHI!
MM!
VEN, HOWEVER, HAS AN EVEN MORE SECRET, EVEN MORE SPECIAL TECHNIQUE THAT IS PERFECT FOR DEFLECTING THE RED LEAF.

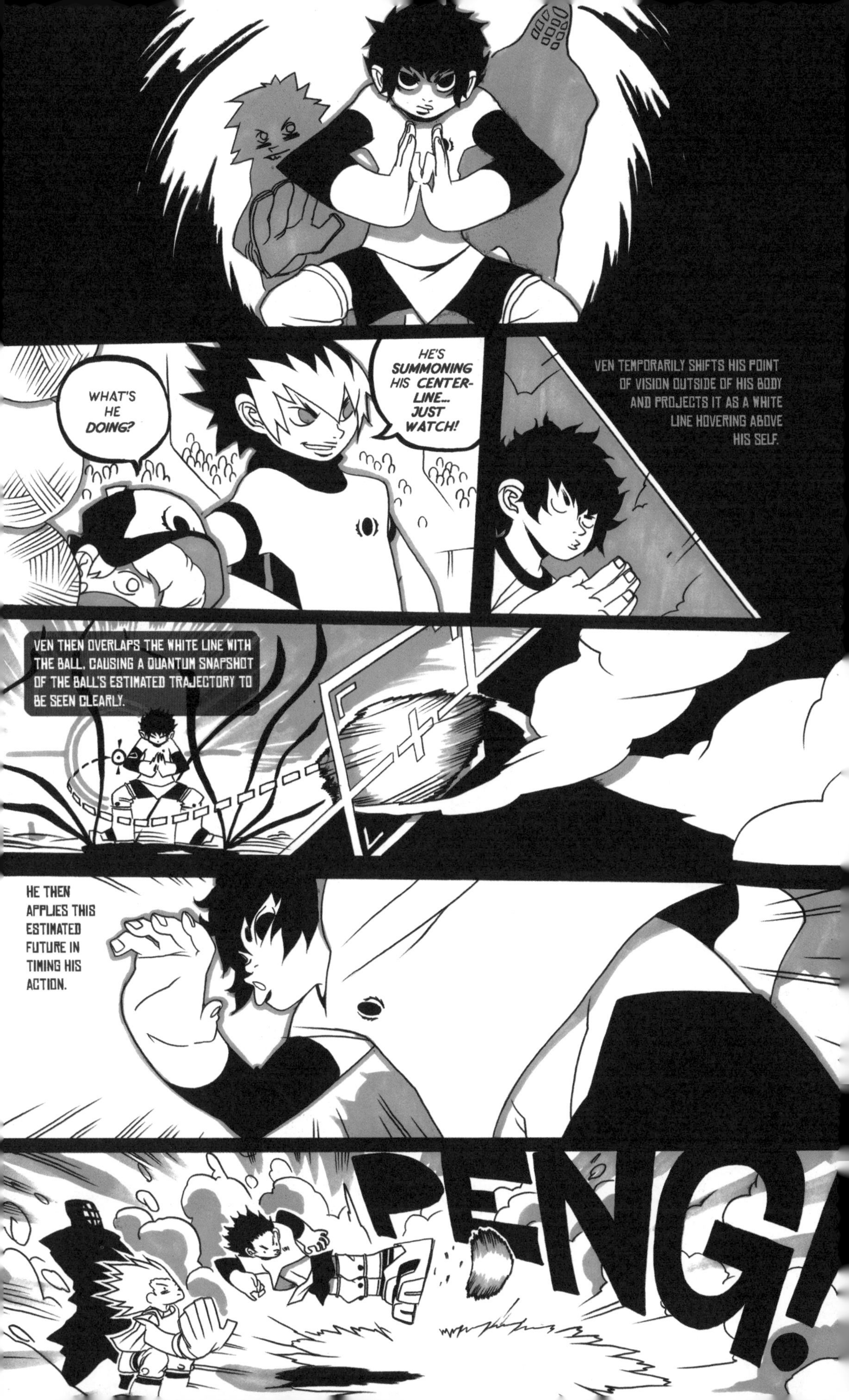
WHAT'S HE DOING?
HE'S SUMMONING HIS CENTER-LINE... JUST WATCH!
VEN TEMPORARILY SHIFTS HIS POINT OF VISION OUTSIDE OF HIS BODY AND PROJECTS IT AS A WHITE LINE HOVERING ABOVE HIS SELF.
VEN THEN OVERLAPS THE WHITE LINE WITH THE BALL, CAUSING A QUANTUM SNAPSHOT OF THE BALL'S ESTIMATED TRAJECTORY TO BE SEEN CLEARLY.
HE THEN APPLIES THIS ESTIMATED FUTURE IN TIMING HIS ACTION.
PENG!

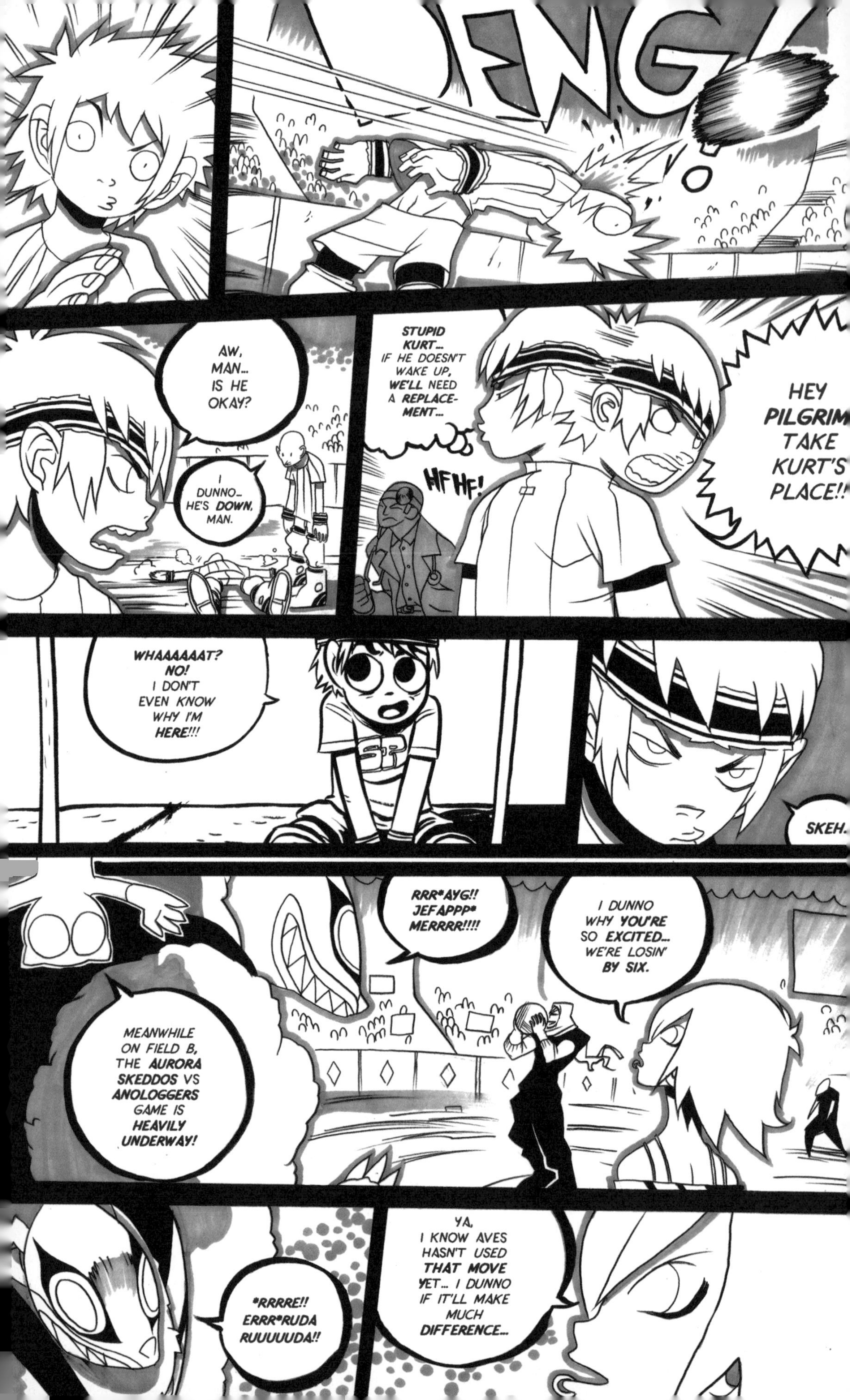

DENG!
AW, MAN... IS HE OKAY?
I DUNNO... HE'S DOWN, MAN.
STUPID KURT... IF HE DOESN'T WAKE UP, WE'LL NEED A REPLACEMENT...
HFHF!
HEY PILGRIM TAKE KURT'S PLACE!!
WHAAAAAAT? NO! I DON'T EVEN KNOW WHY I'M HERE!!!
SKEH.
MEANWHILE ON FIELD B, THE AURORA SKEDDOS VS ANOLOGGERS GAME IS HEAVILY UNDERWAY!
RRR*AYG!! JEFAPPP* MERRRR!!!!
I DUNNO WHY YOU'RE SO EXCITED... WE'RE LOSIN' BY SIX.
*RRRRE!! ERRR*RUDA RUUUUUDA!!
YA, I KNOW AVES HASN'T USED THAT MOVE YET... I DUNNO IF IT'LL MAKE MUCH DIFFERENCE...

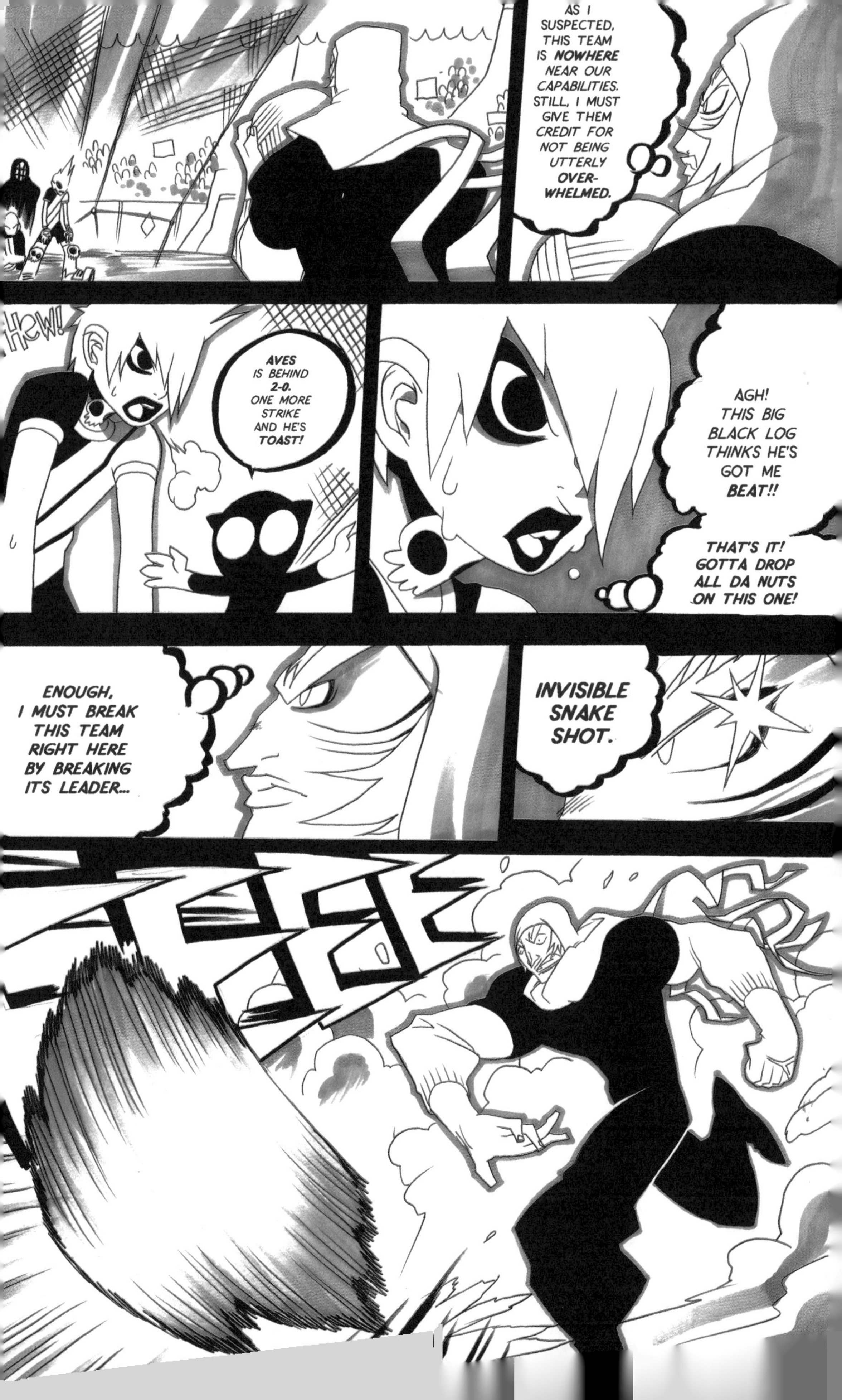
AS I SUSPECTED, THIS TEAM IS NOWHERE NEAR OUR CAPABILITIES. STILL, I MUST GIVE THEM CREDIT FOR NOT BEING UTTERLY OVER-WHELMED.
HEW!
AVES IS BEHIND 2-0. ONE MORE STRIKE AND HE'S TOAST!
AGH! THIS BIG BLACK LOG THINKS HE'S GOT ME BEAT!!
THAT'S IT! GOTTA DROP ALL DA NUTS ON THIS ONE!
ENOUGH, I MUST BREAK THIS TEAM RIGHT HERE BY BREAKING ITS LEADER...
INVISIBLE SNAKE SHOT.

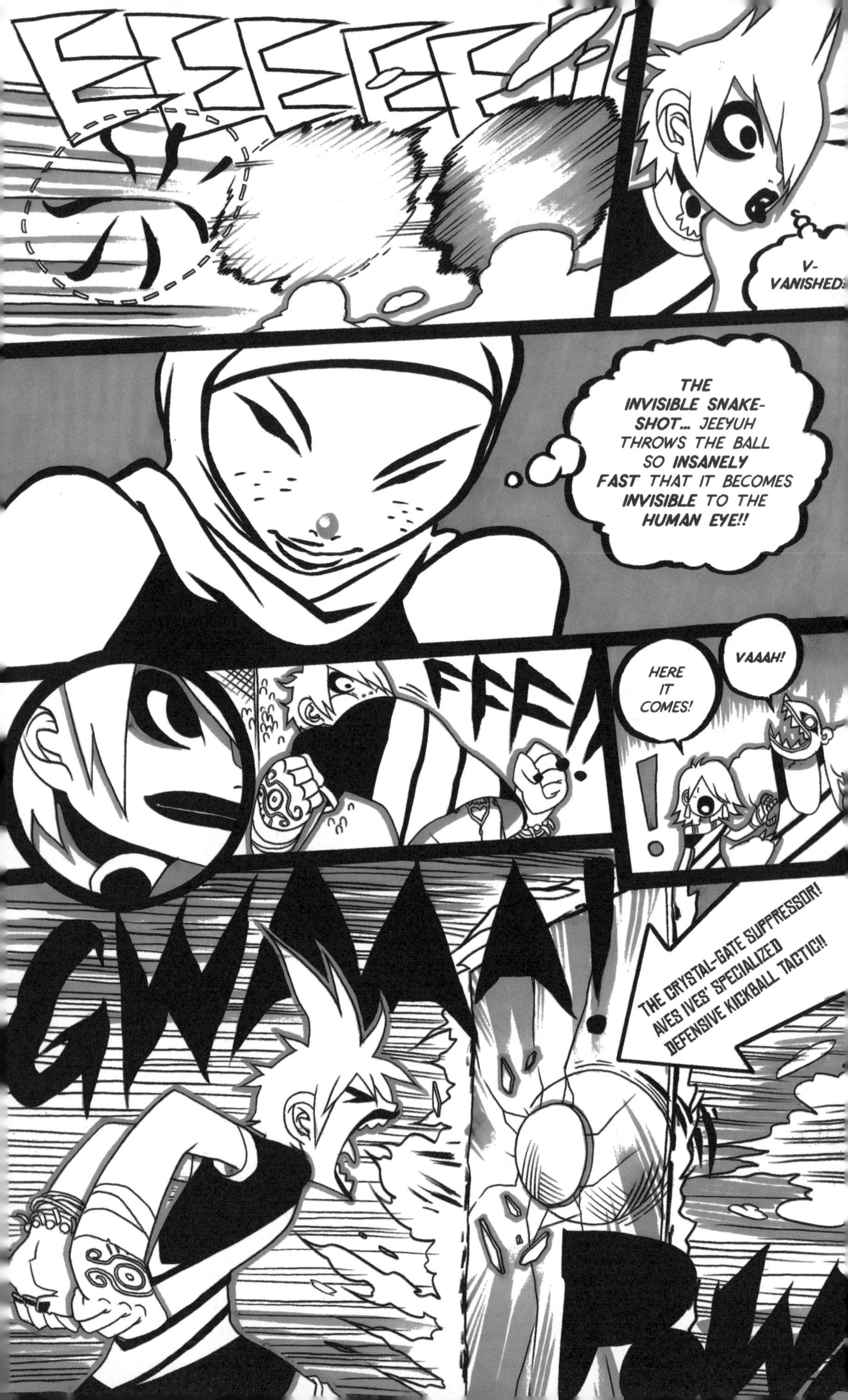
EEEEEEE!!
V-VANISHED!
THE INVISIBLE SNAKE-SHOT... JEEYUH THROWS THE BALL SO INSANELY FAST THAT IT BECOMES INVISIBLE TO THE HUMAN EYE!!
FFF!!
HERE IT COMES!
VAAAH!
GWAAAA!
THE CRYSTAL-GATE SUPPRESSOR! AVES IVES' SPECIALIZED DEFENSIVE KICKBALL TACTIC!!

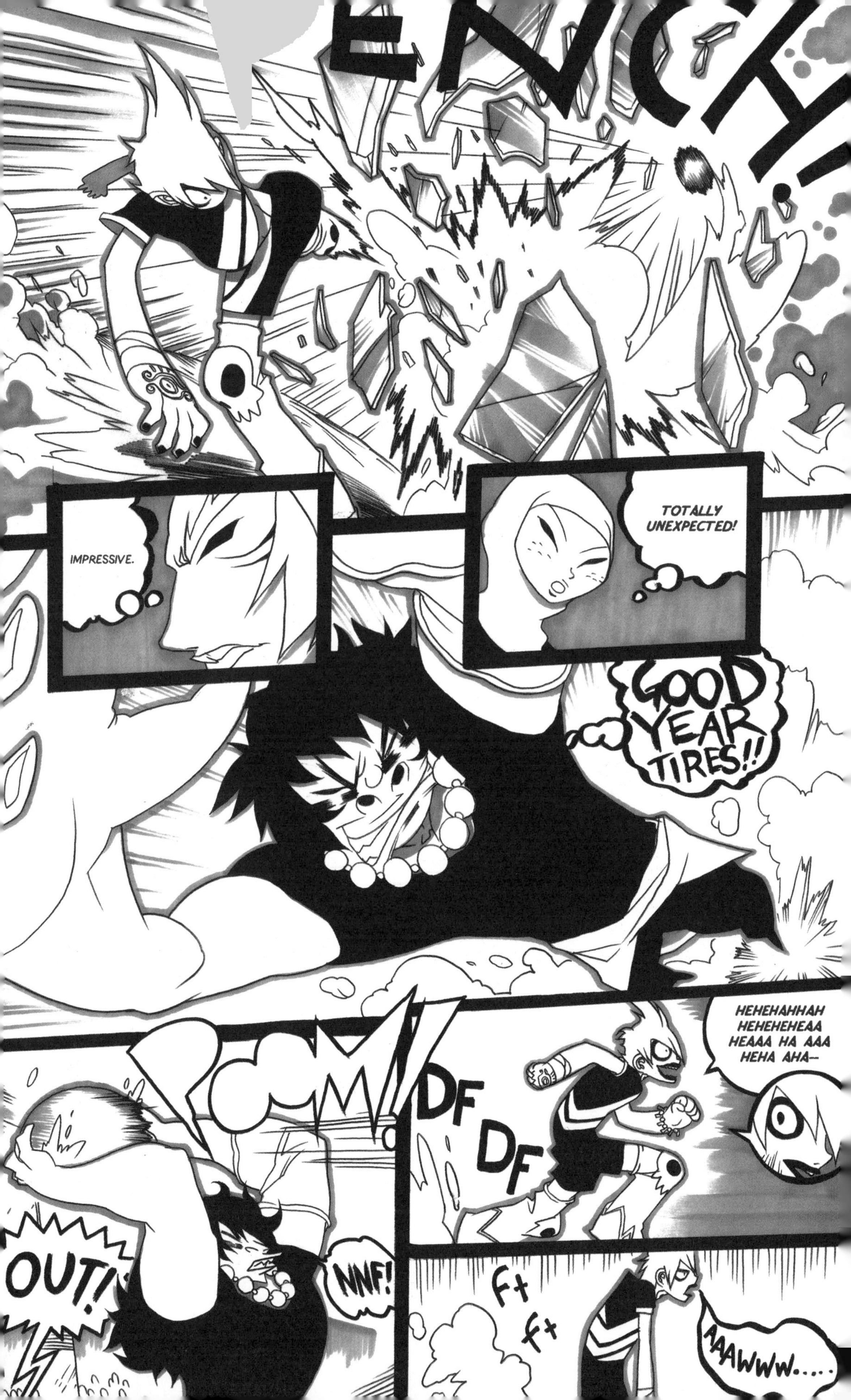
ENCH!
IMPRESSIVE.
TOTALLY UNEXPECTED!
GOOD YEAR TIRES!!
FOOM!
OUT!
NNF!
DF DF
HEHEHAHHAH HEHEHEHEAA HEAAA HA AAA HEHA AHA--
ft ft
AAAWWW.....

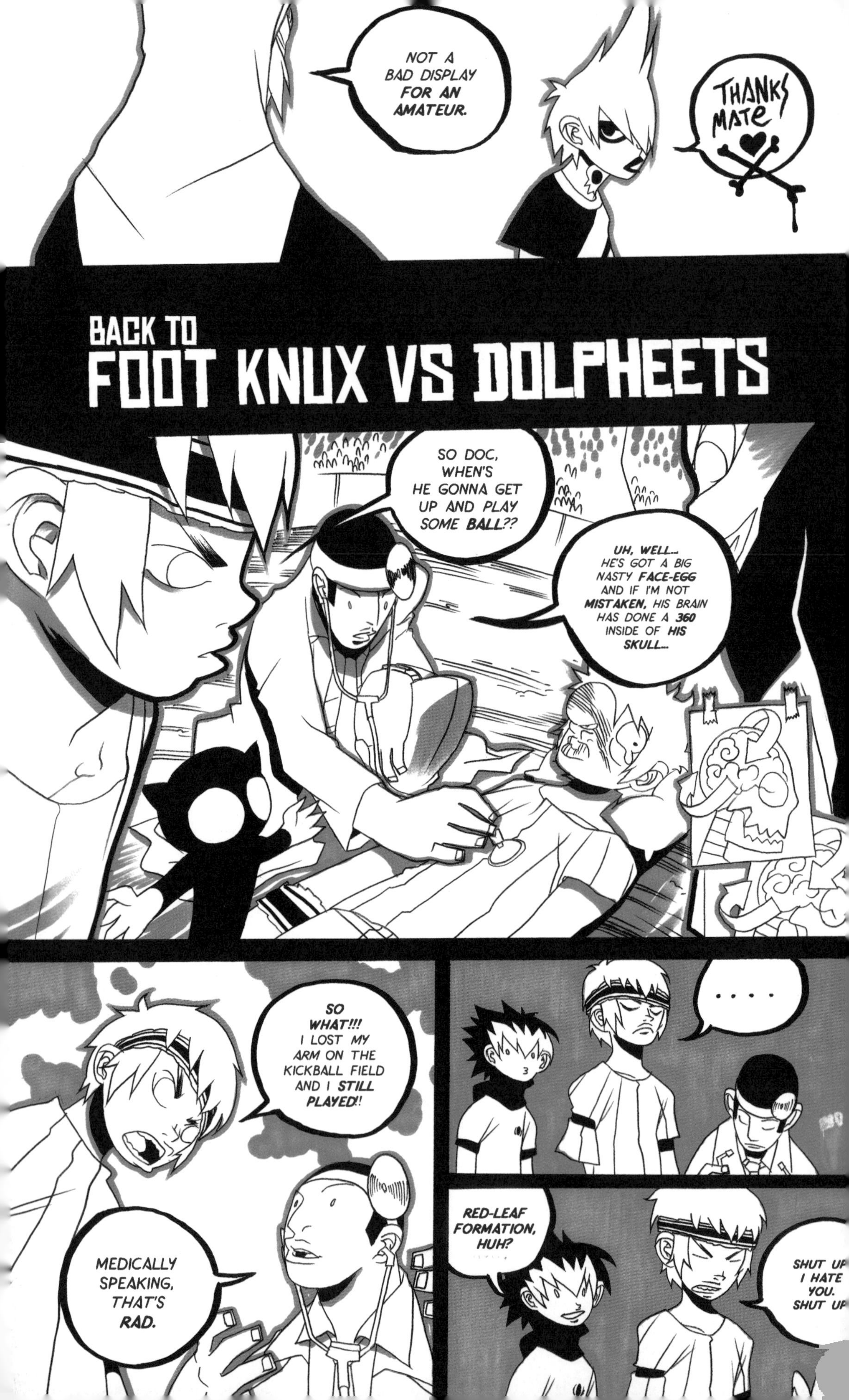
NOT A BAD DISPLAY FOR AN AMATEUR.
THANKS MATE
BACK TO
FOOT KNUX VS DOLPHEETS
SO DOC, WHEN'S HE GONNA GET UP AND PLAY SOME BALL??
UH, WELL... HE'S GOT A BIG NASTY FACE-EGG AND IF I'M NOT MISTAKEN, HIS BRAIN HAS DONE A 360 INSIDE OF HIS SKULL...
SO WHAT!!! I LOST MY ARM ON THE KICKBALL FIELD AND I STILL PLAYED!!
MEDICALLY SPEAKING, THAT'S RAD.
.....
RED-LEAF FORMATION, HUH?
SHUT UP I HATE YOU. SHUT UP

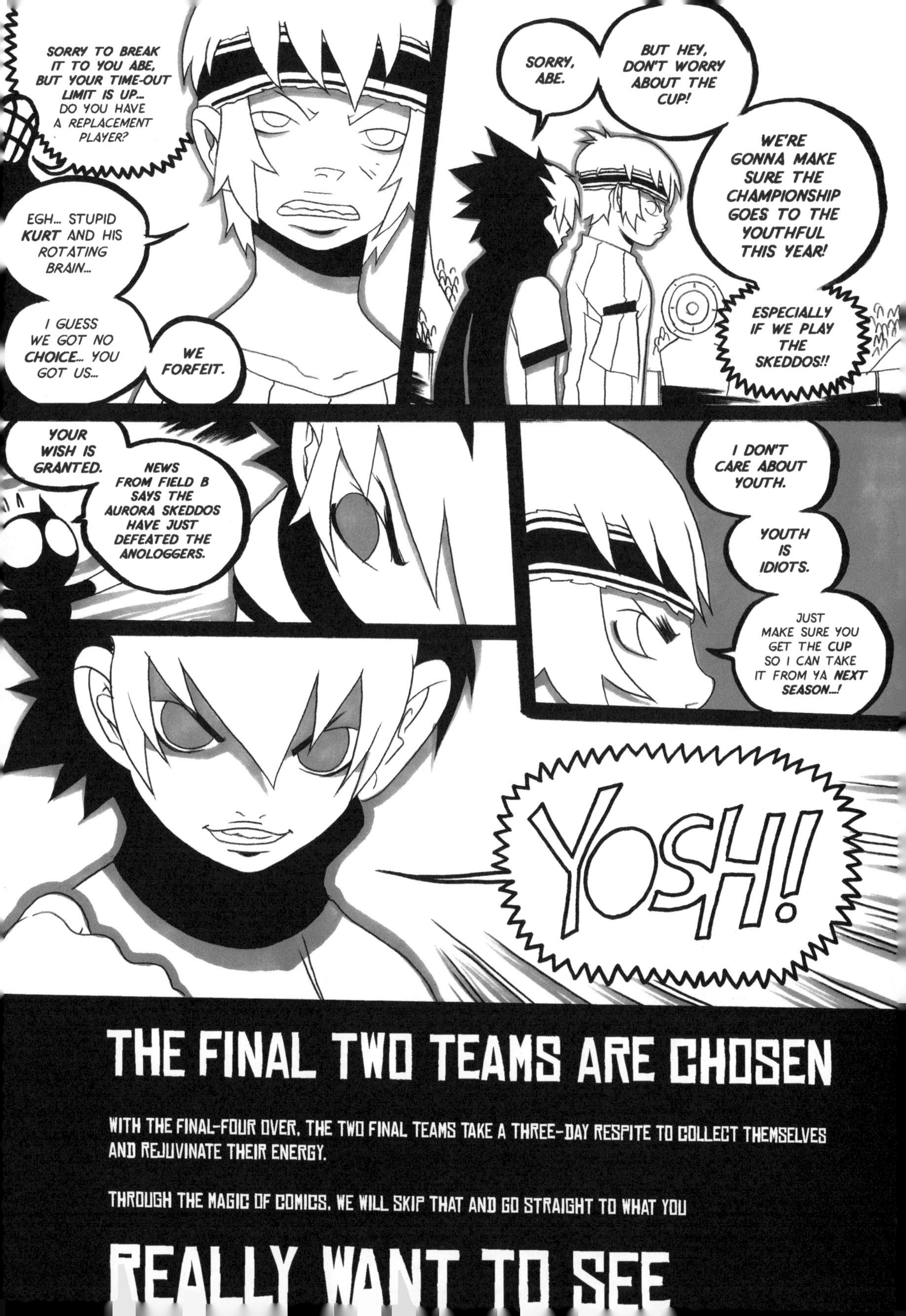
SORRY TO BREAK IT TO YOU ABE, BUT YOUR TIME-OUT LIMIT IS UP... DO YOU HAVE A REPLACEMENT PLAYER?
EGH... STUPID KURT AND HIS ROTATING BRAIN...
I GUESS WE GOT NO CHOICE... YOU GOT US...
WE FORFEIT.
SORRY, ABE.
BUT HEY, DON'T WORRY ABOUT THE CUP!
WE'RE GONNA MAKE SURE THE CHAMPIONSHIP GOES TO THE YOUTHFUL THIS YEAR!
ESPECIALLY IF WE PLAY THE SKEDDOS!!
YOUR WISH IS GRANTED.
NEWS FROM FIELD B SAYS THE AURORA SKEDDOS HAVE JUST DEFEATED THE ANOLOGGERS.
I DON'T CARE ABOUT YOUTH.
YOUTH IS IDIOTS.
JUST MAKE SURE YOU GET THE CUP SO I CAN TAKE IT FROM YA NEXT SEASON...!
YOSH!

THE FINAL TWO TEAMS ARE CHOSEN

WITH THE FINAL-FOUR OVER, THE TWO FINAL TEAMS TAKE A THREE-DAY RESPITE TO COLLECT THEMSELVES AND REJUVINATE THEIR ENERGY.

THROUGH THE MAGIC OF COMICS, WE WILL SKIP THAT AND GO STRAIGHT TO WHAT YOU

REALLY WANT TO SEE

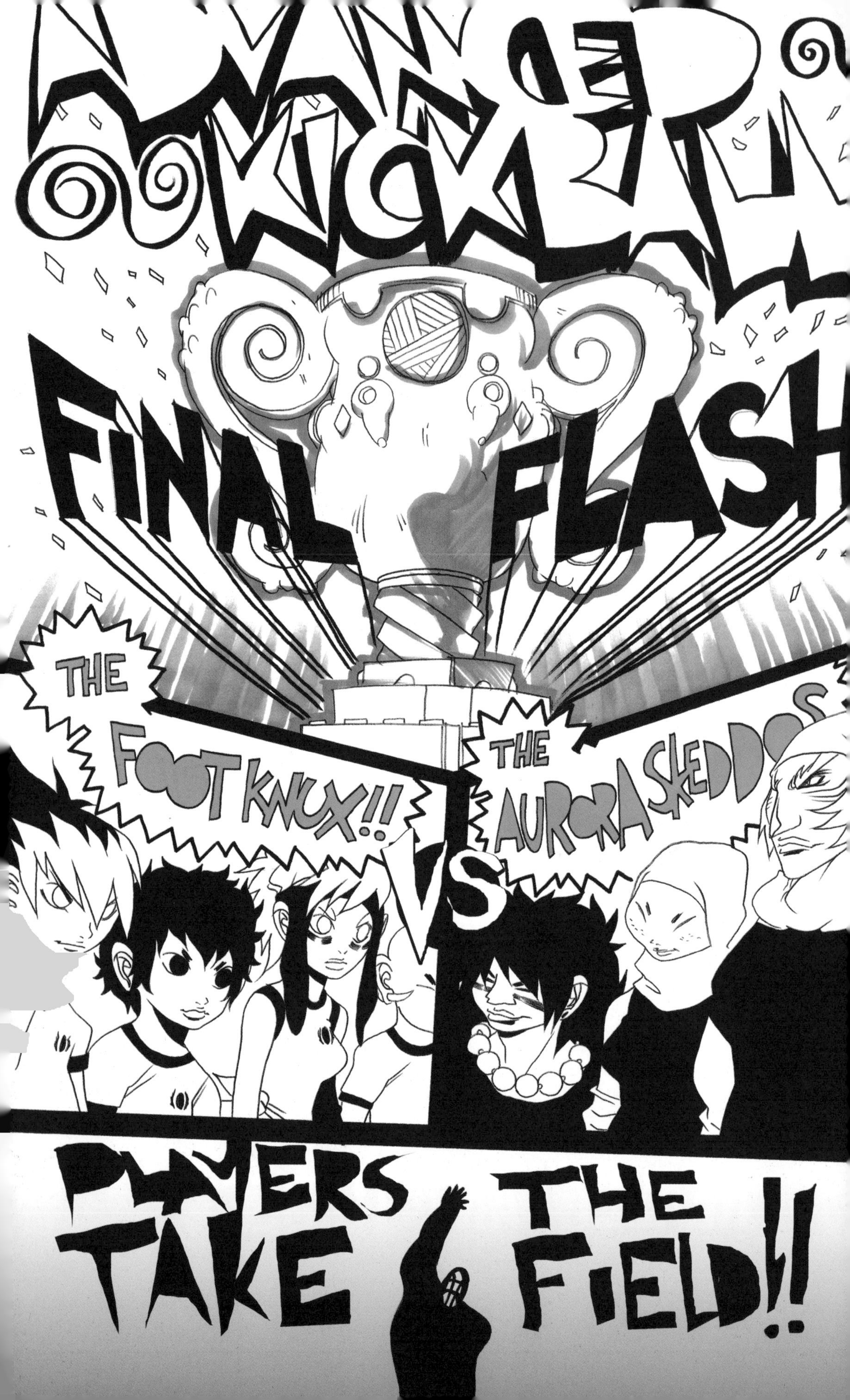
FINAL FLASH
THE
FOOT KNUX!!
VS
THE
AURORA SKEDDOS
PLAYERS TAKE THE FIELD!!

ANTICIPATION COMPARABLE TO TWELVE-TON ATOMIC ROCKETS JETTISONS A PAYLOAD OF PRE-ACTION-STIMULUS UPON ALL 450,000 SLO-MOZ ADJUSTED HUMAN HEADS WITHIN COASTALVANIA STADIUM.

INCLUDED IN THE HEAD COUNT ARE THE 12 CRANIUMS OF EACH FOOT KNUX AND AURORA SKEDDO PLAYER. NO ONE IS EXEMPT FROM THIS MAGICAL HAPPENING.

THEY EACH TAKE A BRIEF SCAN OF THE SITUATION. THEY REMEMBER WHAT IT TOOK TO COME THIS FAR.

THEY SLIP INTO THE ZONE. THEY ARE ZONED.

FEP! FEP!

FIRST KICK; GLEFF SHUJO OF THE AROURA SKEDDOS!

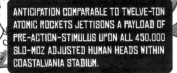

KRAK!

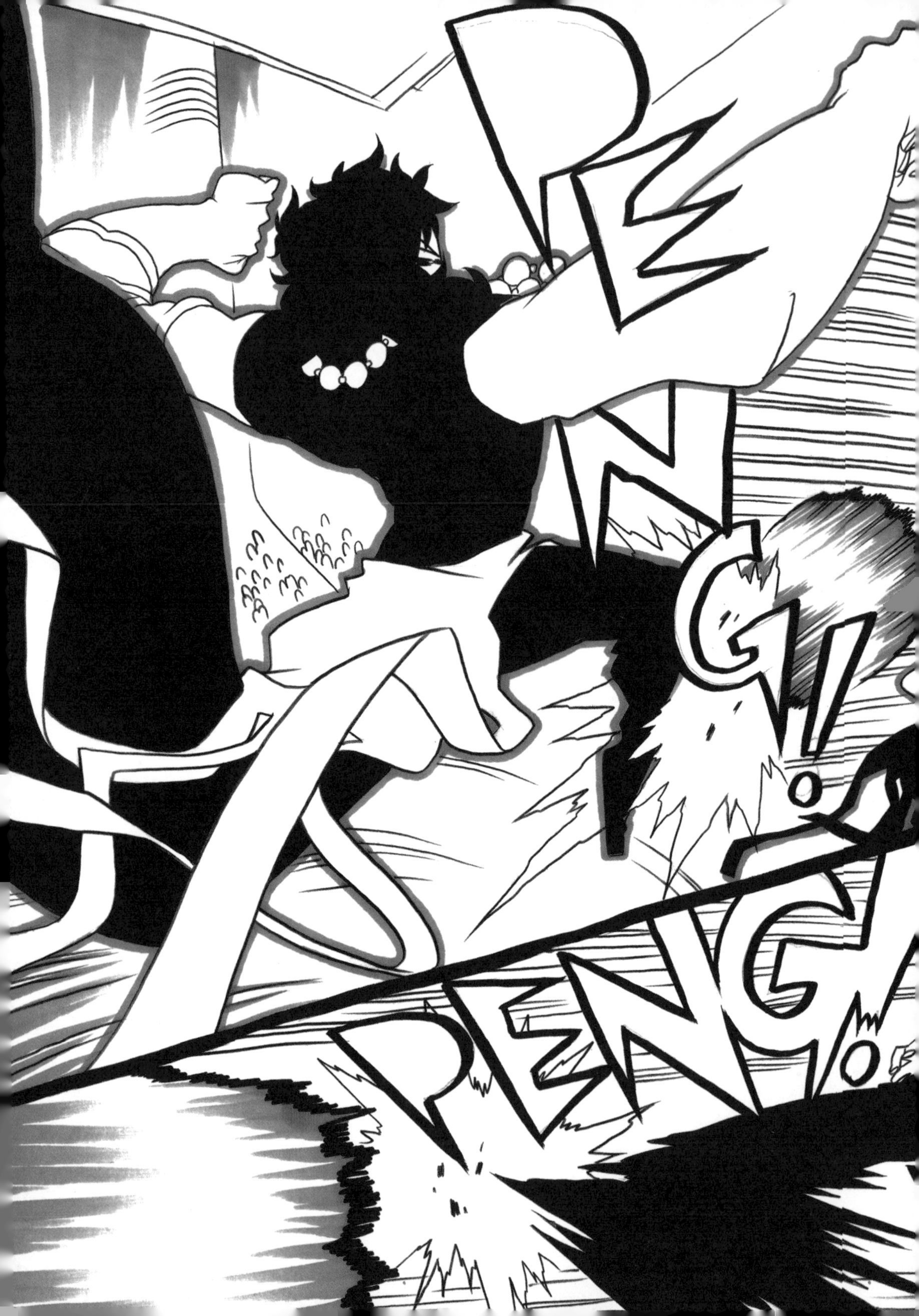
PENG!!
PENG!

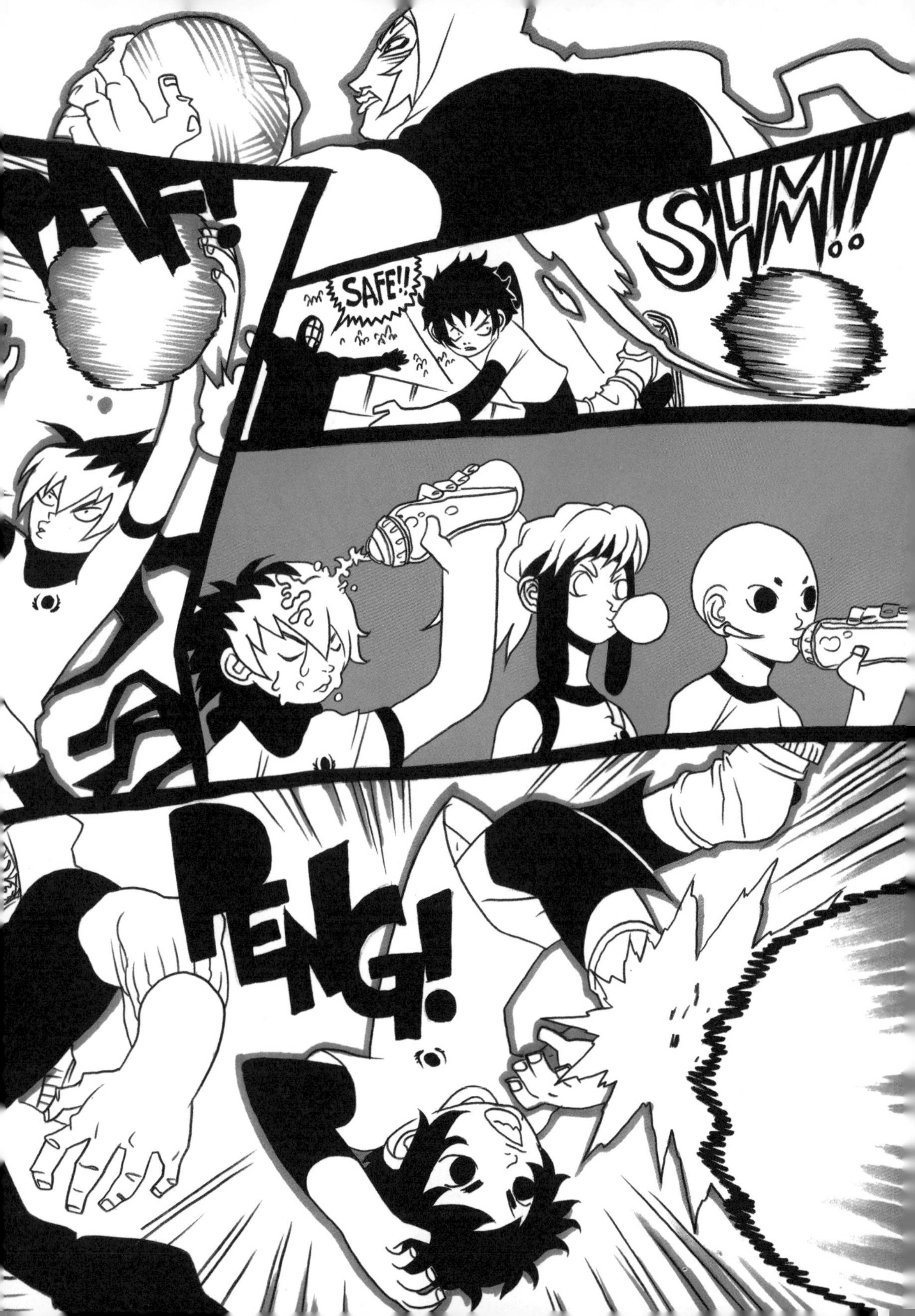
PAF!
SWM!!
SAFE!!
PENG!

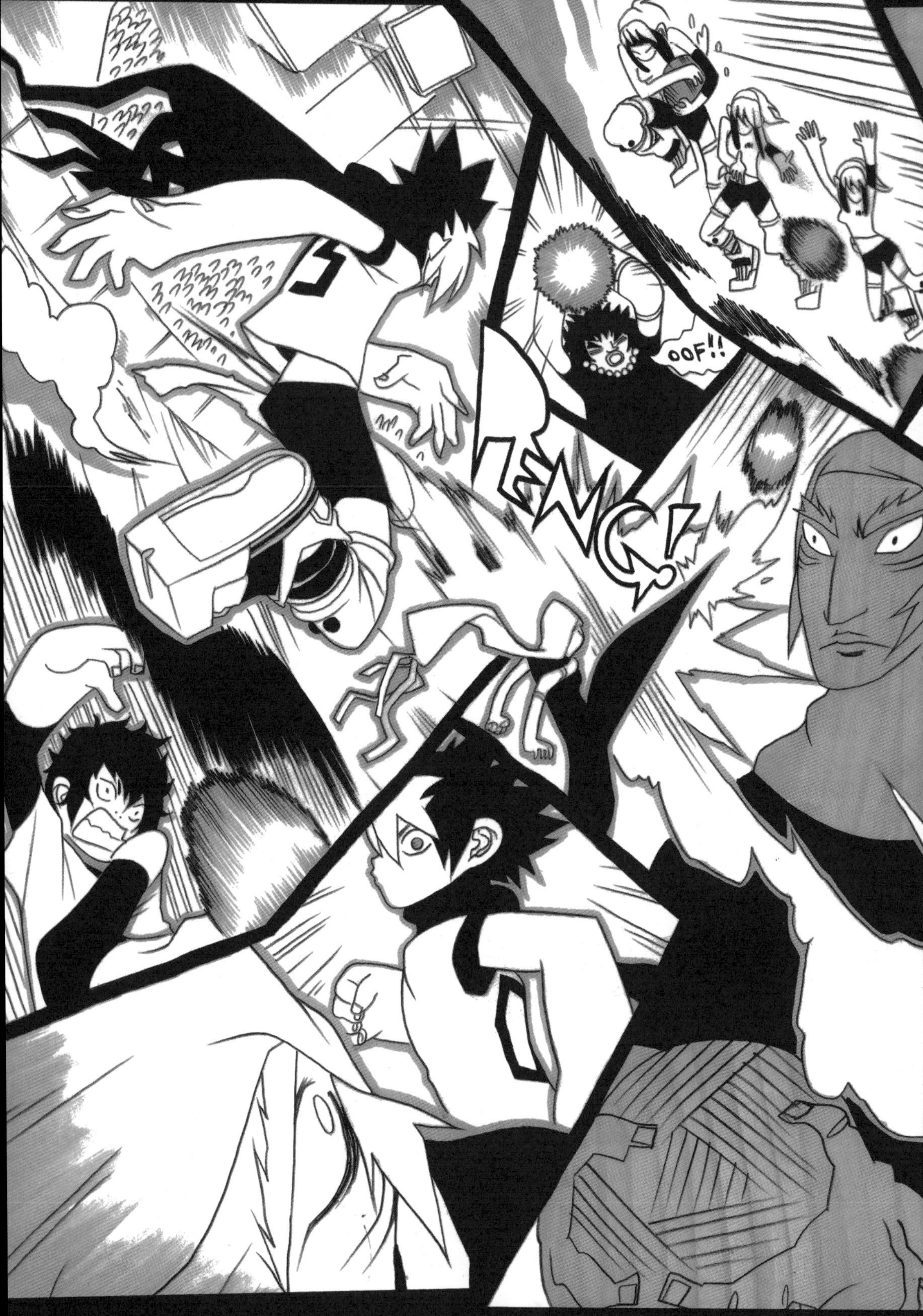
OOF!!

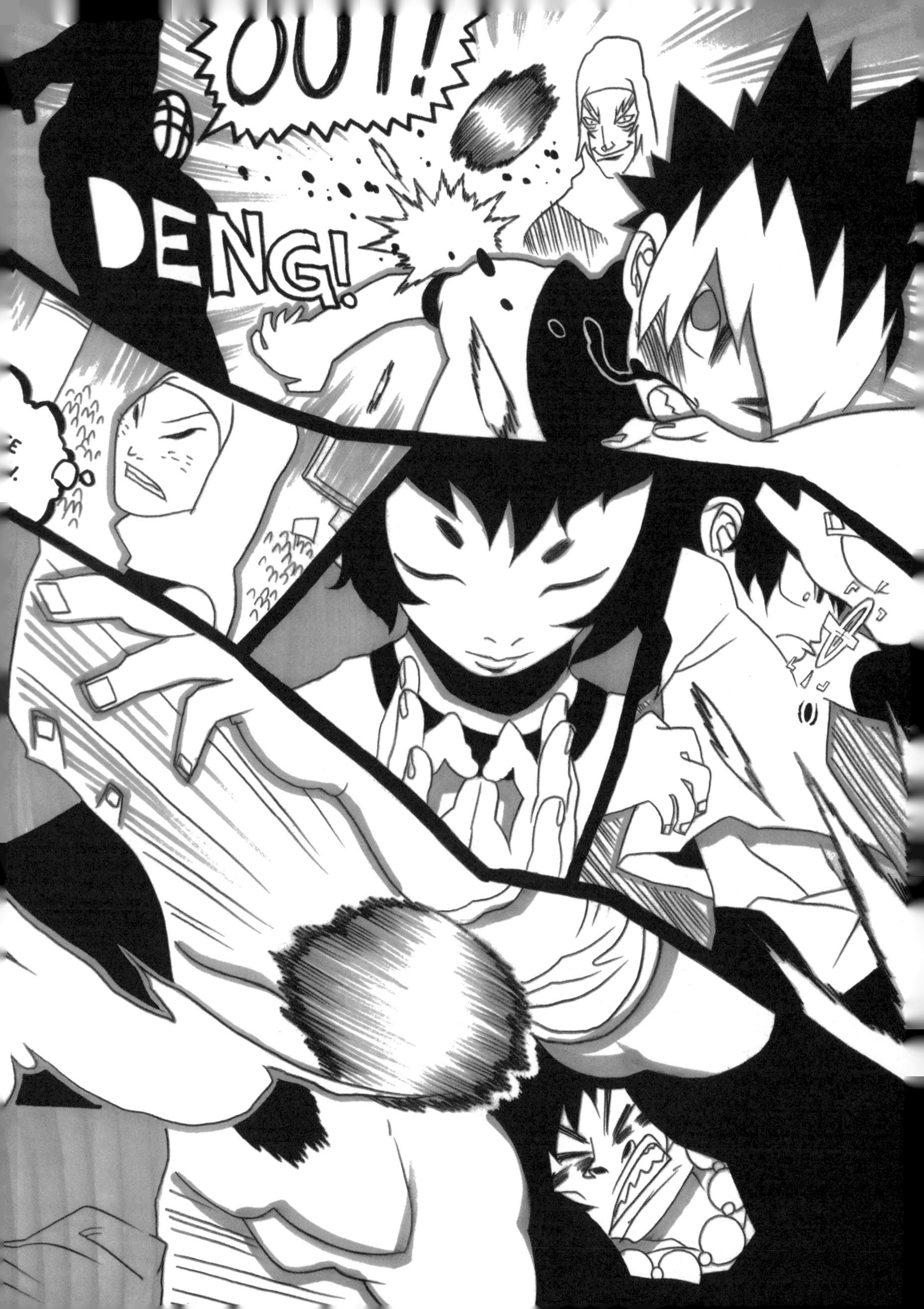
OUT!
DENG!

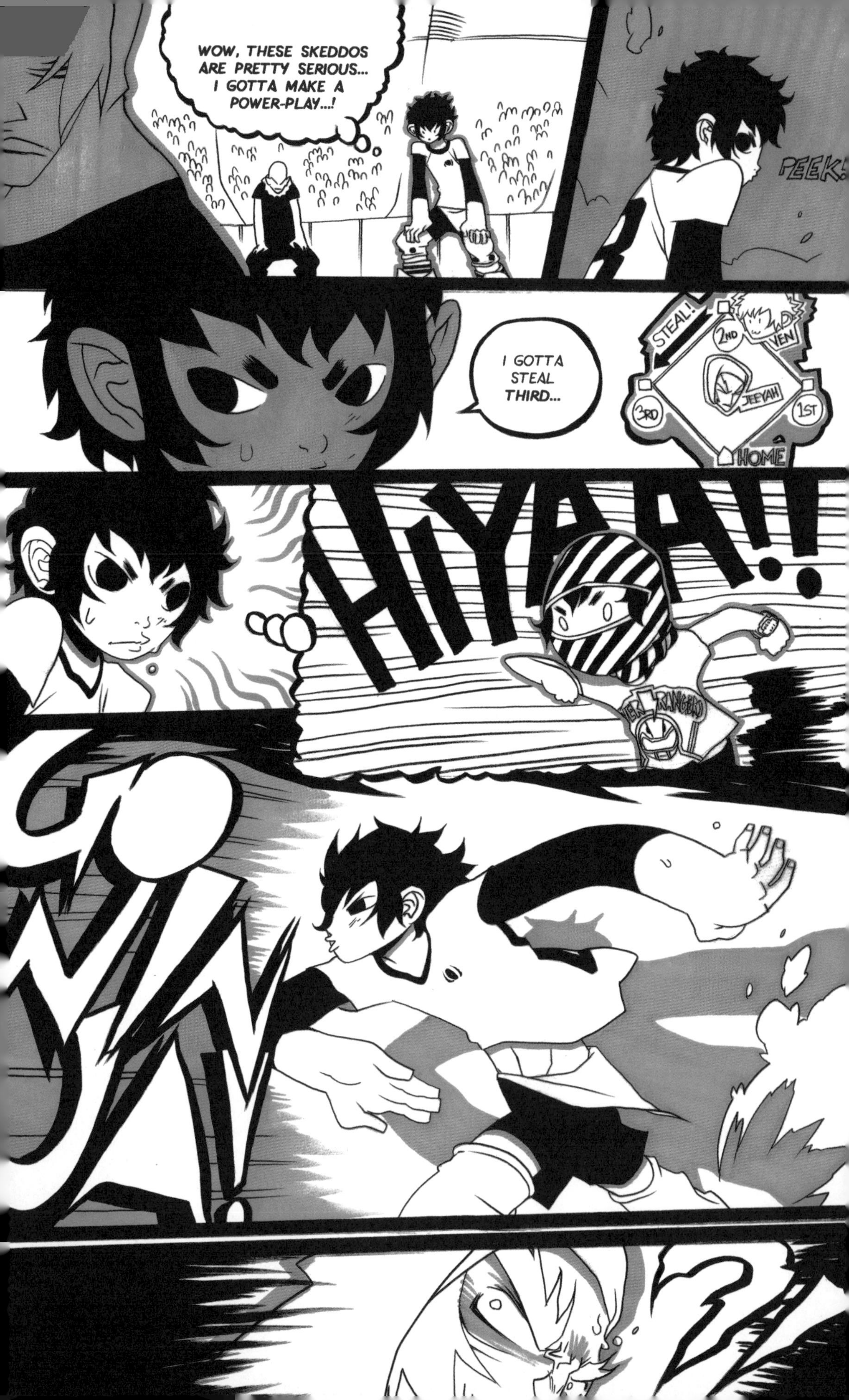
WOW, THESE SKEDDOS ARE PRETTY SERIOUS... I GOTTA MAKE A POWER-PLAY...!
PEEK!
I GOTTA STEAL THIRD...
STEAL!
2ND
VEN
JEEYAH
3RD
1ST
HOME
HIYAA!!

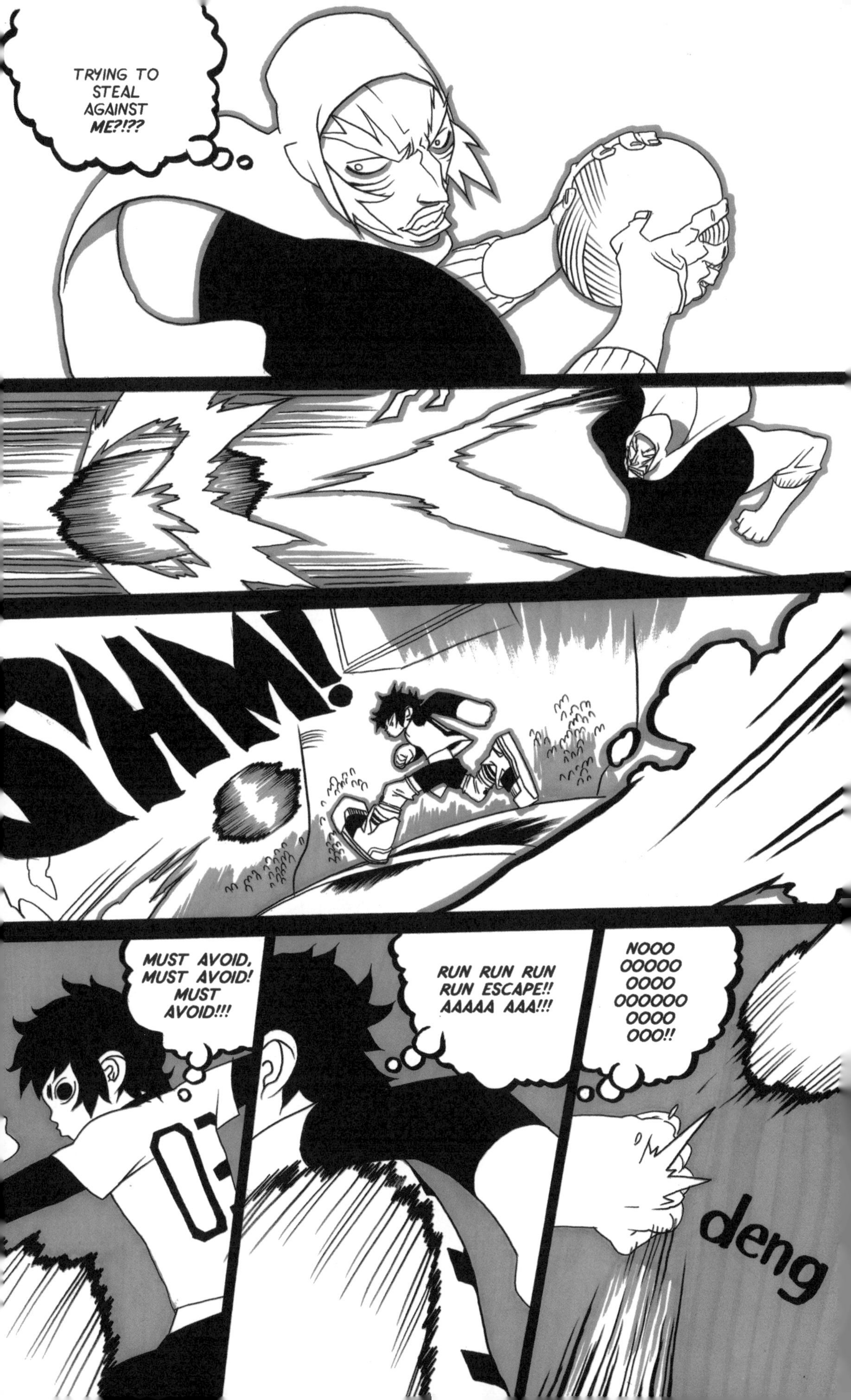
TRYING TO STEAL AGAINST ME?!??
MUST AVOID, MUST AVOID! MUST AVOID!!!
RUN RUN RUN RUN ESCAPE!! AAAAA AAA!!!
NOOO OOOOO OOOO OOOOOO OOOO OOO!!
deng

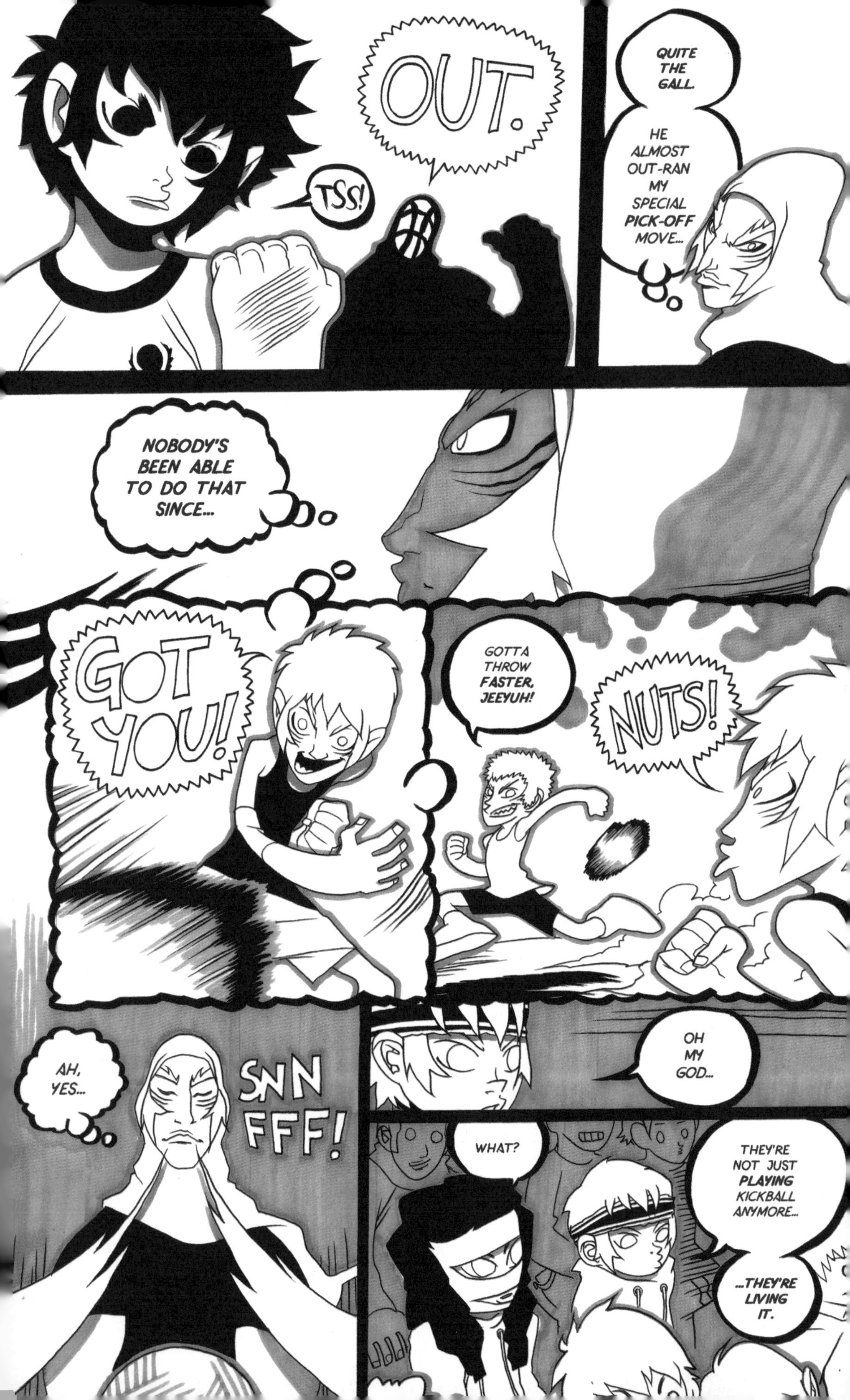
OUT.
TSS!
QUITE THE GALL.
HE ALMOST OUT-RAN MY SPECIAL PICK-OFF MOVE...
NOBODY'S BEEN ABLE TO DO THAT SINCE...
GOT YOU!
GOTTA THROW FASTER, JEEYUH!
NUTS!
AH, YES...
SNN FFF!
OH MY GOD...
WHAT?
THEY'RE NOT JUST PLAYING KICKBALL ANYMORE...
...THEY'RE LIVING IT.

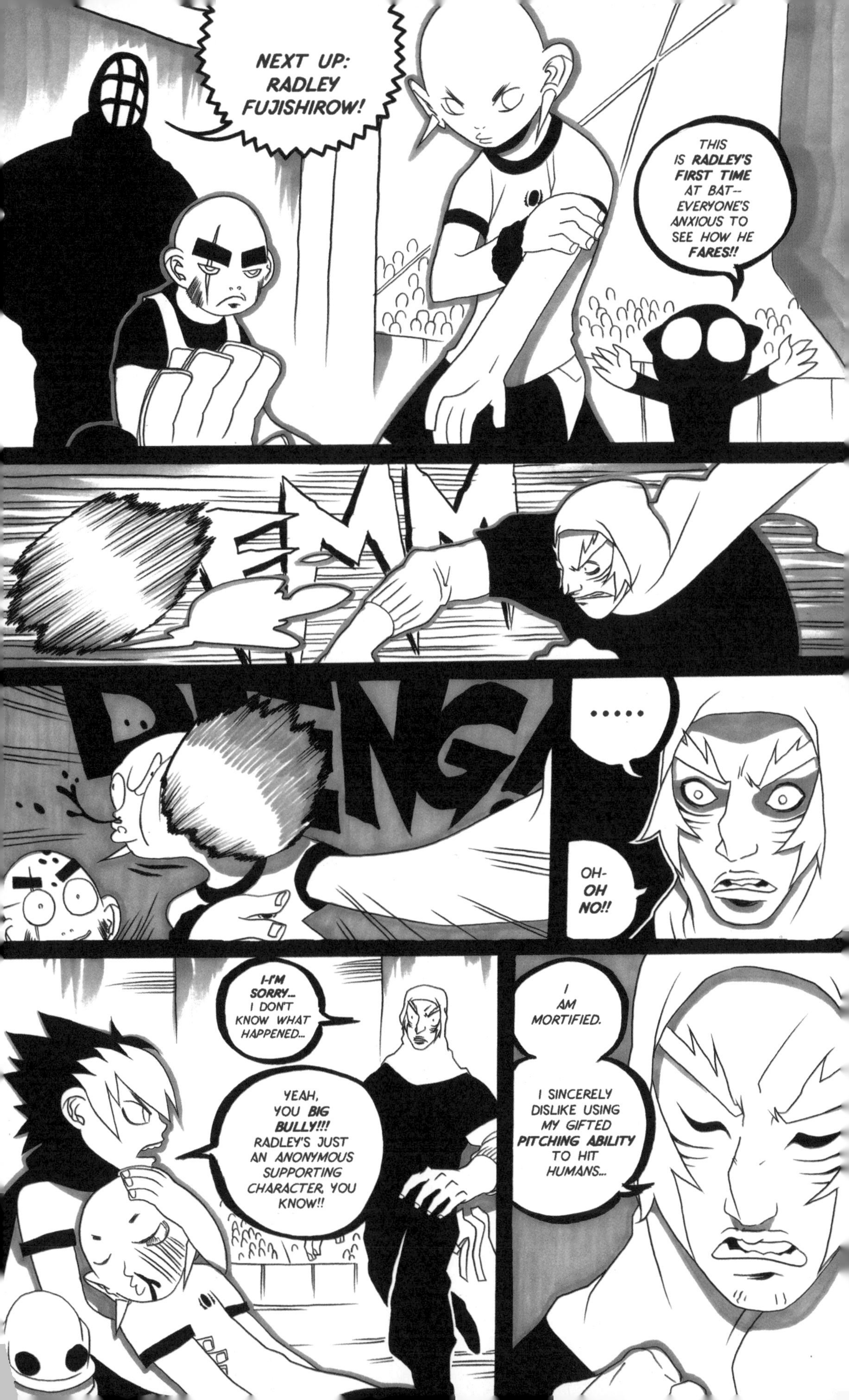
NEXT UP: RADLEY FUJISHIROW!
THIS IS RADLEY'S FIRST TIME AT BAT-- EVERYONE'S ANXIOUS TO SEE HOW HE FARES!!
.....
OH- OH NO!!
I-I'M SORRY... I DON'T KNOW WHAT HAPPENED...
YEAH, YOU BIG BULLY!!! RADLEY'S JUST AN ANONYMOUS SUPPORTING CHARACTER, YOU KNOW!!
I AM MORTIFIED.
I SINCERELY DISLIKE USING MY GIFTED PITCHING ABILITY TO HIT HUMANS...

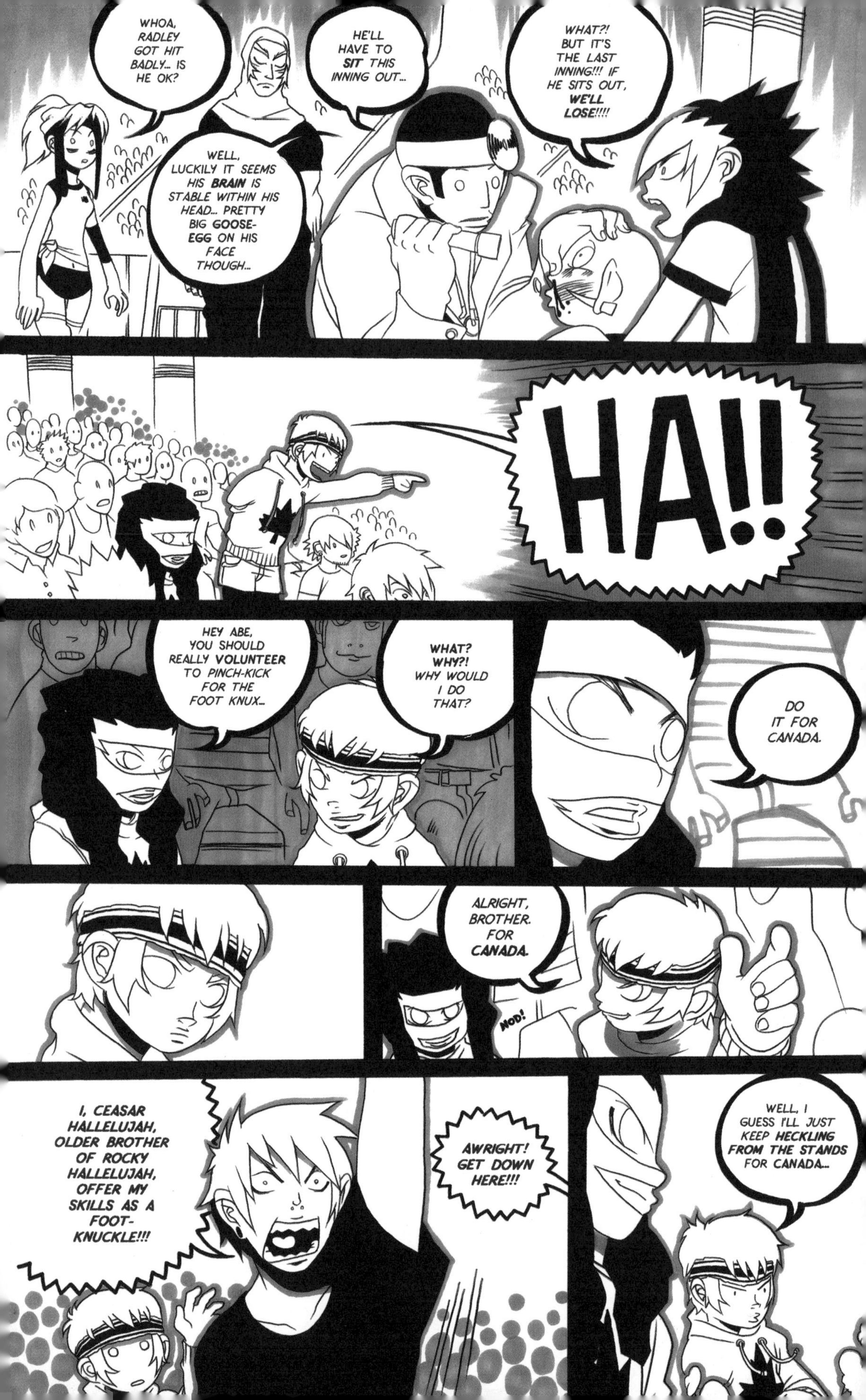
WHOA, RADLEY GOT HIT BADLY... IS HE OK?
HE'LL HAVE TO SIT THIS INNING OUT...
WELL, LUCKILY IT SEEMS HIS BRAIN IS STABLE WITHIN HIS HEAD... PRETTY BIG GOOSE-EGG ON HIS FACE THOUGH...
WHAT?! BUT IT'S THE LAST INNING!!! IF HE SITS OUT, WE'LL LOSE!!!!
HA!!
HEY ABE, YOU SHOULD REALLY VOLUNTEER TO PINCH-KICK FOR THE FOOT KNUX...
WHAT? WHY?! WHY WOULD I DO THAT?
DO IT FOR CANADA.
ALRIGHT, BROTHER. FOR CANADA.
NOD!
I, CEASAR HALLELUJAH, OLDER BROTHER OF ROCKY HALLELUJAH, OFFER MY SKILLS AS A FOOT-KNUCKLE!!!
AWRIGHT! GET DOWN HERE!!!
WELL, I GUESS I'LL JUST KEEP HECKLING FROM THE STANDS FOR CANADA...

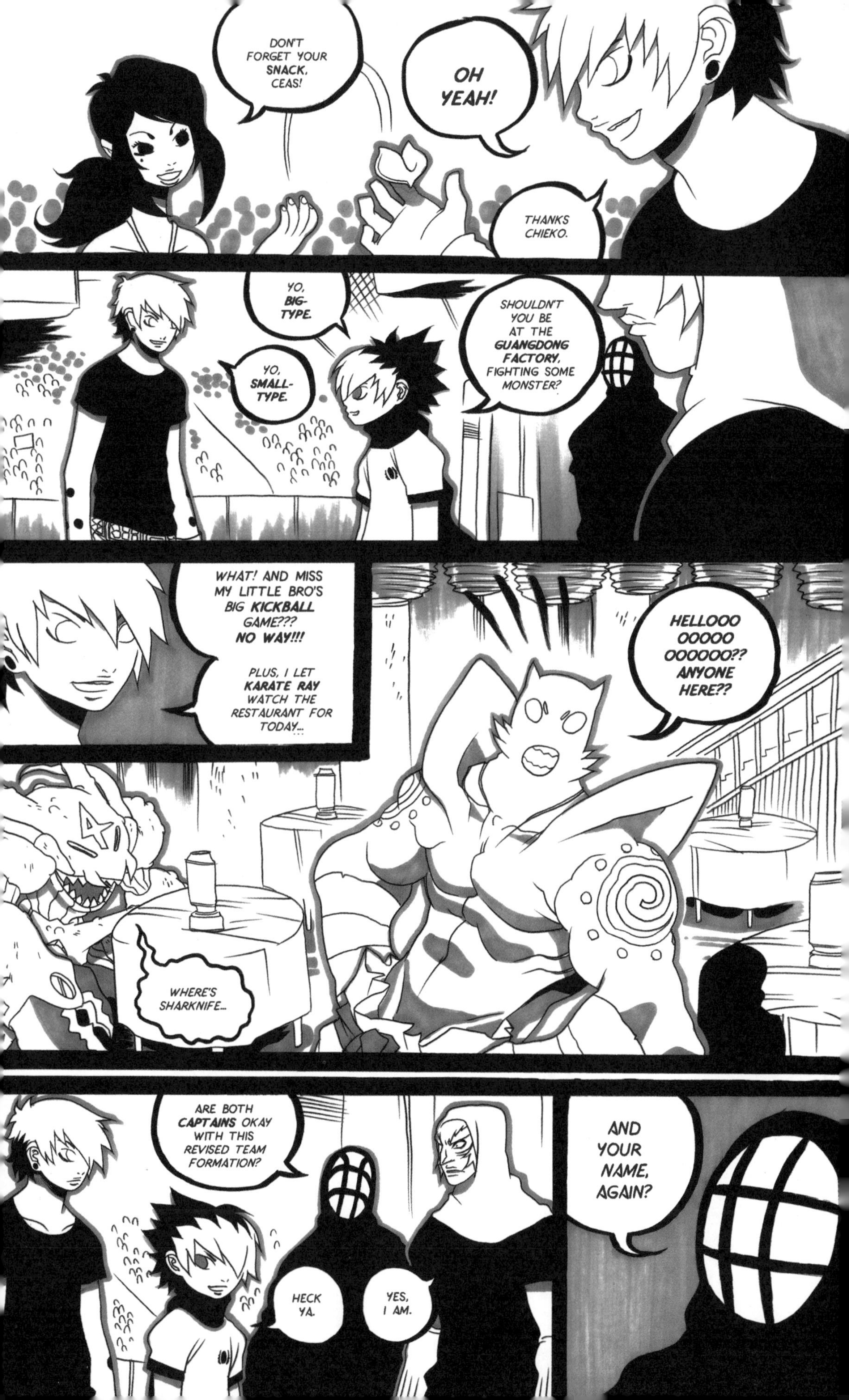
DON'T FORGET YOUR SNACK, CEAS!
OH YEAH!
THANKS CHIEKO.
YO, BIG-TYPE.
YO, SMALL-TYPE.
SHOULDN'T YOU BE AT THE GUANGDONG FACTORY, FIGHTING SOME MONSTER?
WHAT! AND MISS MY LITTLE BRO'S BIG KICKBALL GAME??? NO WAY!!!
PLUS, I LET KARATE RAY WATCH THE RESTAURANT FOR TODAY...
HELLOOO OOOOO OOOOOO?? ANYONE HERE??
WHERE'S SHARKNIFE...
ARE BOTH CAPTAINS OKAY WITH THIS REVISED TEAM FORMATION?
HECK YA.
YES, I AM.
AND YOUR NAME, AGAIN?

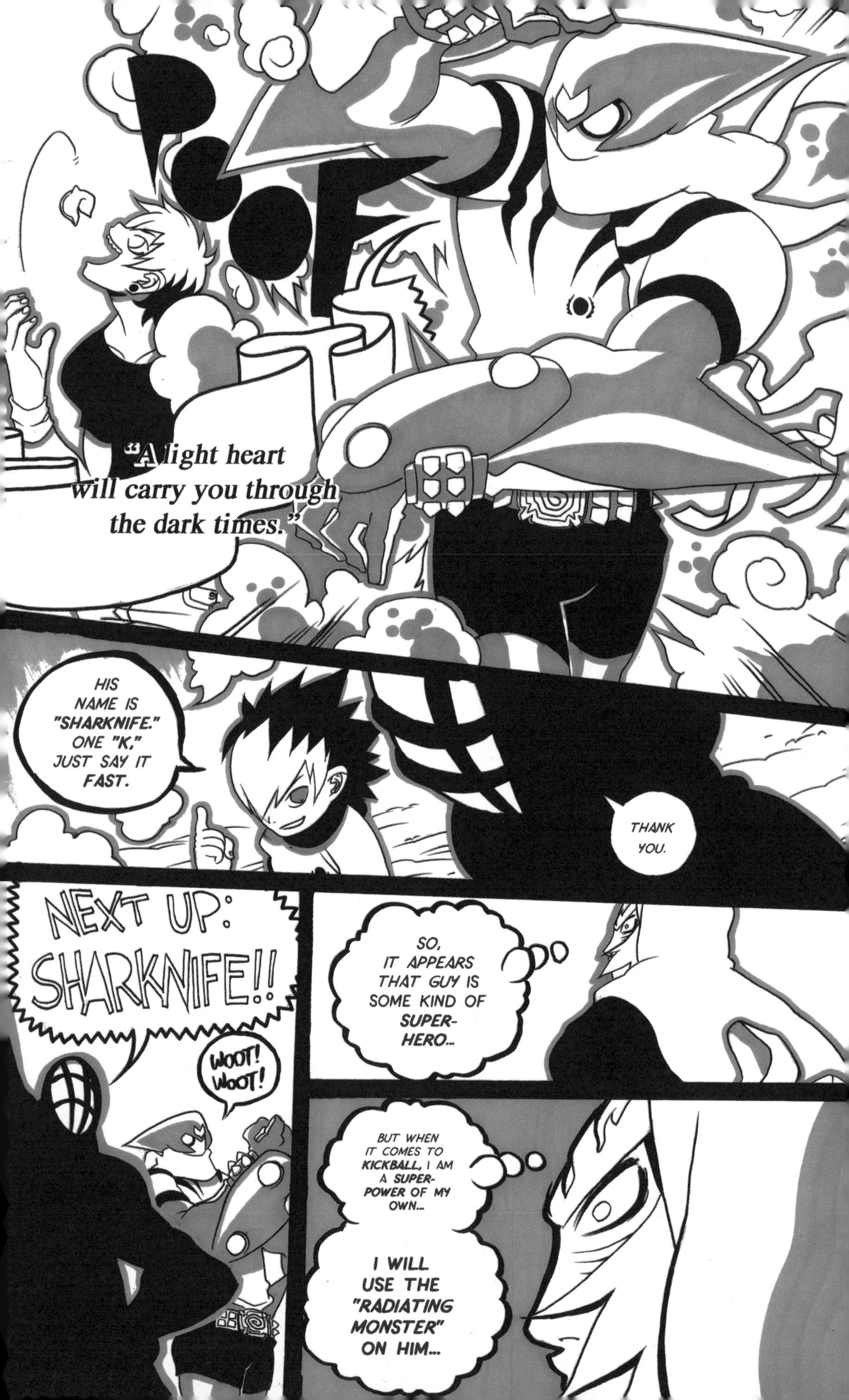
POOF
"A light heart
will carry you through
the dark times."
HIS NAME IS "SHARKNIFE." ONE "K," JUST SAY IT FAST.
THANK YOU.
NEXT UP: SHARKNIFE!!
WOOT! WOOT!
SO, IT APPEARS THAT GUY IS SOME KIND OF SUPER-HERO...
BUT WHEN IT COMES TO KICKBALL, I AM A SUPER-POWER OF MY OWN...
I WILL USE THE "RADIATING MONSTER" ON HIM...

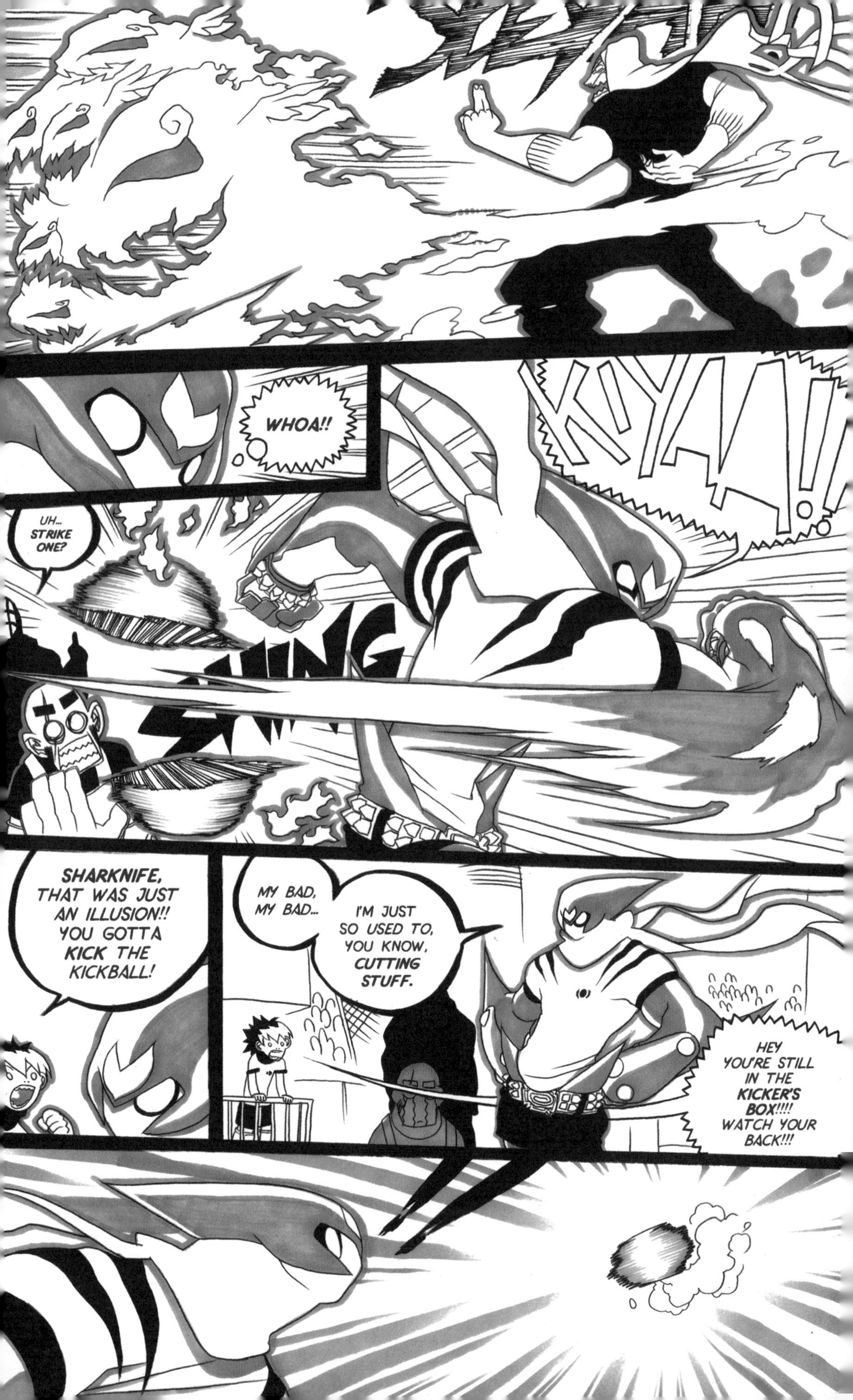
WHOA!!
KIYAA!!
UH... STRIKE ONE?
SHING
SHING
SHARKNIFE, THAT WAS JUST AN ILLUSION!! YOU GOTTA KICK THE KICKBALL!
MY BAD, MY BAD...
I'M JUST SO USED TO, YOU KNOW, CUTTING STUFF.
HEY YOU'RE STILL IN THE KICKER'S BOX!!!! WATCH YOUR BACK!!!

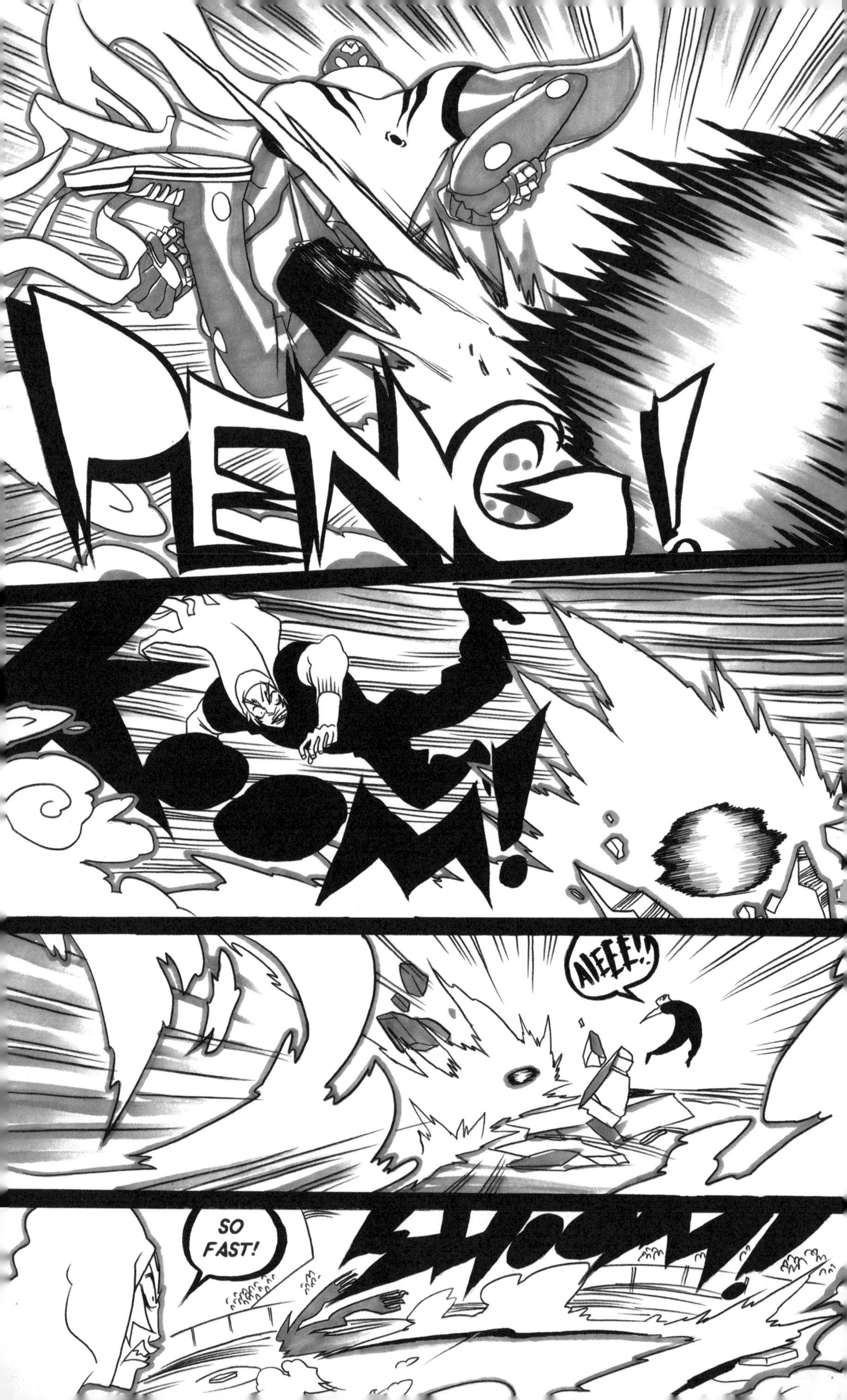
PENG!
KROOM!
AIEEE!
SO FAST!
SHOOM!

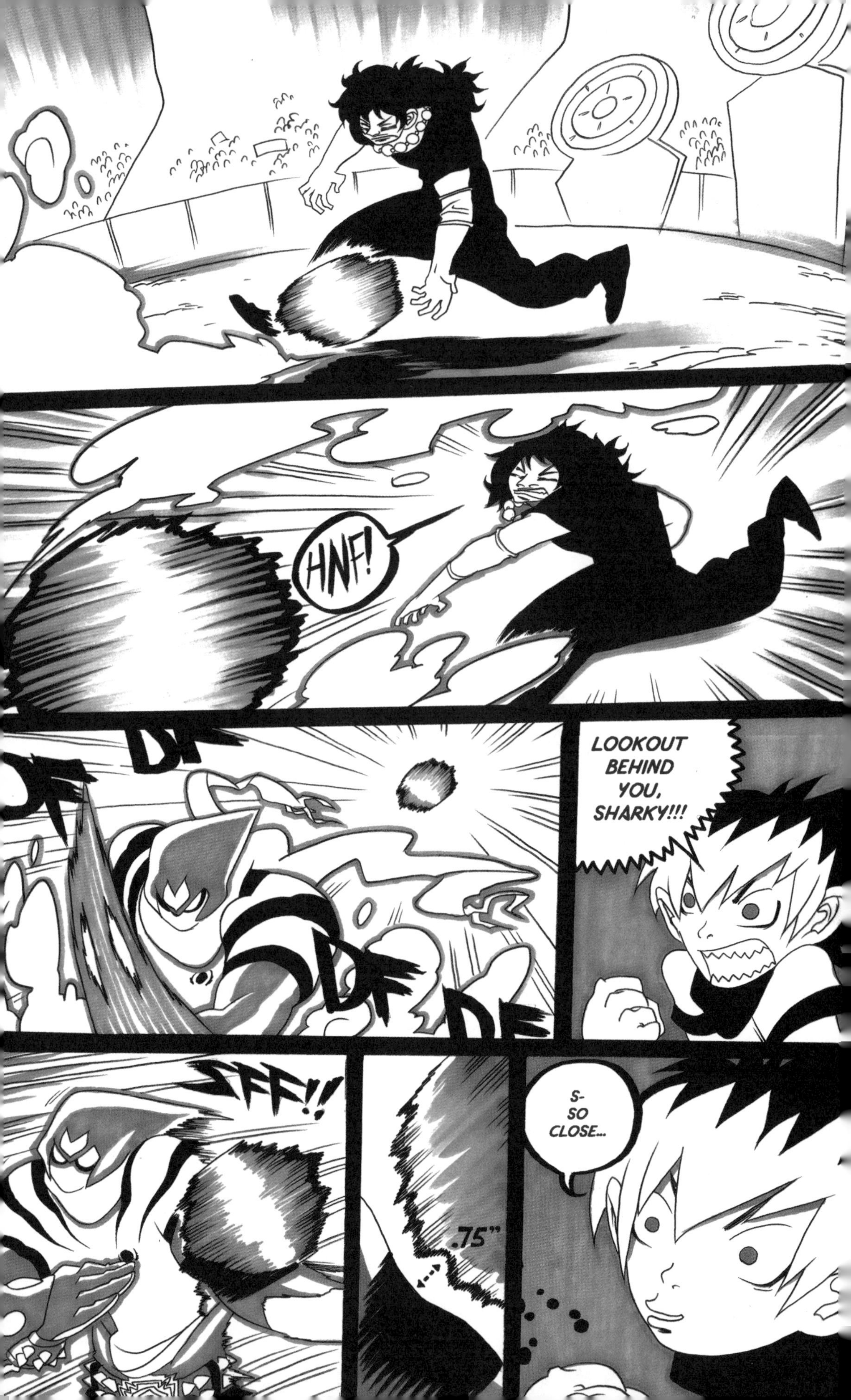
HNF!
LOOKOUT BEHIND YOU, SHARKY!!!
S- SO CLOSE...
.75"

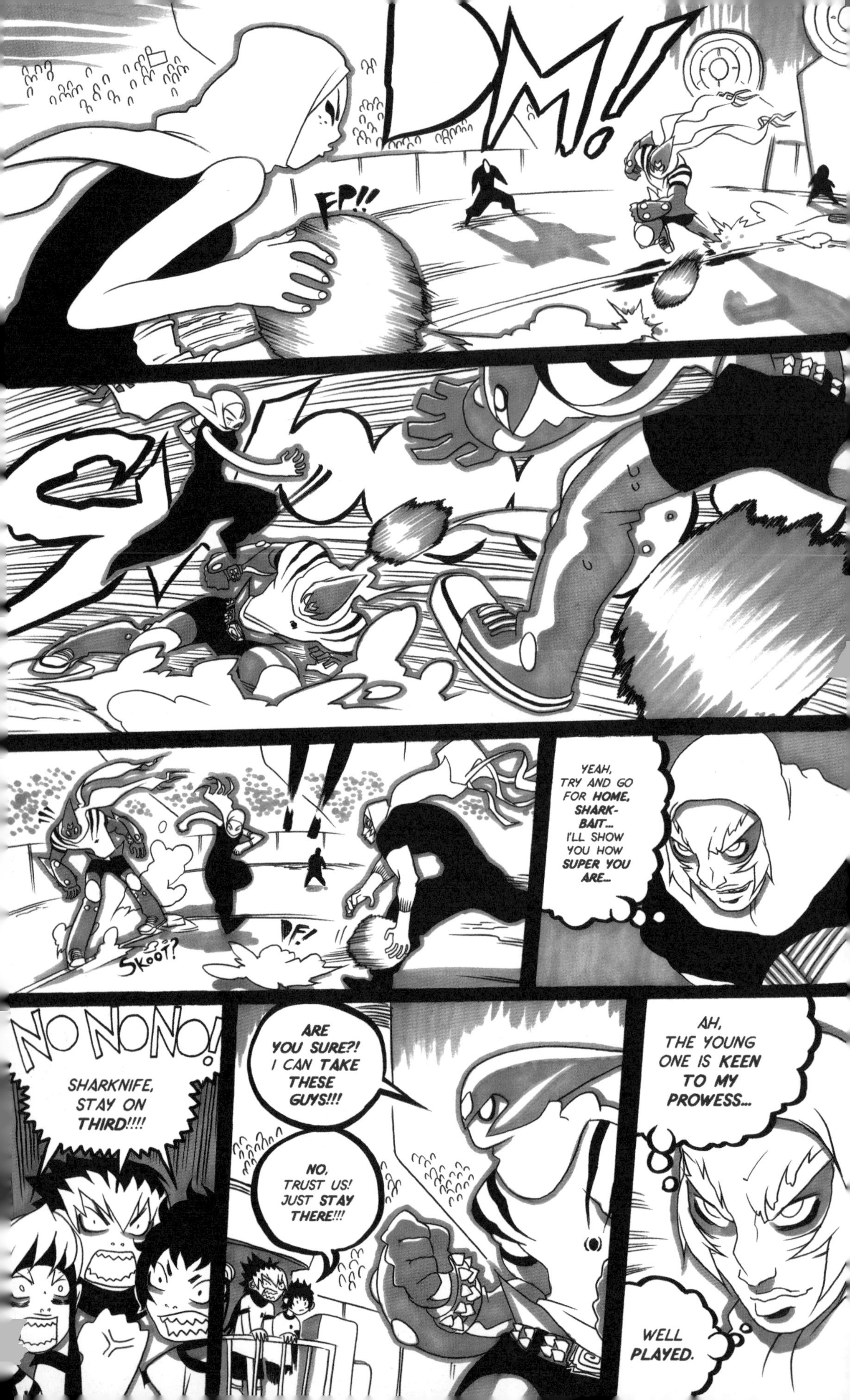
DM!
FP!!
SKOOT?
PF!
YEAH, TRY AND GO FOR HOME, SHARK-BAIT... I'LL SHOW YOU HOW SUPER YOU ARE...
NO NO NO!
SHARKNIFE, STAY ON THIRD!!!!
ARE YOU SURE?! I CAN TAKE THESE GUYS!!!
NO, TRUST US! JUST STAY THERE!!!
AH, THE YOUNG ONE IS KEEN TO MY PROWESS...
WELL PLAYED.

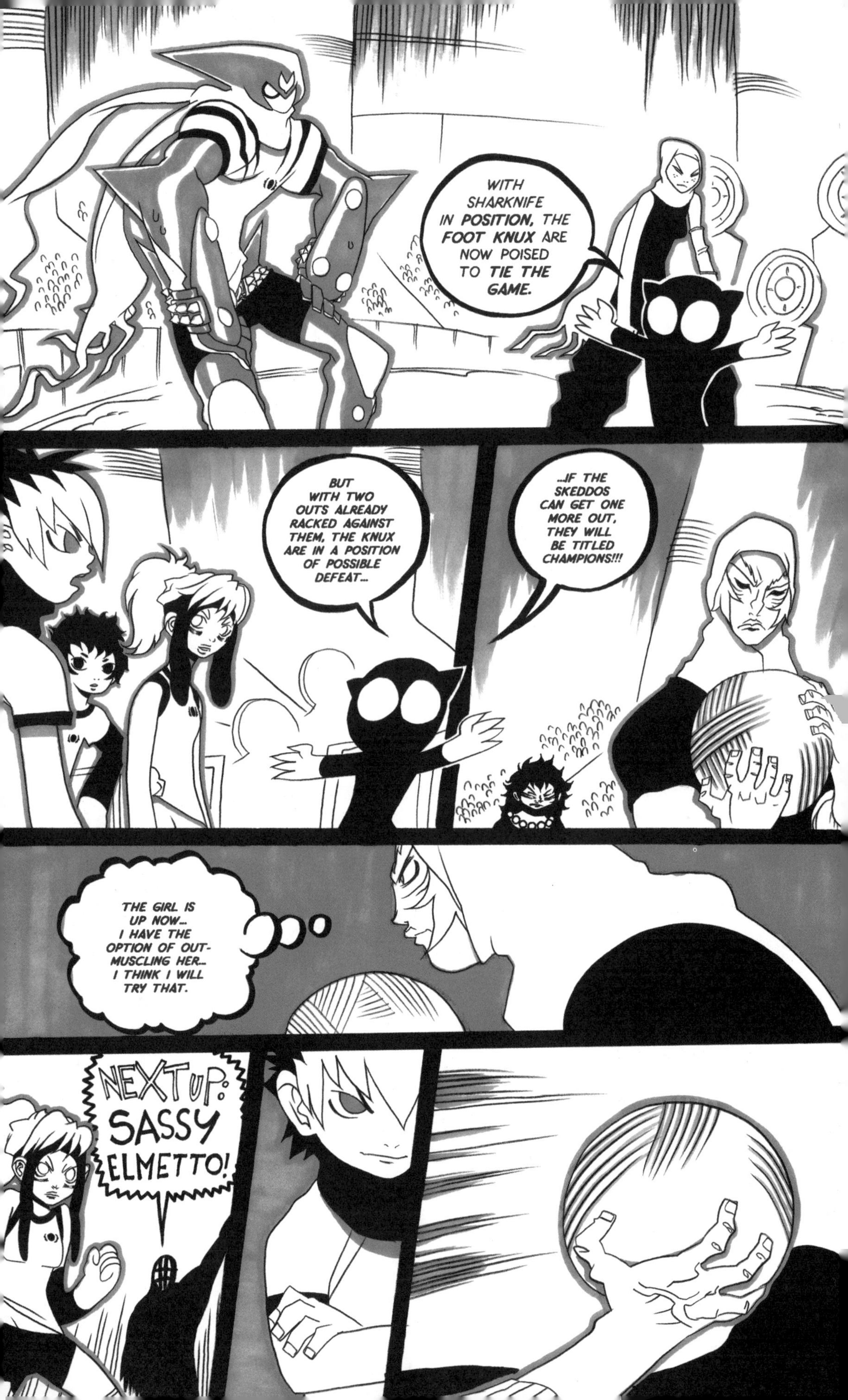
WITH SHARKNIFE IN POSITION, THE FOOT KNUX ARE NOW POISED TO TIE THE GAME.
BUT WITH TWO OUTS ALREADY RACKED AGAINST THEM, THE KNUX ARE IN A POSITION OF POSSIBLE DEFEAT...
...IF THE SKEDDOS CAN GET ONE MORE OUT, THEY WILL BE TITLED CHAMPIONS!!!
THE GIRL IS UP NOW... I HAVE THE OPTION OF OUT-MUSCLING HER... I THINK I WILL TRY THAT.
NEXT UP: SASSY ELMETTO!

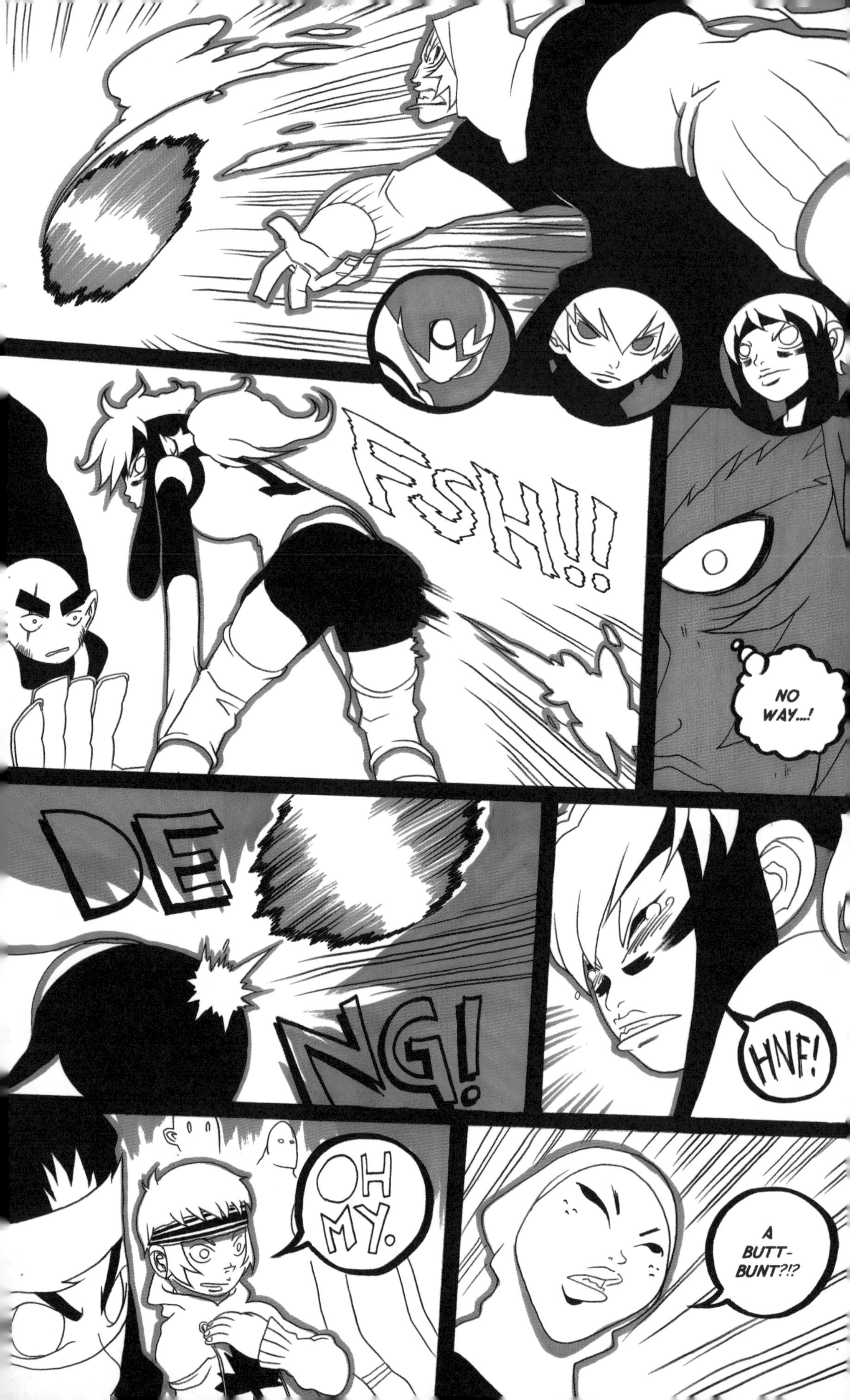
FSH!!
NO WAY...!
DE
NG!
HNF!
OH MY.
A BUTT-BUNT?!?

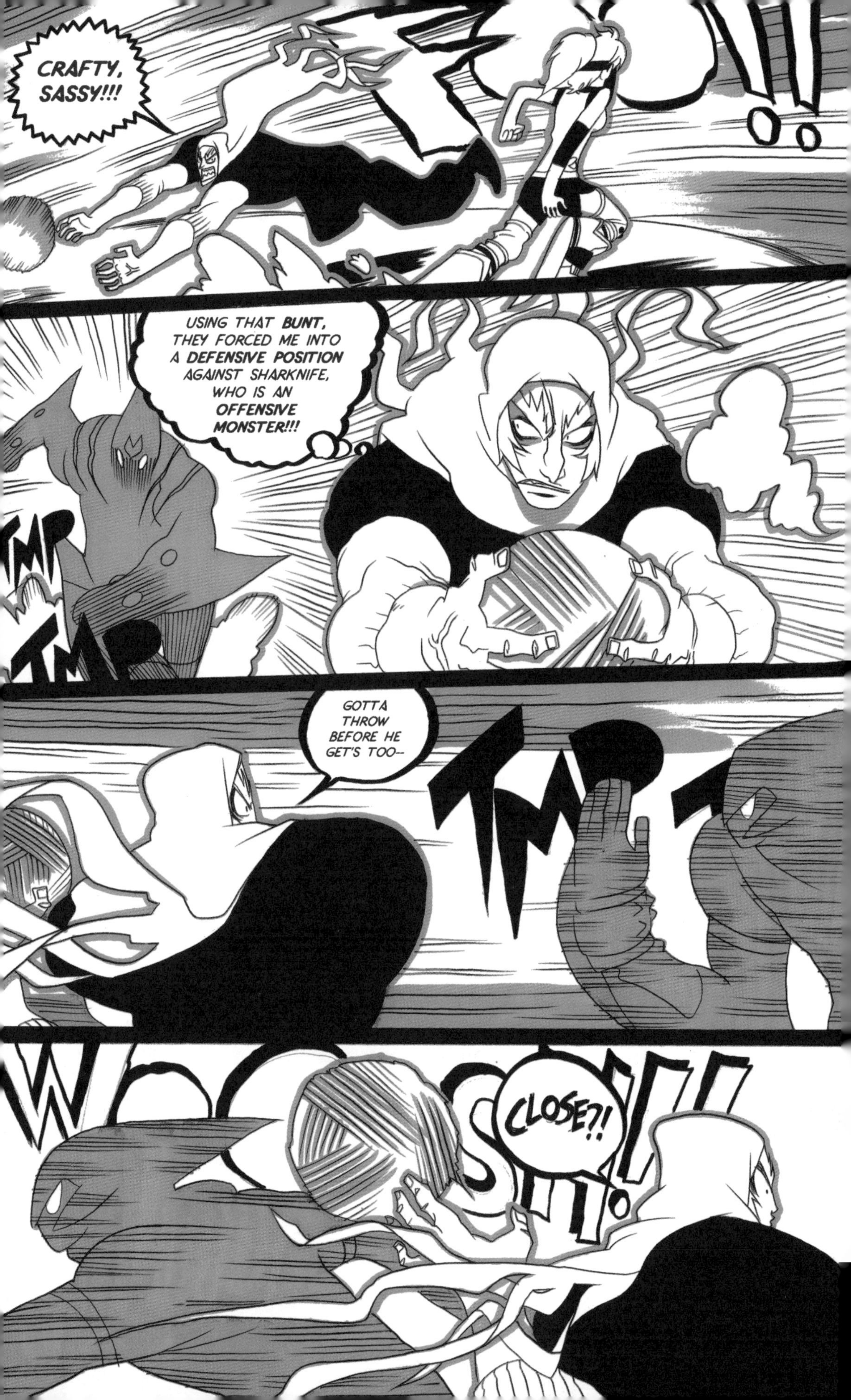
CRAFTY, SASSY!!!
USING THAT BUNT, THEY FORCED ME INTO A DEFENSIVE POSITION AGAINST SHARKNIFE, WHO IS AN OFFENSIVE MONSTER!!!
TMP
TMP
GOTTA THROW BEFORE HE GET'S TOO--
TMP
CLOSE?!

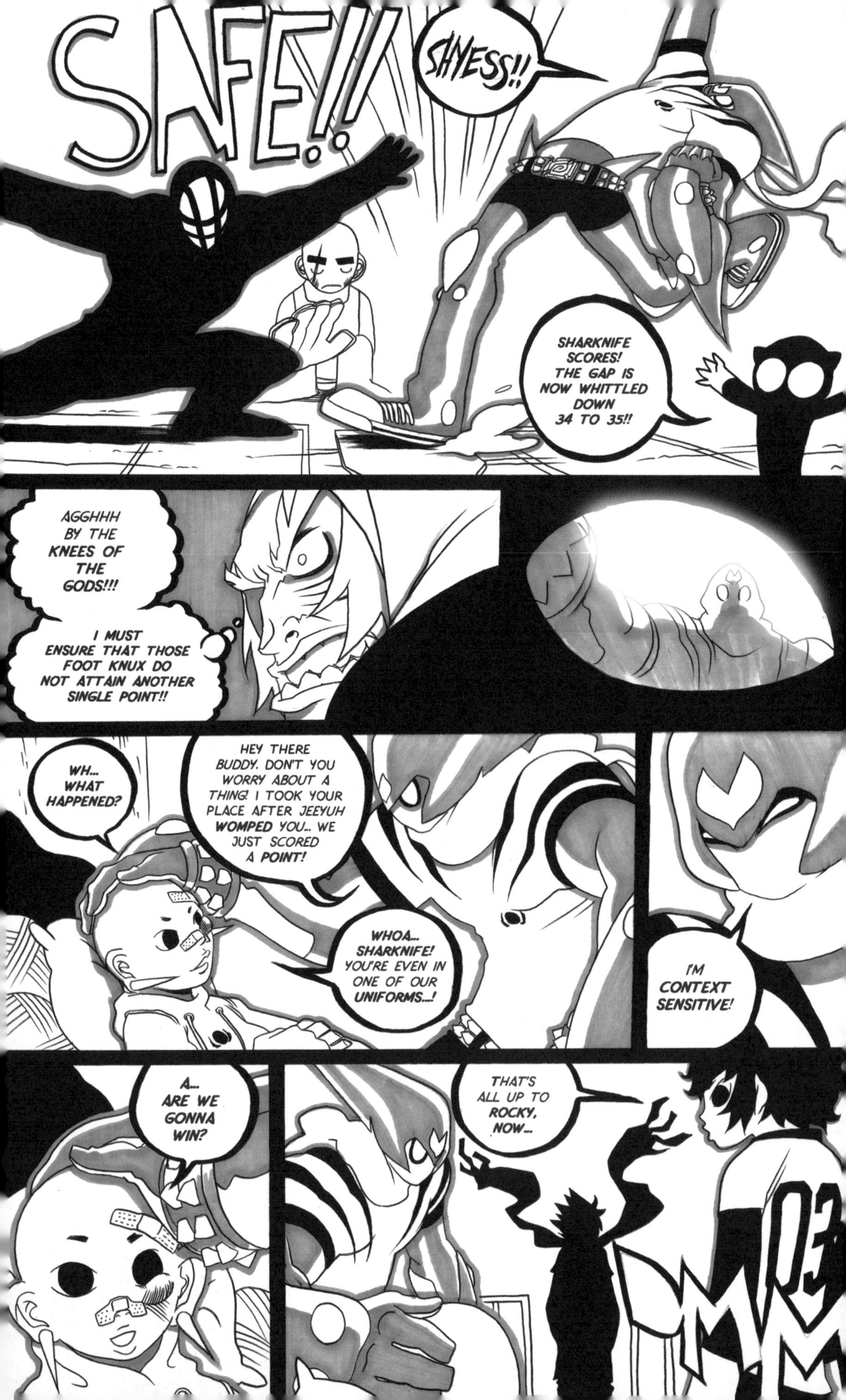
SAFE!!
SHYESS!!
SHARKNIFE SCORES! THE GAP IS NOW WHITTLED DOWN 34 TO 35!!
AGGHHH BY THE KNEES OF THE GODS!!!
I MUST ENSURE THAT THOSE FOOT KNUX DO NOT ATTAIN ANOTHER SINGLE POINT!!
WH... WHAT HAPPENED?
HEY THERE BUDDY. DON'T YOU WORRY ABOUT A THING! I TOOK YOUR PLACE AFTER JEEYUH WOMPED YOU... WE JUST SCORED A POINT!
WHOA... SHARKNIFE! YOU'RE EVEN IN ONE OF OUR UNIFORMS...!
I'M CONTEXT SENSITIVE!
A... ARE WE GONNA WIN?
THAT'S ALL UP TO ROCKY, NOW...
03

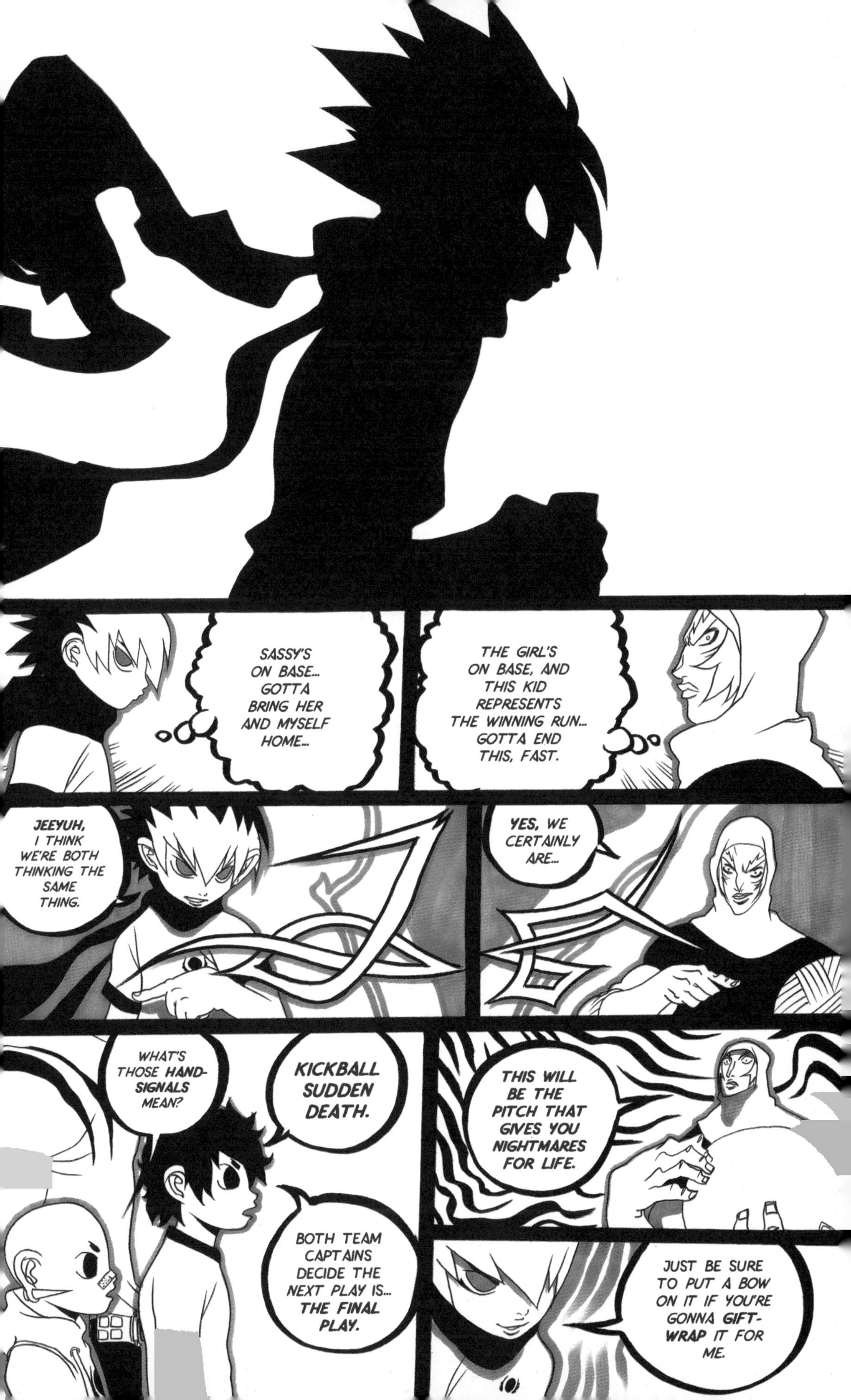
SASSY'S ON BASE... GOTTA BRING HER AND MYSELF HOME...
THE GIRL'S ON BASE, AND THIS KID REPRESENTS THE WINNING RUN... GOTTA END THIS, FAST.
JEEYUH, I THINK WE'RE BOTH THINKING THE SAME THING.
YES, WE CERTAINLY ARE...
WHAT'S THOSE HAND-SIGNALS MEAN?
KICKBALL SUDDEN DEATH.
BOTH TEAM CAPTAINS DECIDE THE NEXT PLAY IS... THE FINAL PLAY.
THIS WILL BE THE PITCH THAT GIVES YOU NIGHTMARES FOR LIFE.
JUST BE SURE TO PUT A BOW ON IT IF YOU'RE GONNA GIFT-WRAP IT FOR ME.

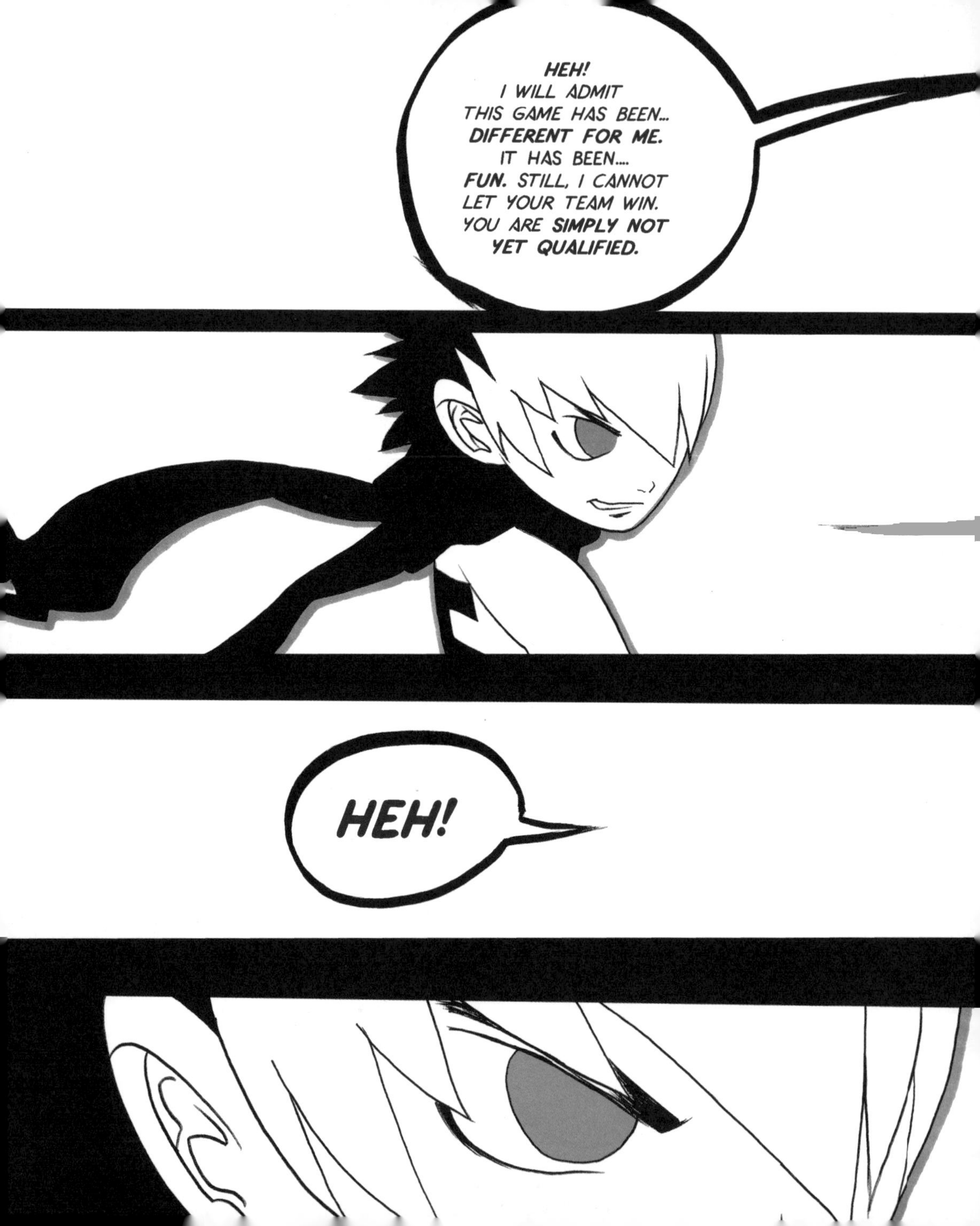
HEH! I WILL ADMIT THIS GAME HAS BEEN... DIFFERENT FOR ME. IT HAS BEEN.... FUN. STILL, I CANNOT LET YOUR TEAM WIN. YOU ARE SIMPLY NOT YET QUALIFIED.
HEH!

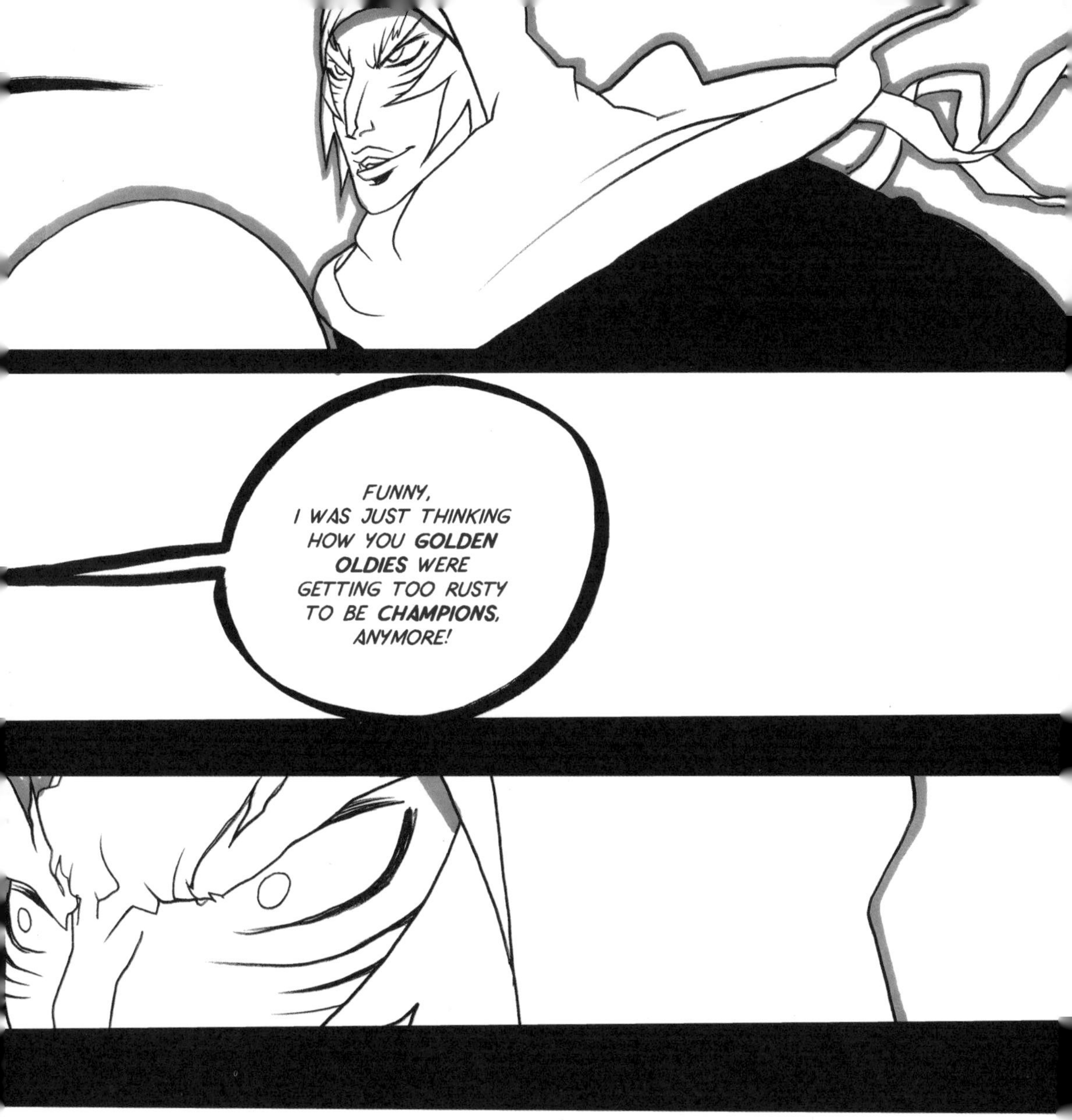
FUNNY, I WAS JUST THINKING HOW YOU GOLDEN OLDIES WERE GETTING TOO RUSTY TO BE CHAMPIONS, ANYMORE!

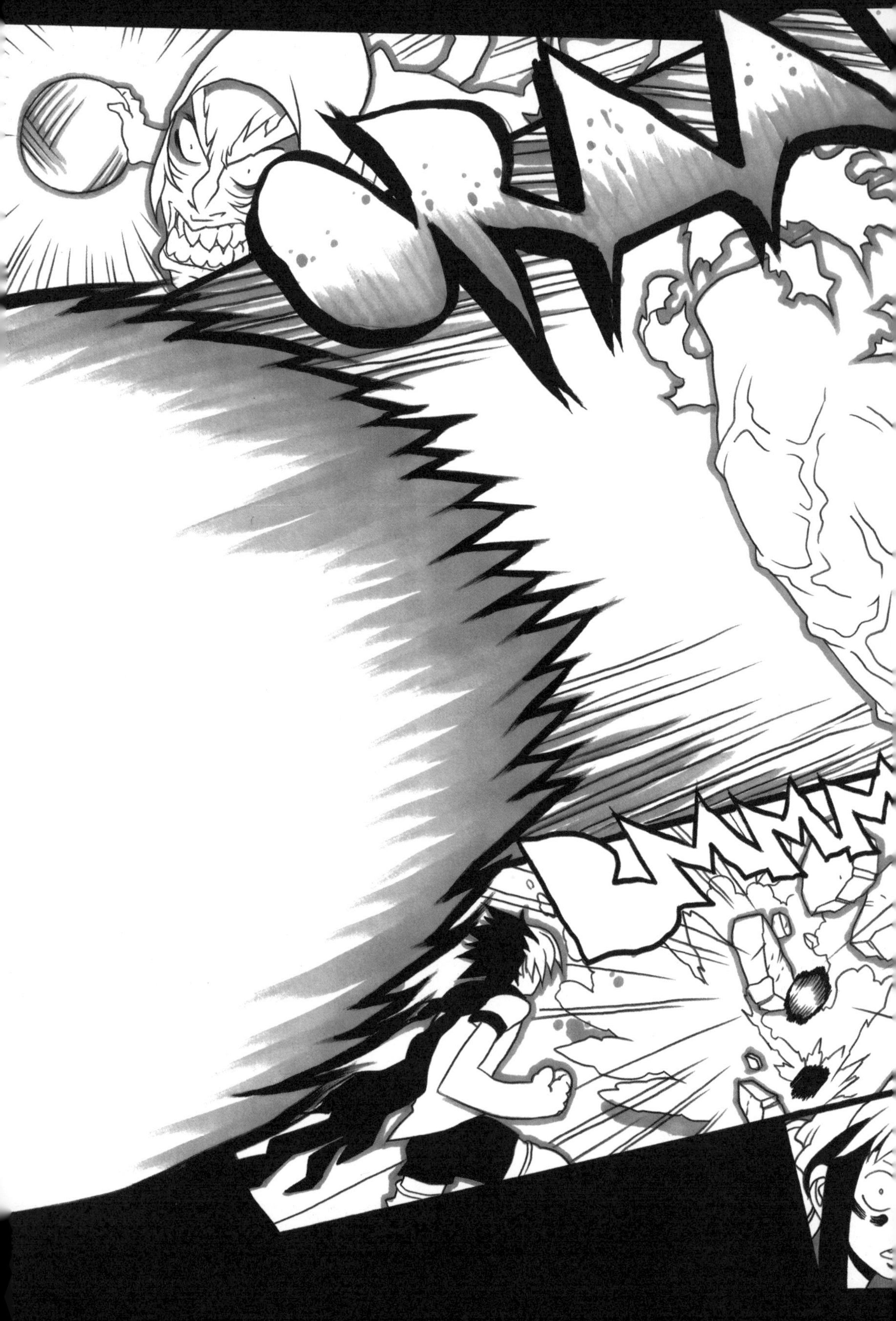

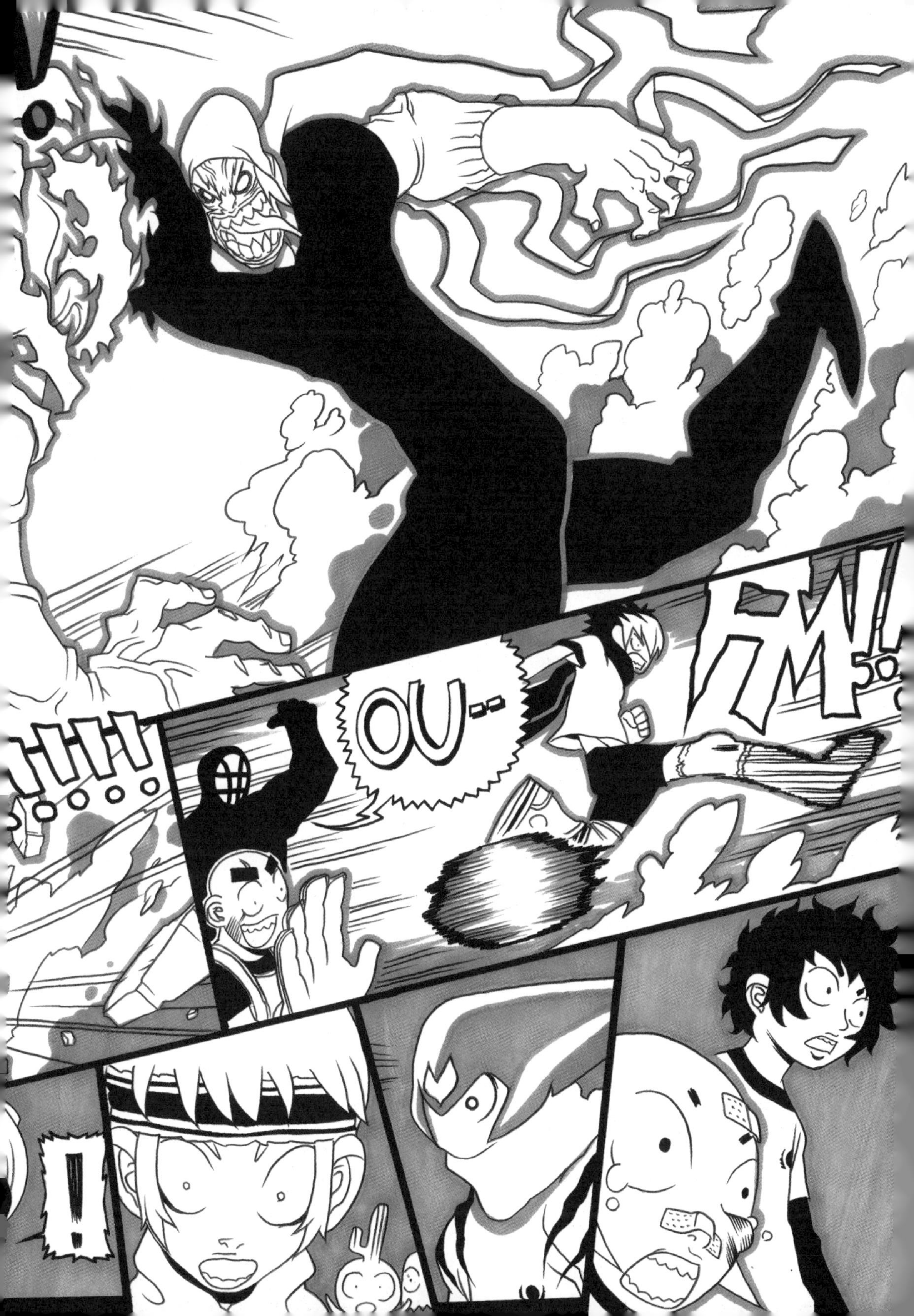

OU--

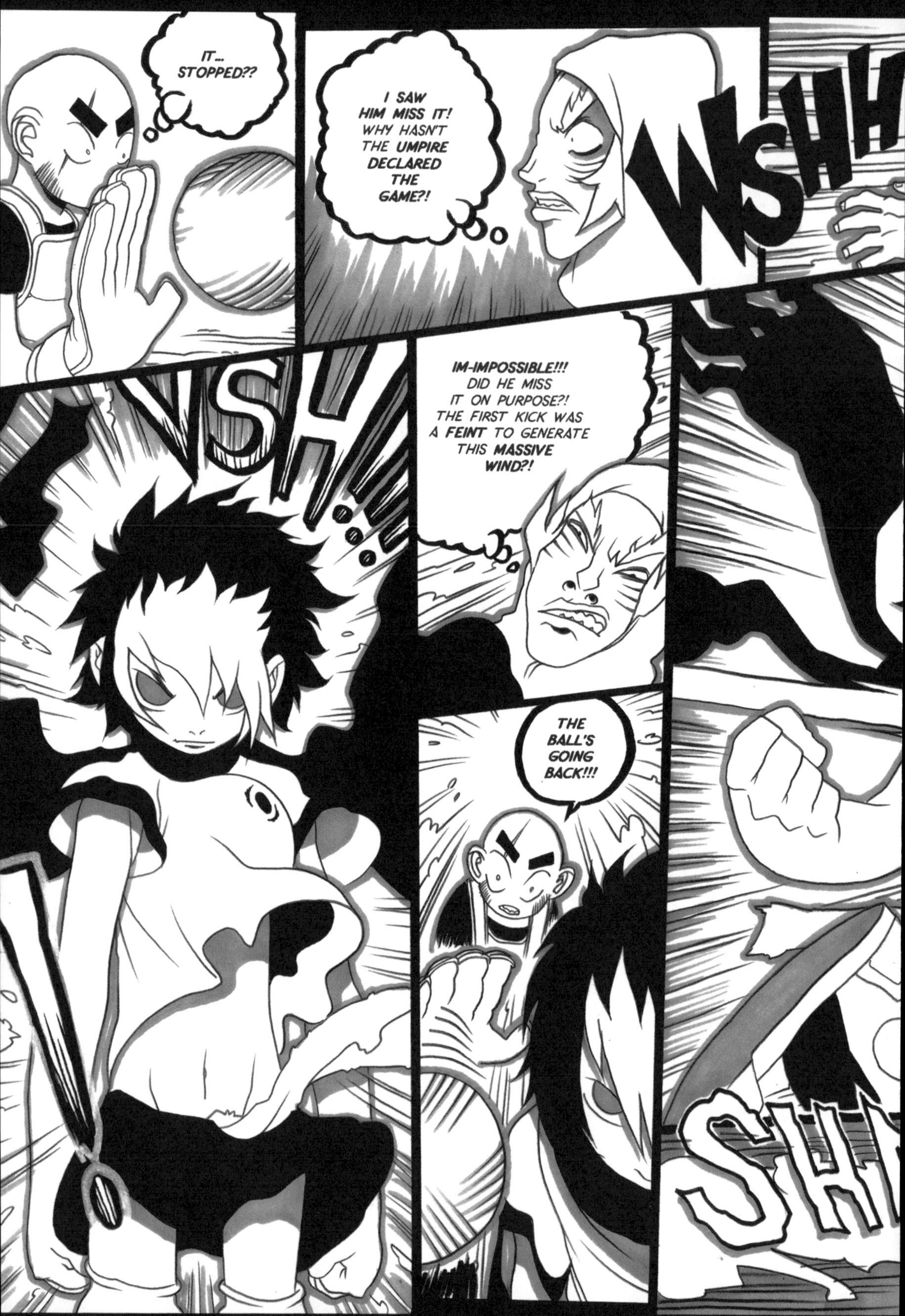

IT... STOPPED??
I SAW HIM MISS IT! WHY HASN'T THE UMPIRE DECLARED THE GAME?!
WSHH
WSH!!!
IM-IMPOSSIBLE!!! DID HE MISS IT ON PURPOSE?! THE FIRST KICK WAS A FEINT TO GENERATE THIS MASSIVE WIND?!
THE BALL'S GOING BACK!!!
SHH

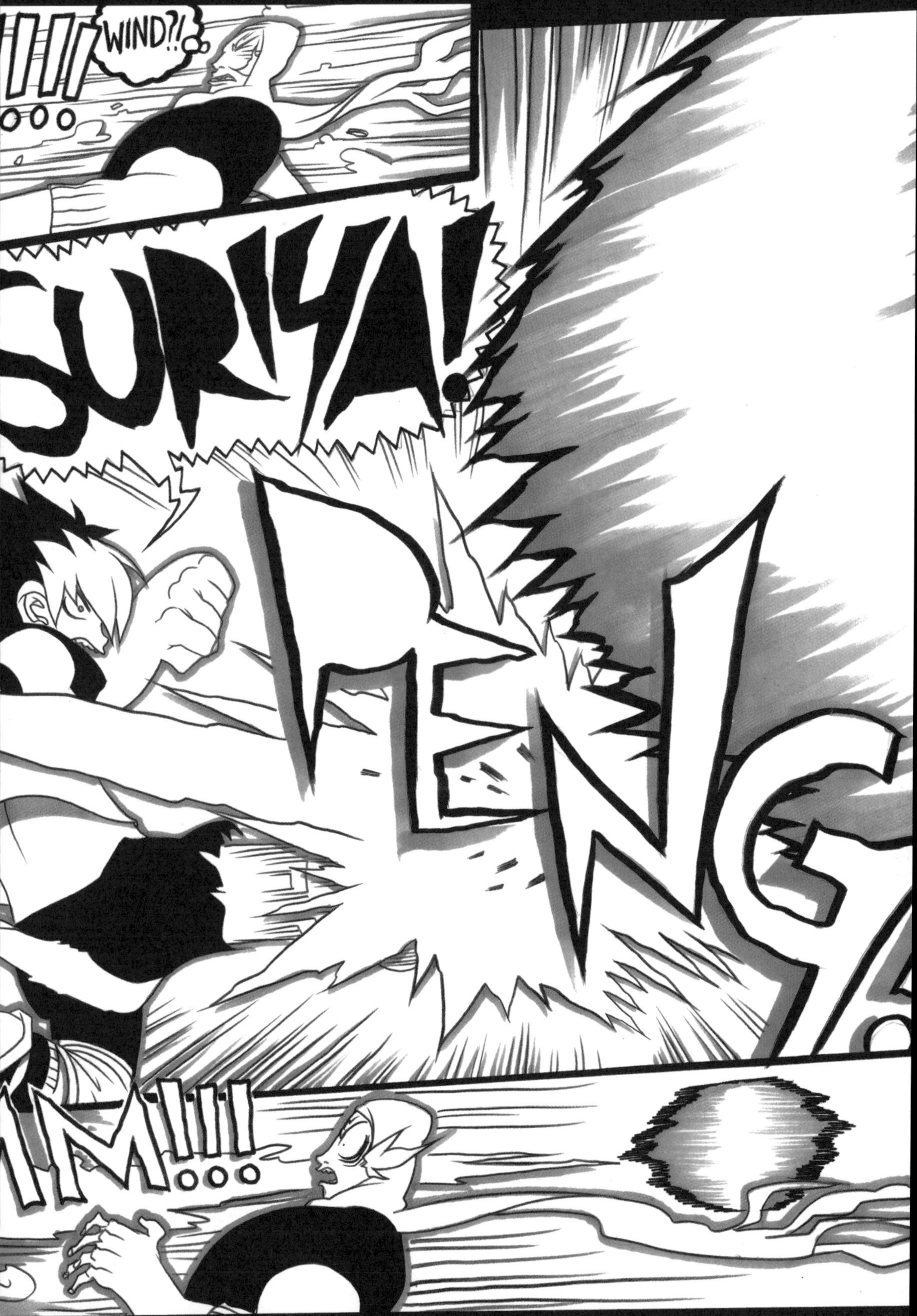

WIND?!
SURIYA!
DING

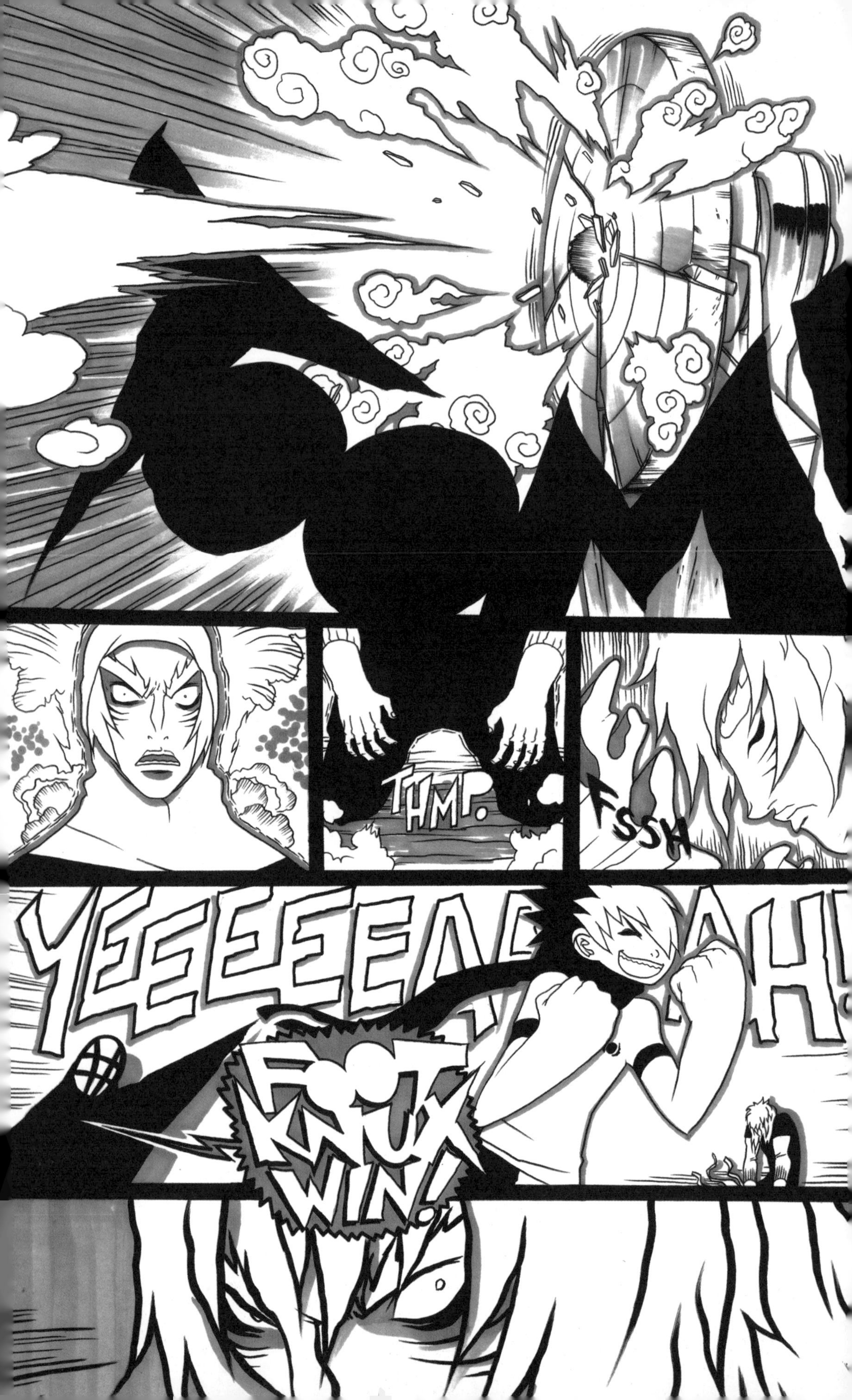
THMP.
FSSH
YEEEEEAAH!
FOOT KNUX WIN!

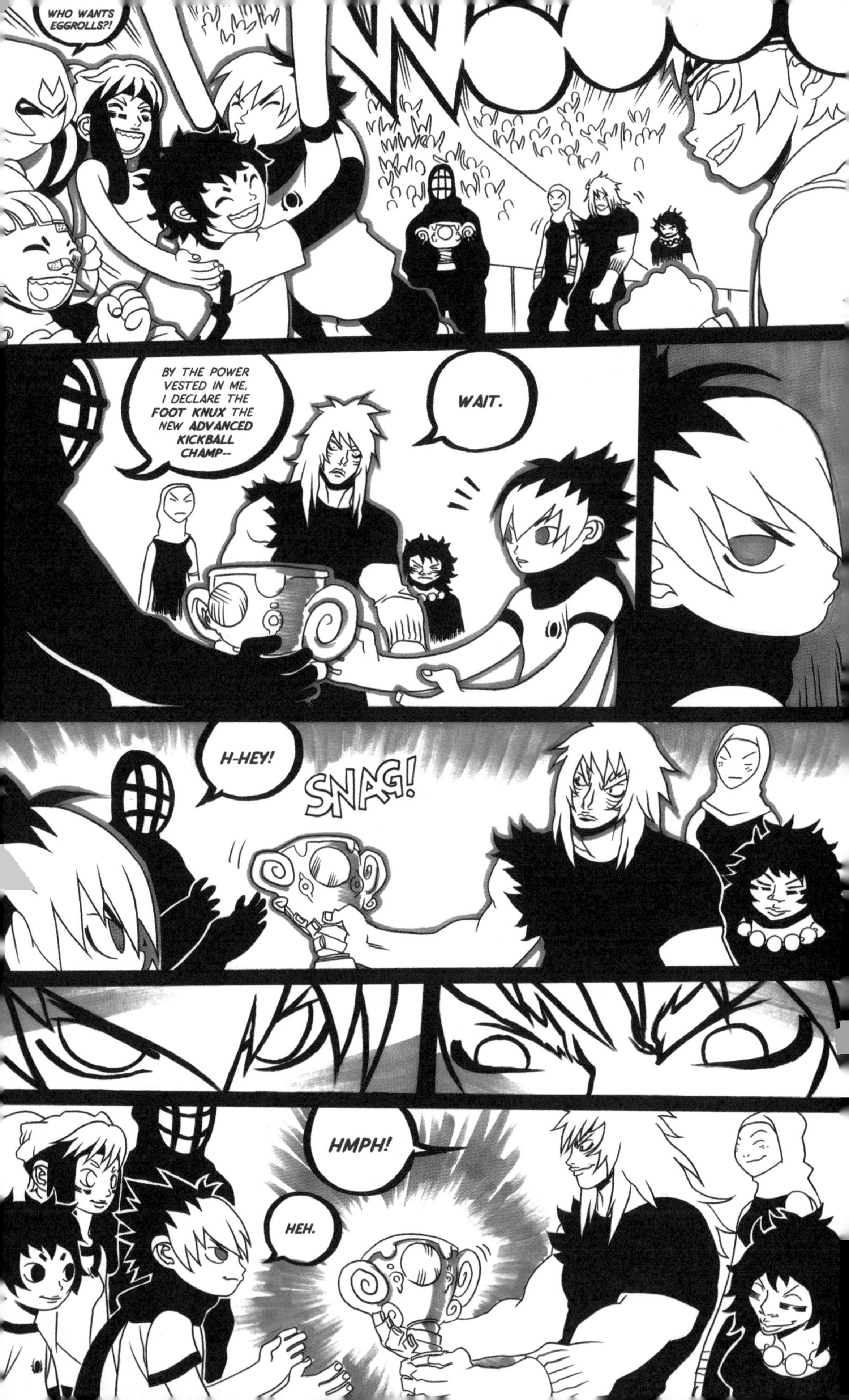
WHO WANTS EGGROLLS?!
WOOO
BY THE POWER VESTED IN ME, I DECLARE THE FOOT KNUX THE NEW ADVANCED KICKBALL CHAMP--
WAIT.
H-HEY!
SNAG!
HMPH!
HEH.

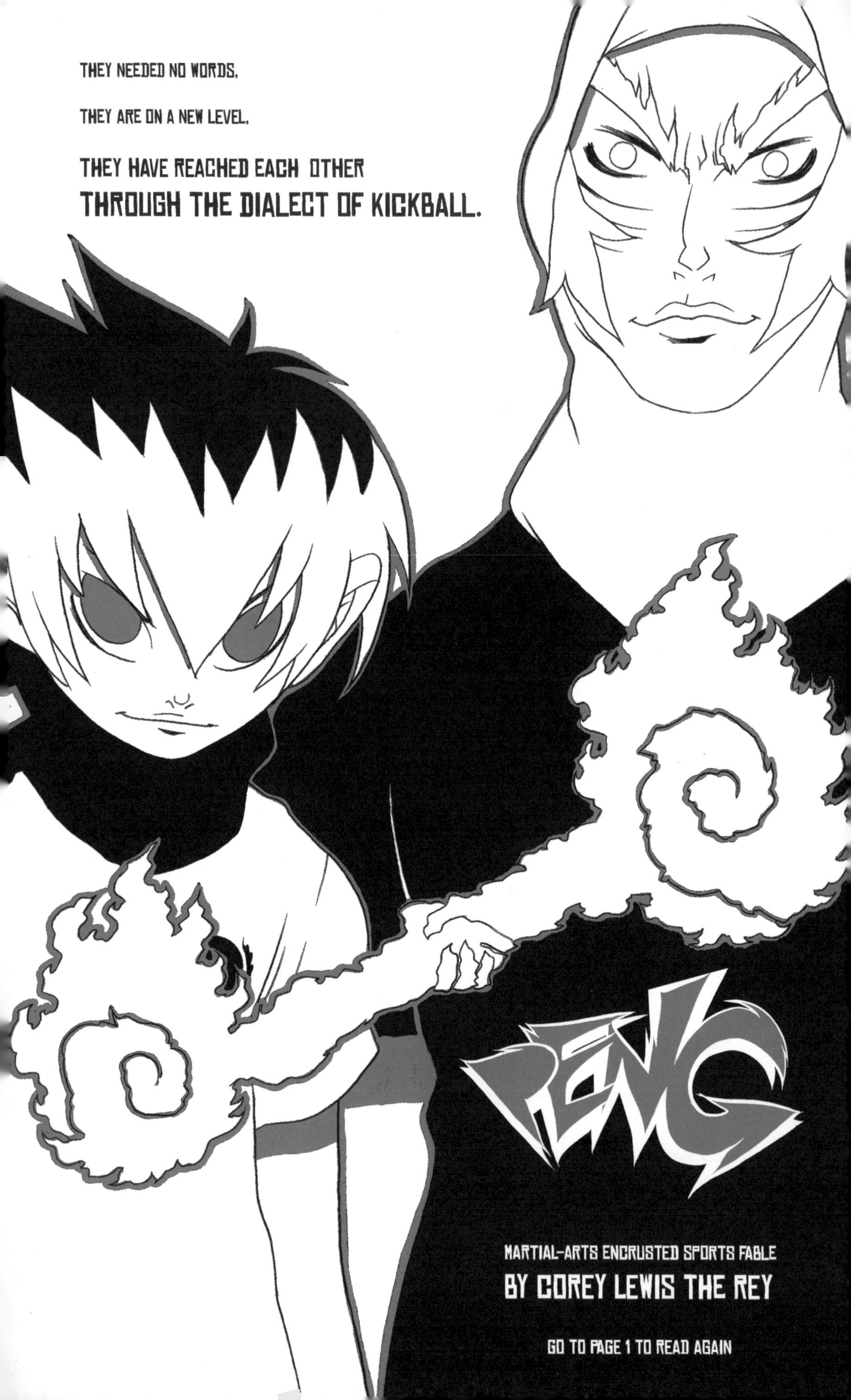
THEY NEEDED NO WORDS.
THEY ARE ON A NEW LEVEL.
THEY HAVE REACHED EACH OTHER
THROUGH THE DIALECT OF KICKBALL.
MARTIAL-ARTS ENCRUSTED SPORTS FABLE
BY COREY LEWIS THE REY
GO TO PAGE 1 TO READ AGAIN

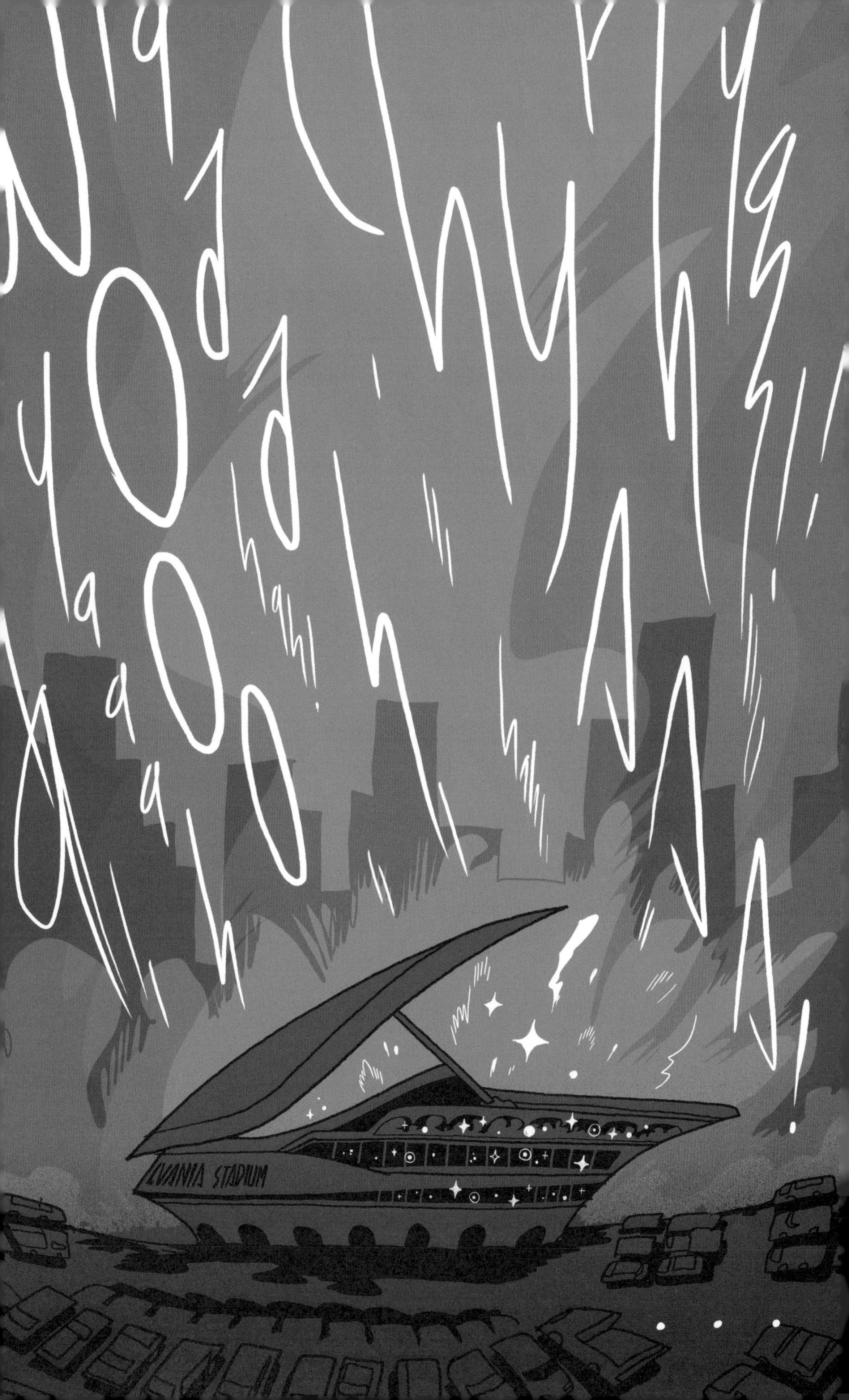
LVANIA STADIUM

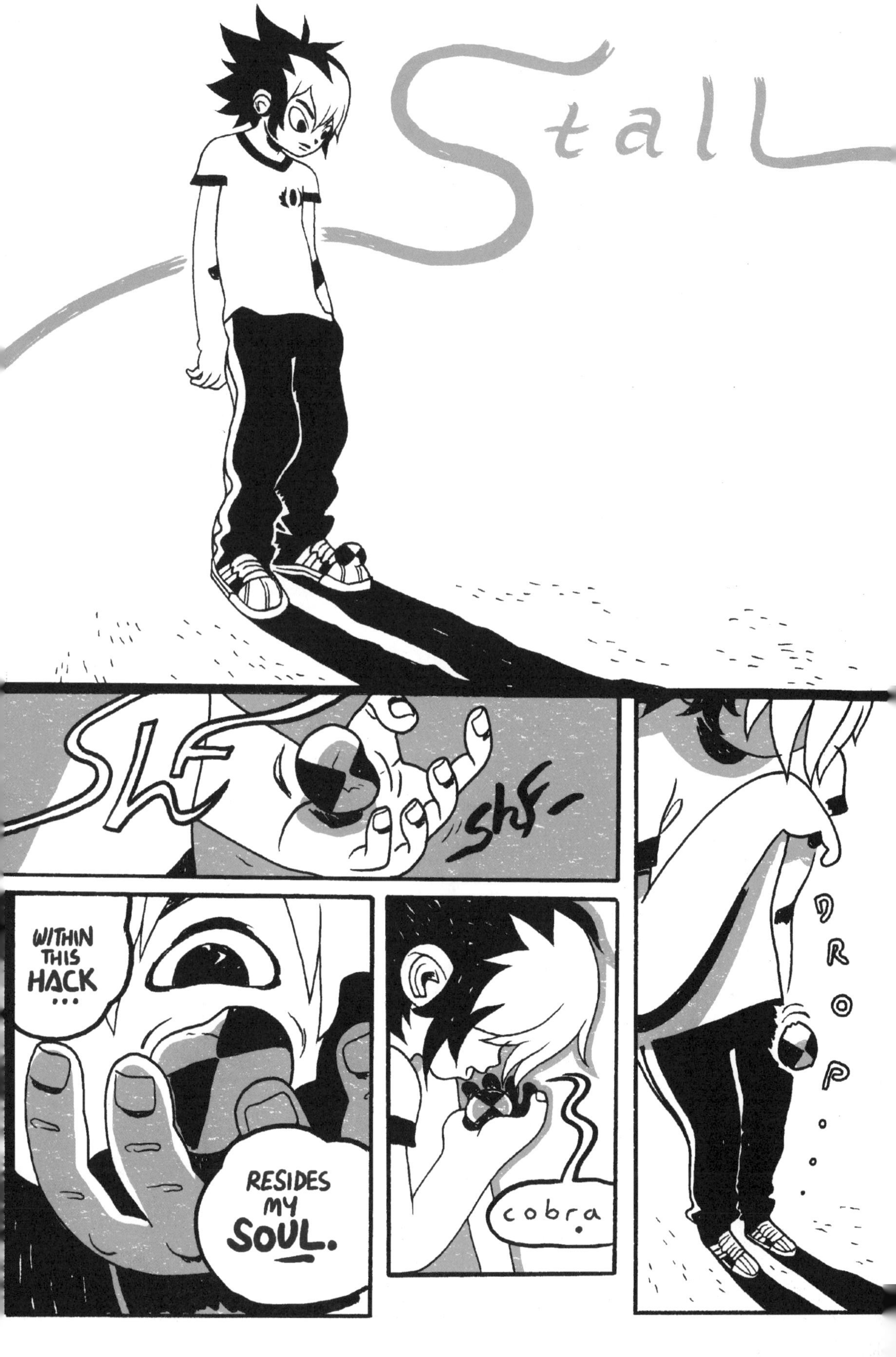

Stall
Shf
shf-
WITHIN THIS HACK...
RESIDES MY SOUL.
cobra.
DROP...

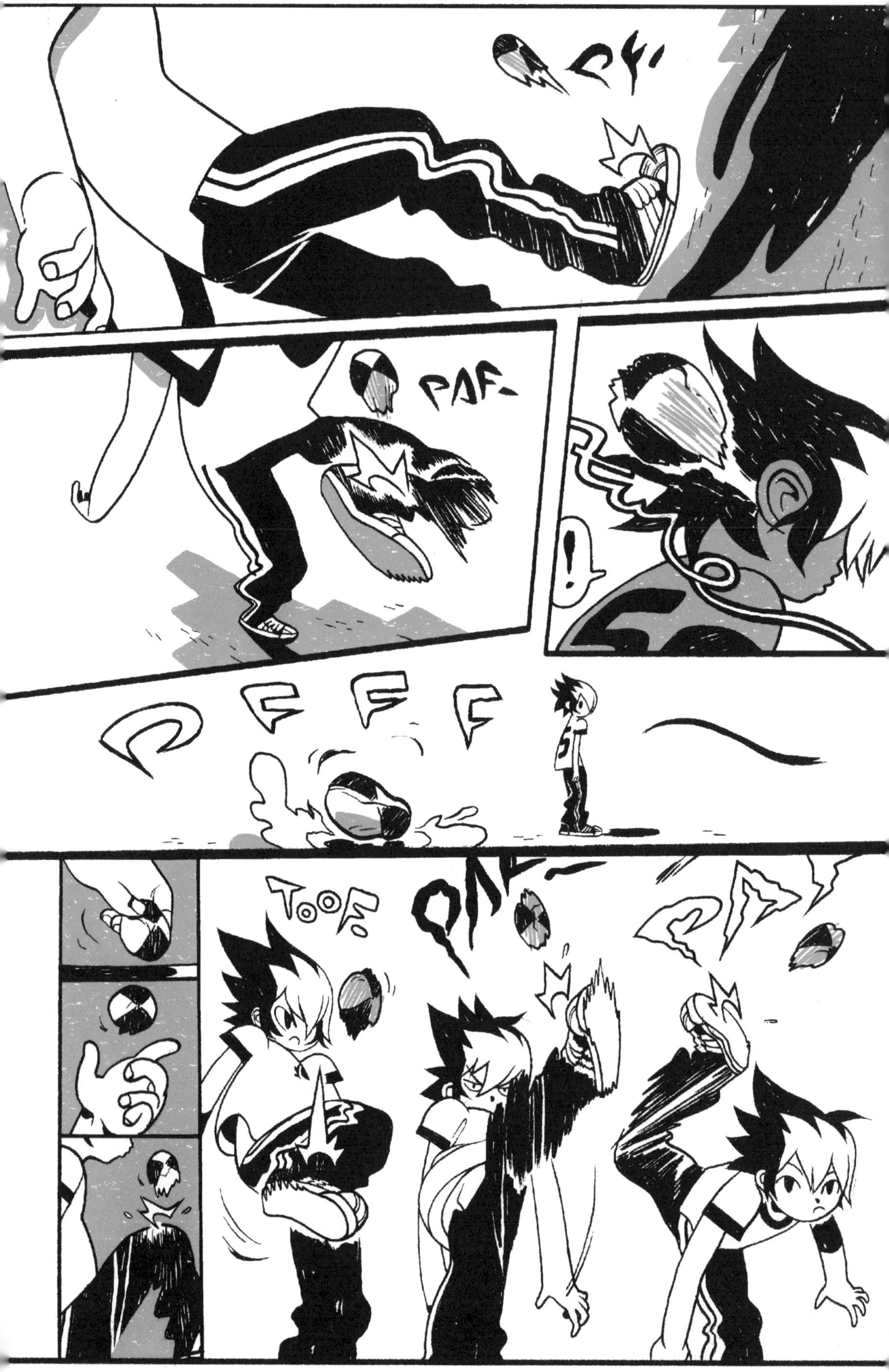
PAF-
!
TOOF

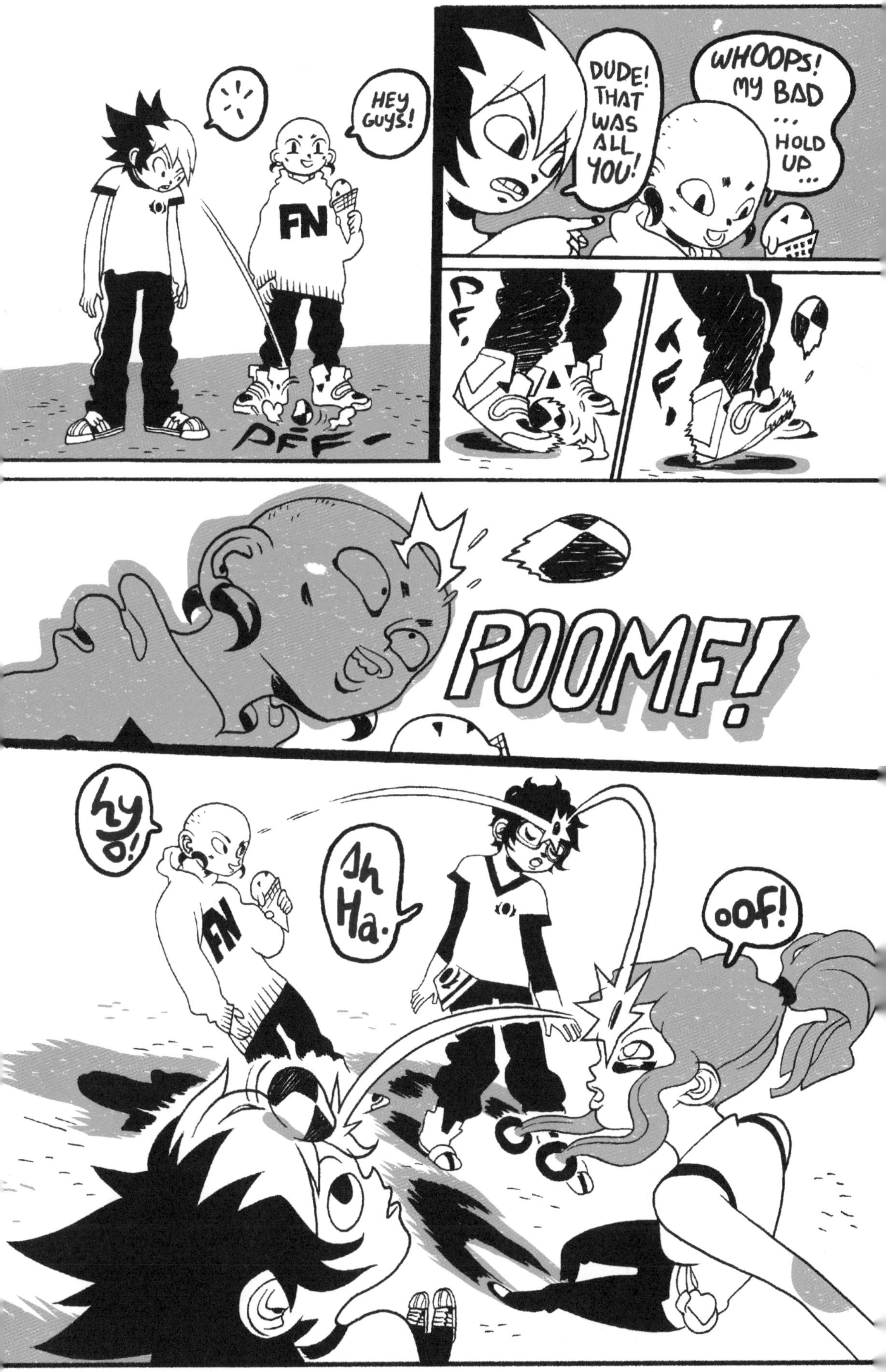
HEY GUYS!
PFF-
DUDE! THAT WAS ALL YOU!
WHOOPS! MY BAD ... HOLD UP...
POOMF!
hyo!
Ah Ha.
oOF!

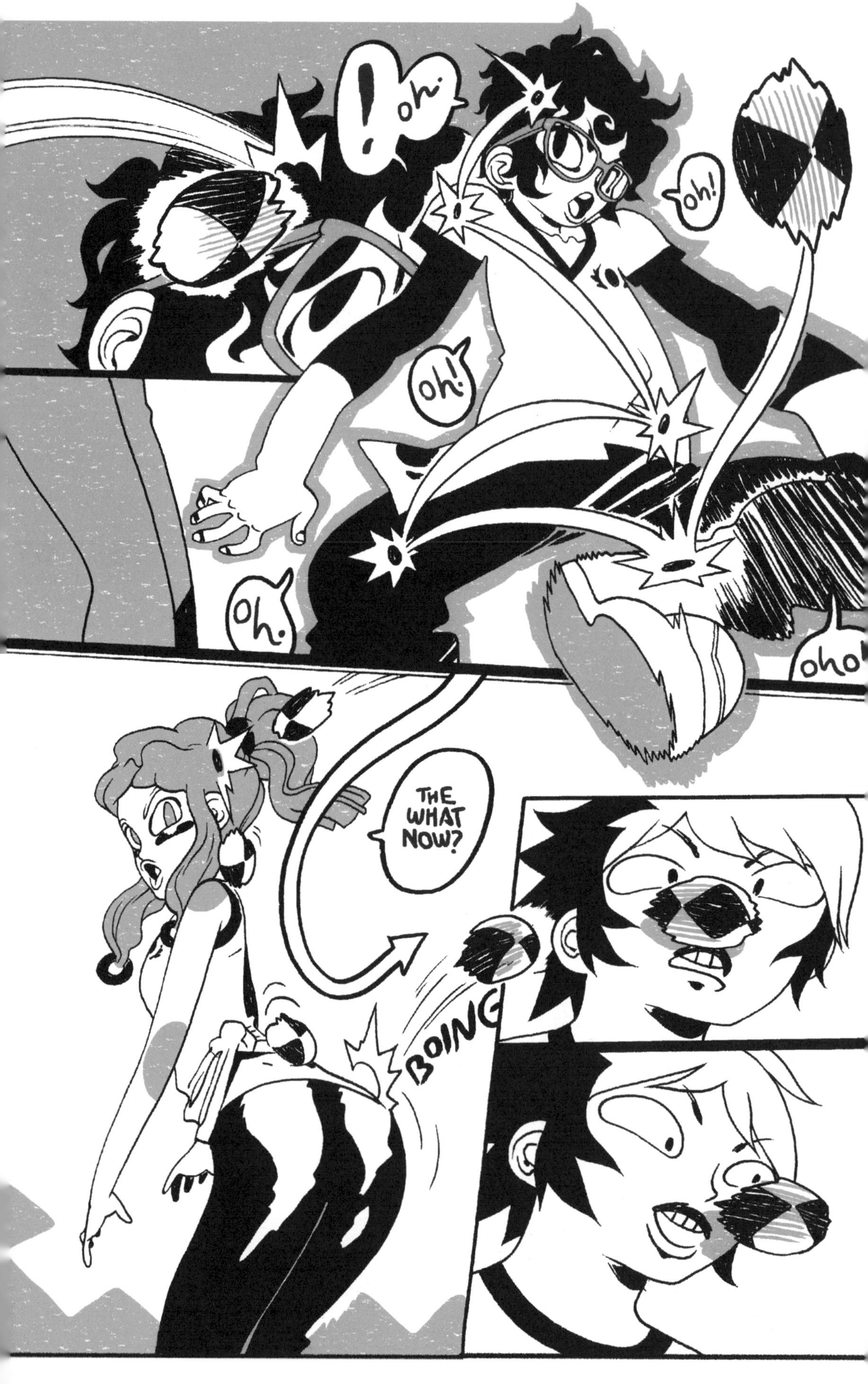
!
oh.
oh!
oh!
oh.
oho!
THE WHAT NOW?
BOING

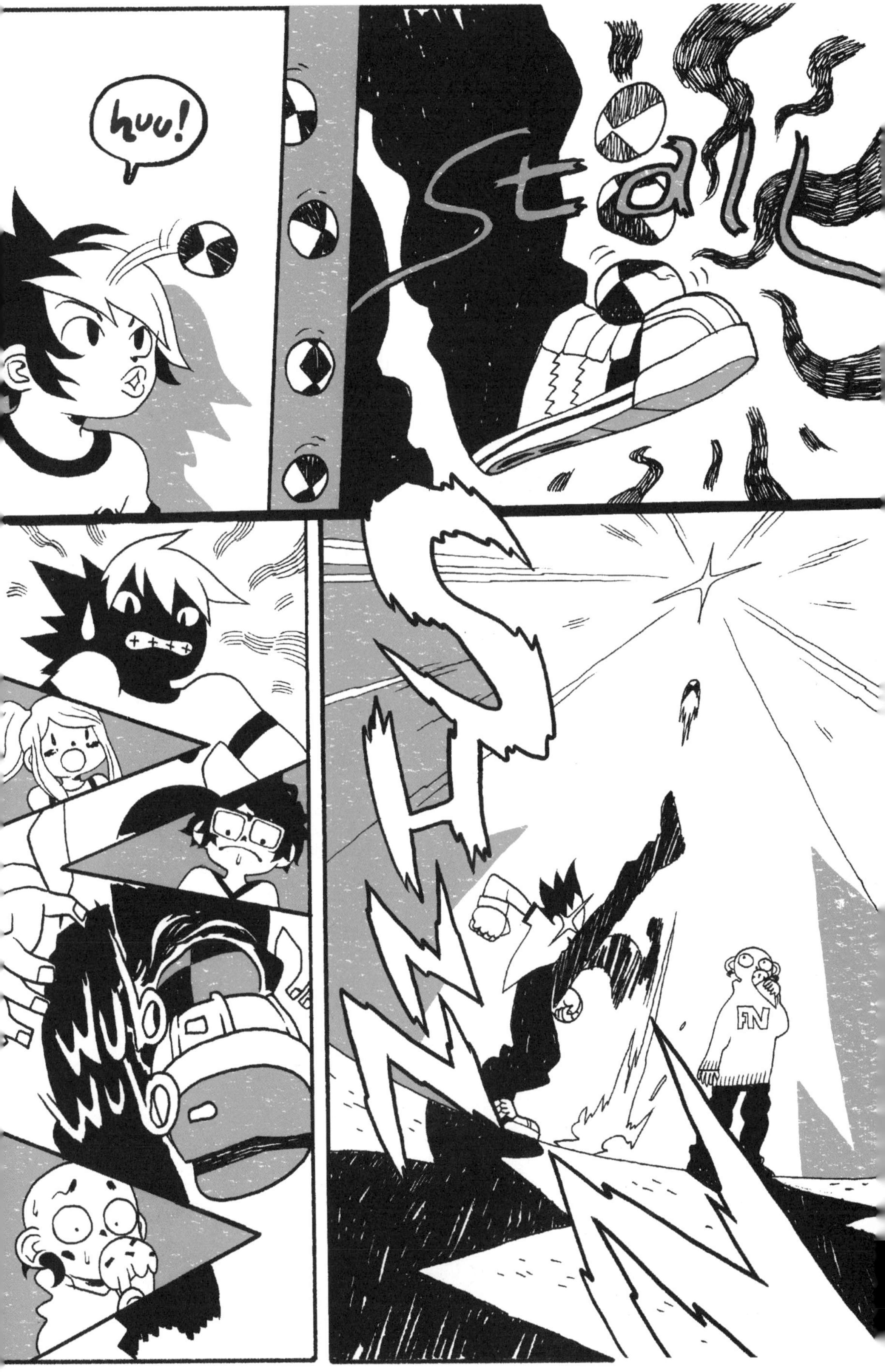

huu!
Stall
wub
wub
FN

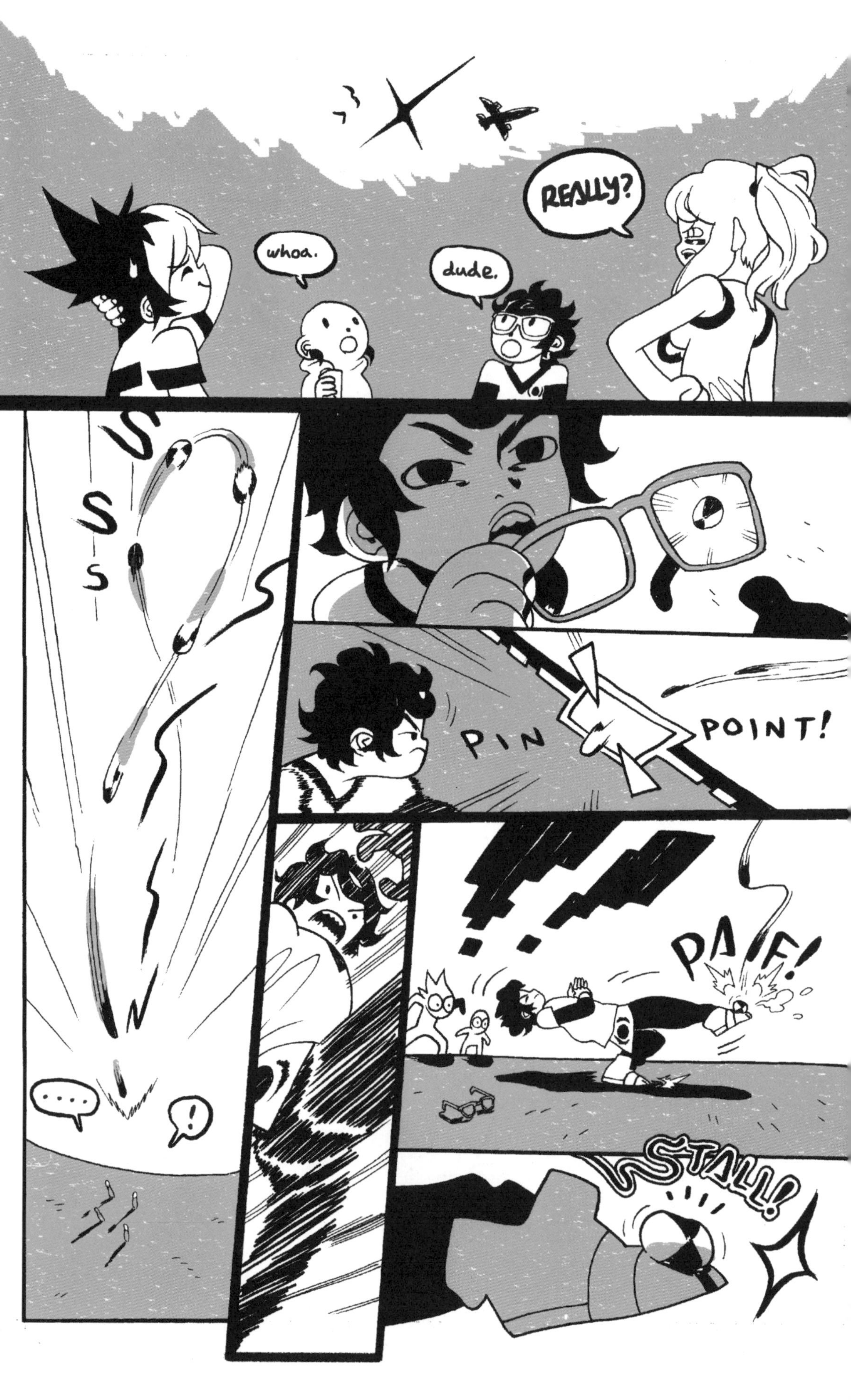
whoa.
dude.
REALLY?
S
S
S
....
!
PIN POINT!
PAF!
WSTALL!

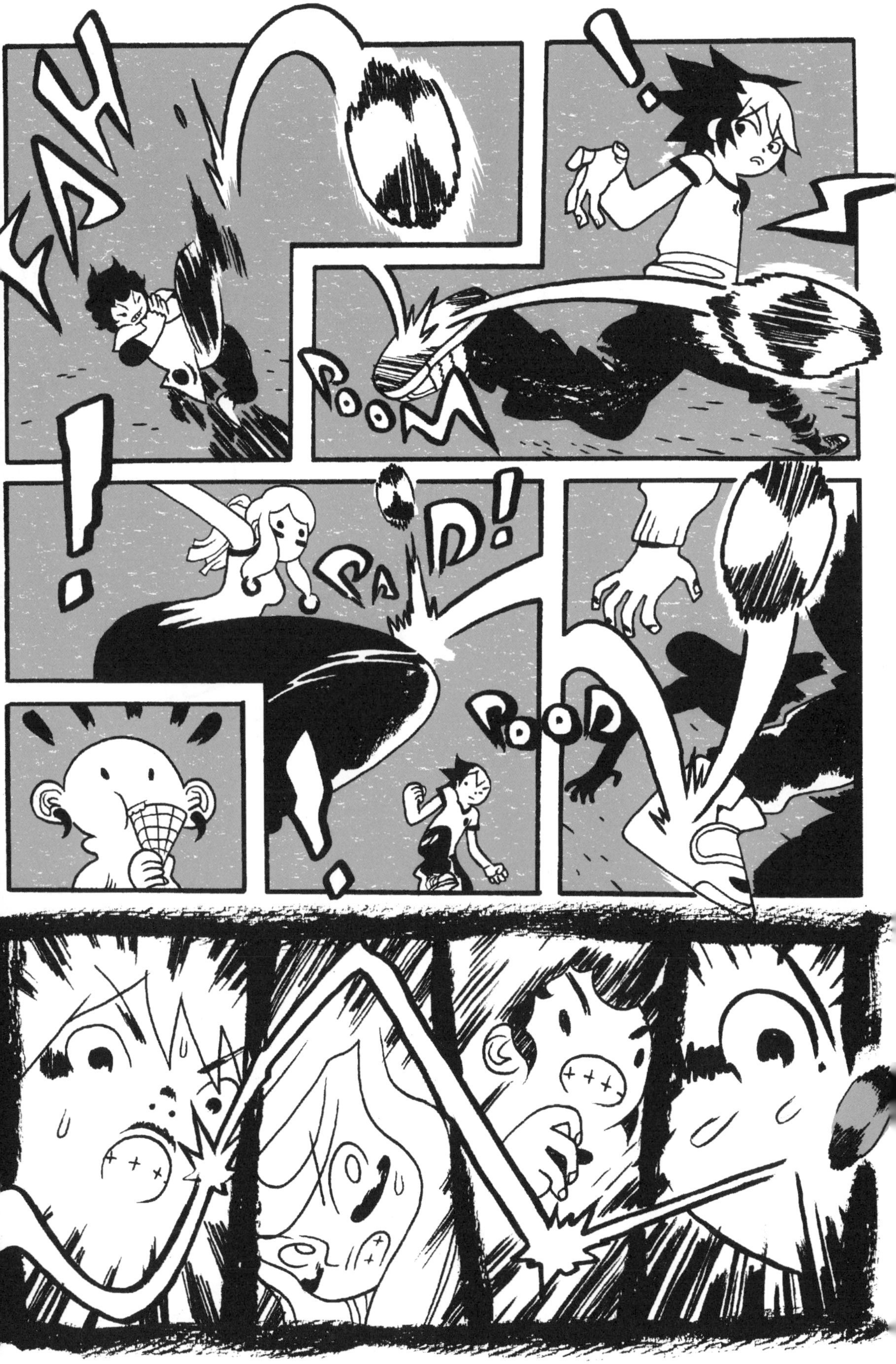
POOM
PAD!
POOD

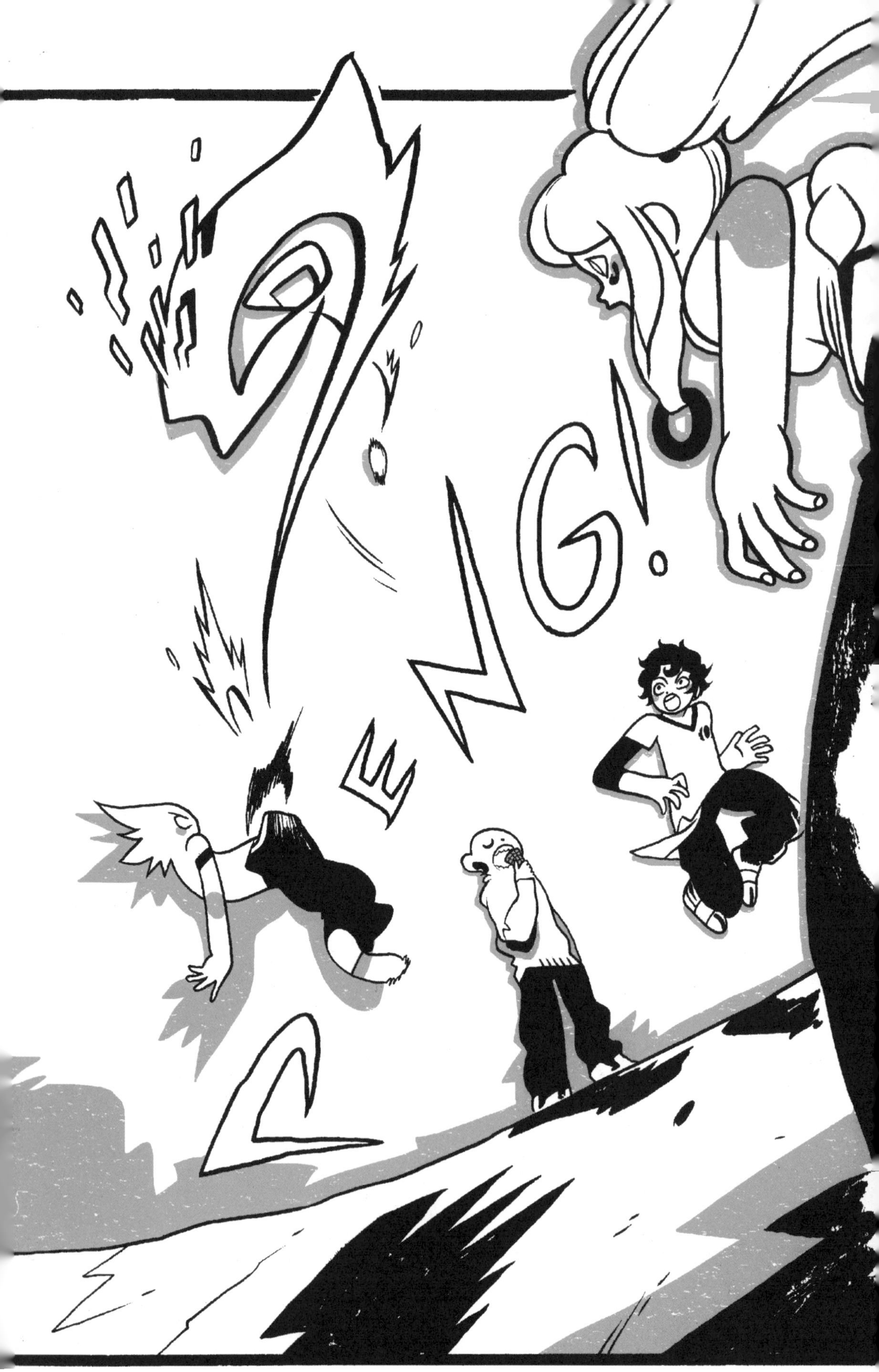
ENG!

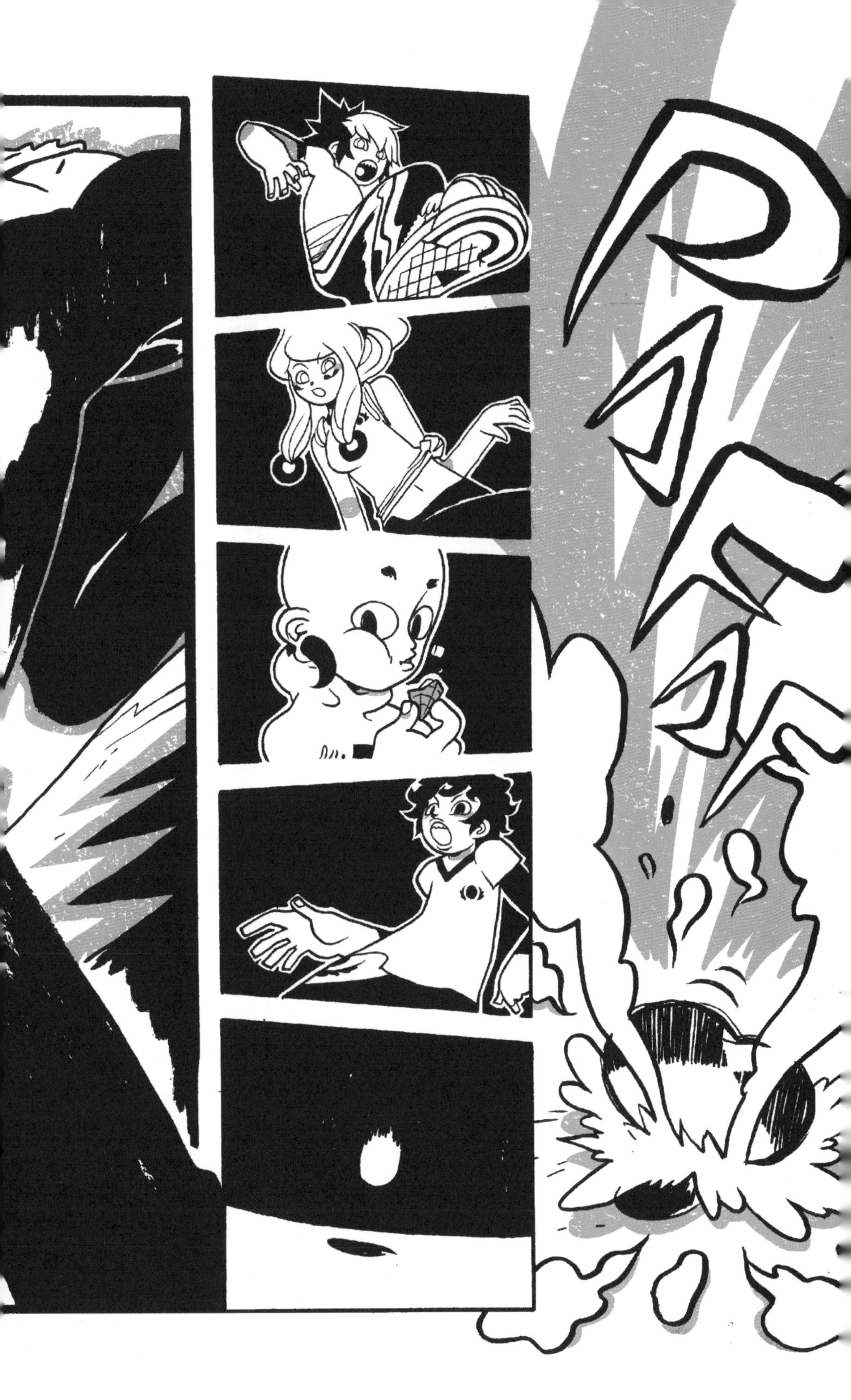

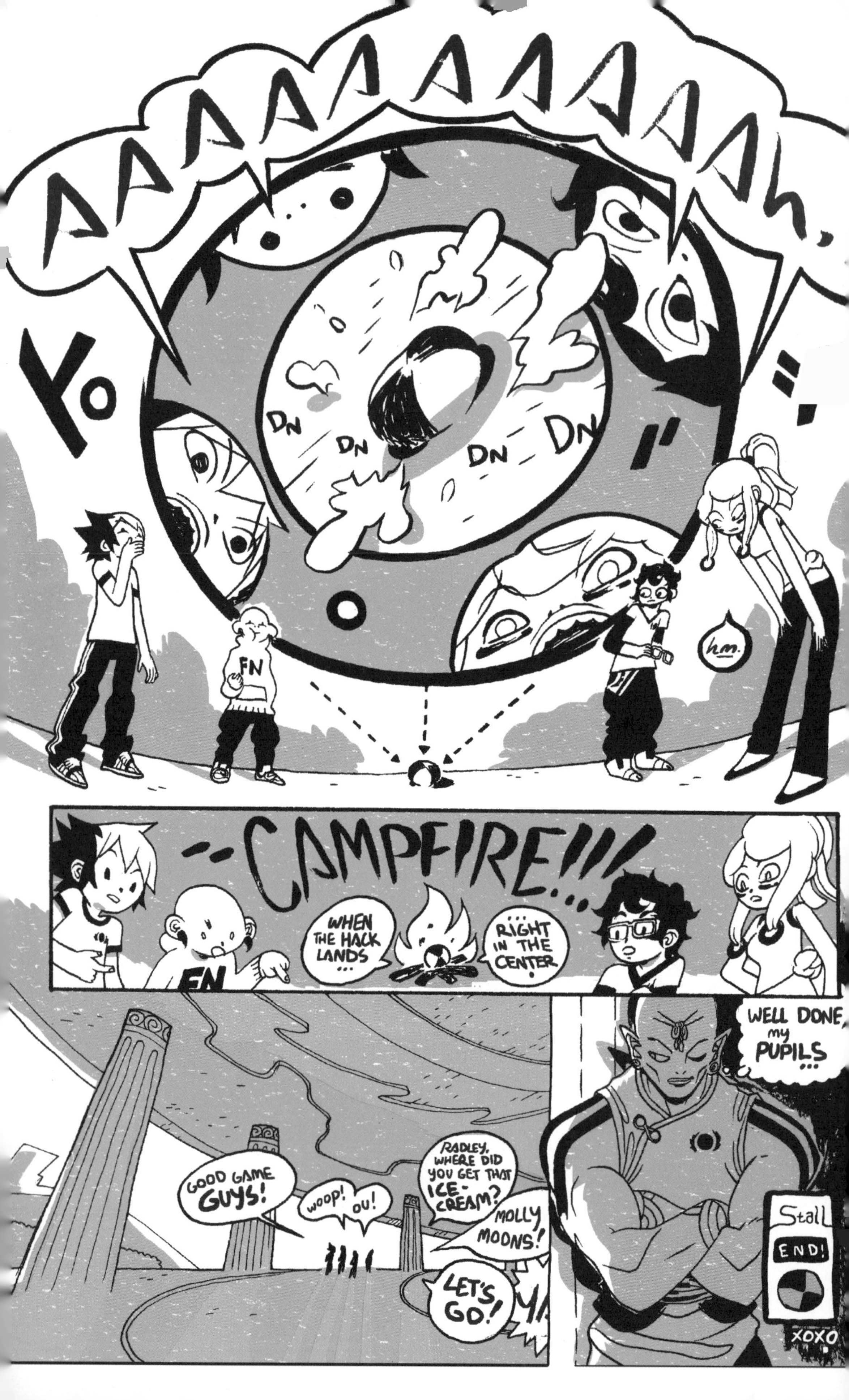

YOAAAAAAAAAAAh,!!
DN DN DN DN
hm.
--CAMPFIRE!!!...
WHEN THE HACK LANDS...
...RIGHT IN THE CENTER.
WELL DONE, my PUPILS...
GOOD GAME GUYS!
woop! ou!
RADLEY, WHERE DID YOU GET THAT ICE-CREAM?
MOLLY MOONS!
LET'S GO!
Stall
END!
XOXO

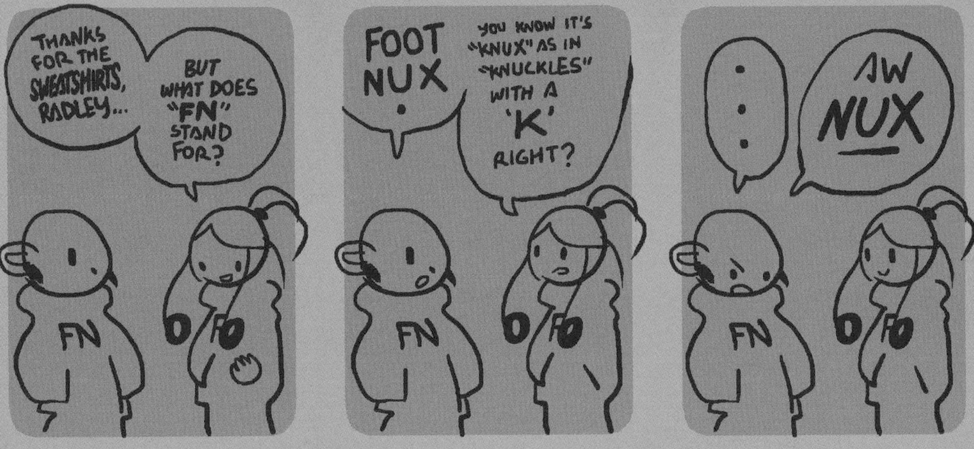
THANKS FOR THE SWEATSHIRTS, RADLEY...
BUT WHAT DOES "FN" STAND FOR?
FOOT NUX.
YOU KNOW IT'S "KNUX" AS IN "KNUCKLES" WITH A 'K' RIGHT?
...
AW NUX

PENG!
MOAR COMIN!

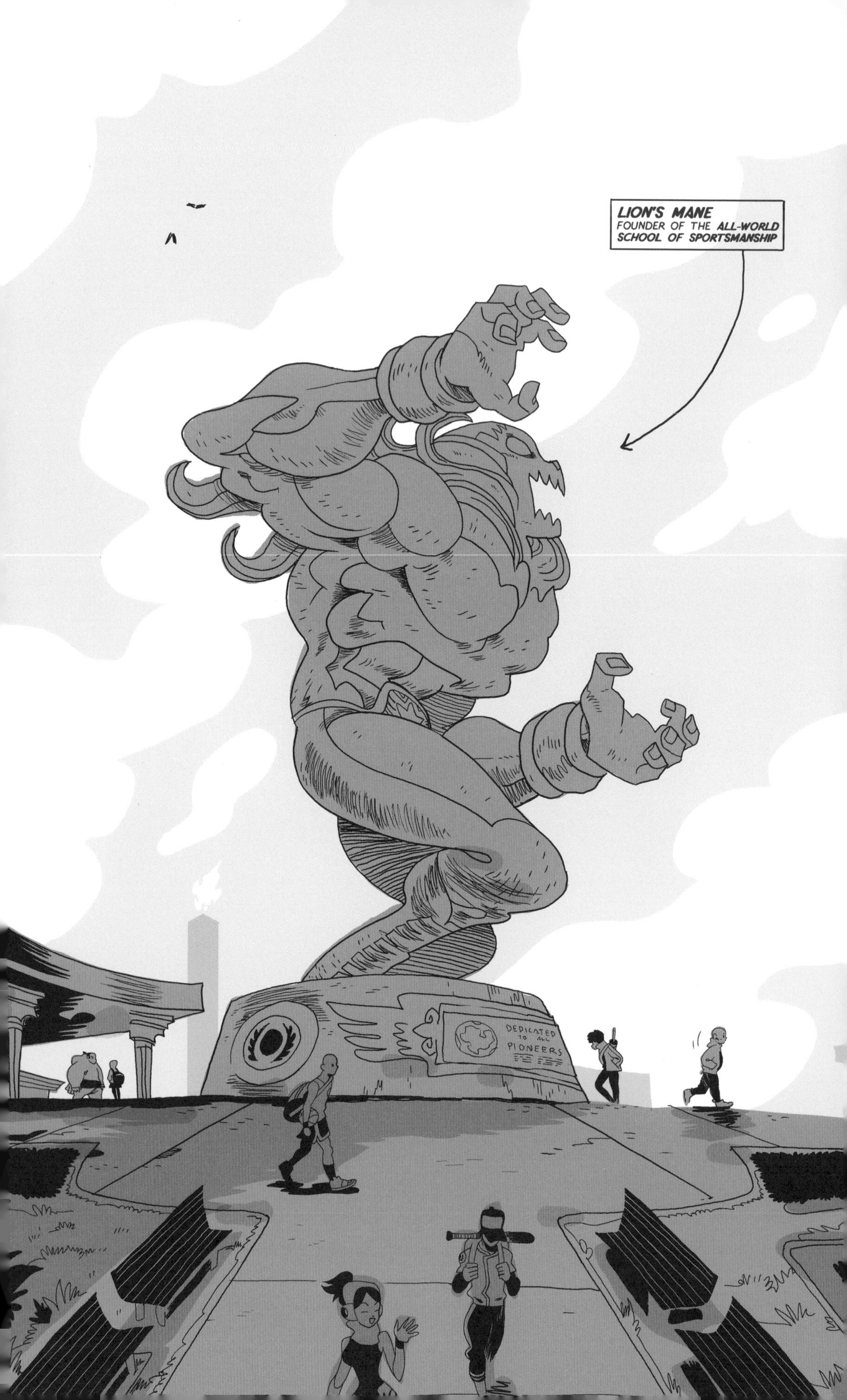
LION'S MANE
FOUNDER OF THE ALL-WORLD SCHOOL OF SPORTSMANSHIP
DEDICATED TO ALL PIONEERS

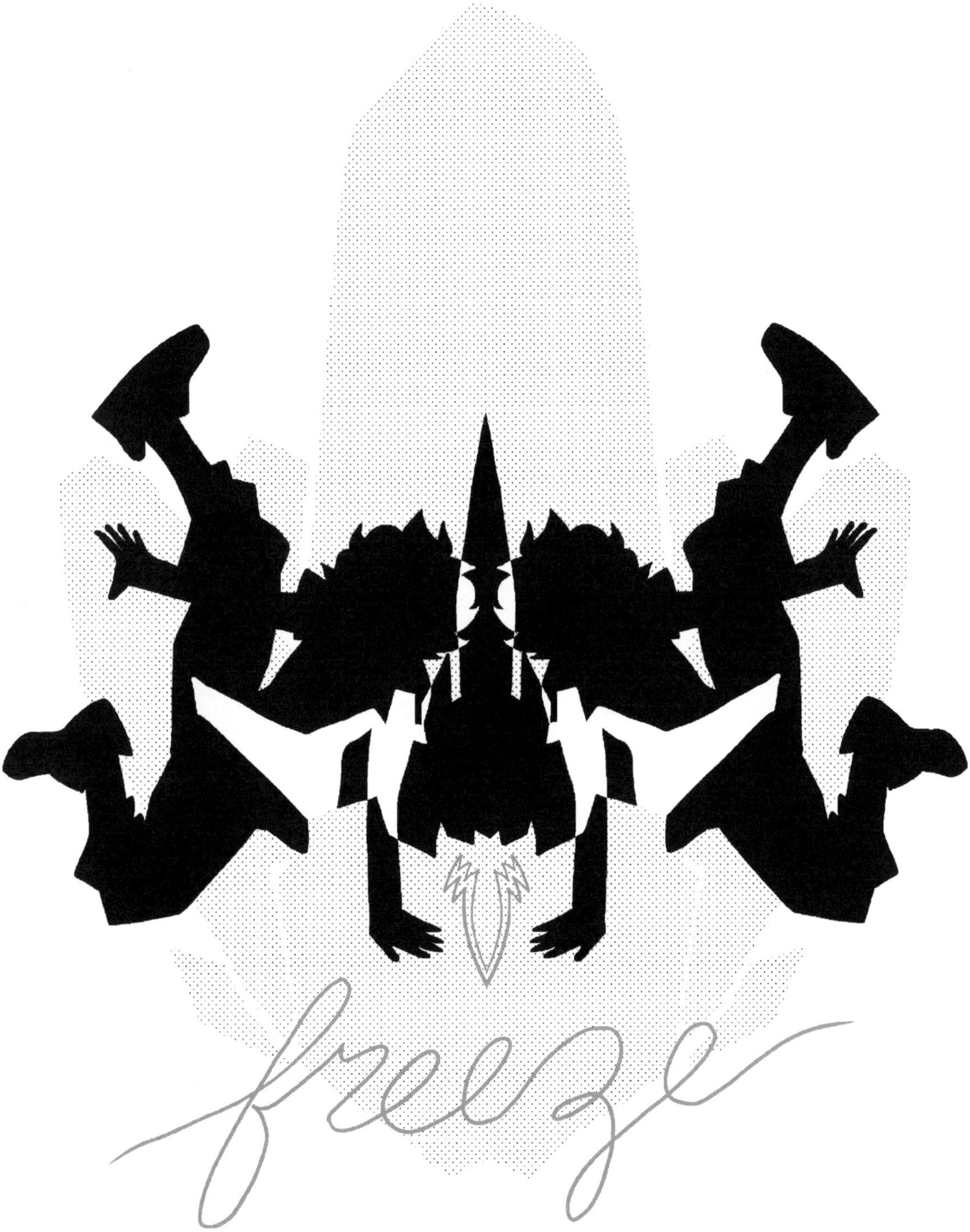
freeze

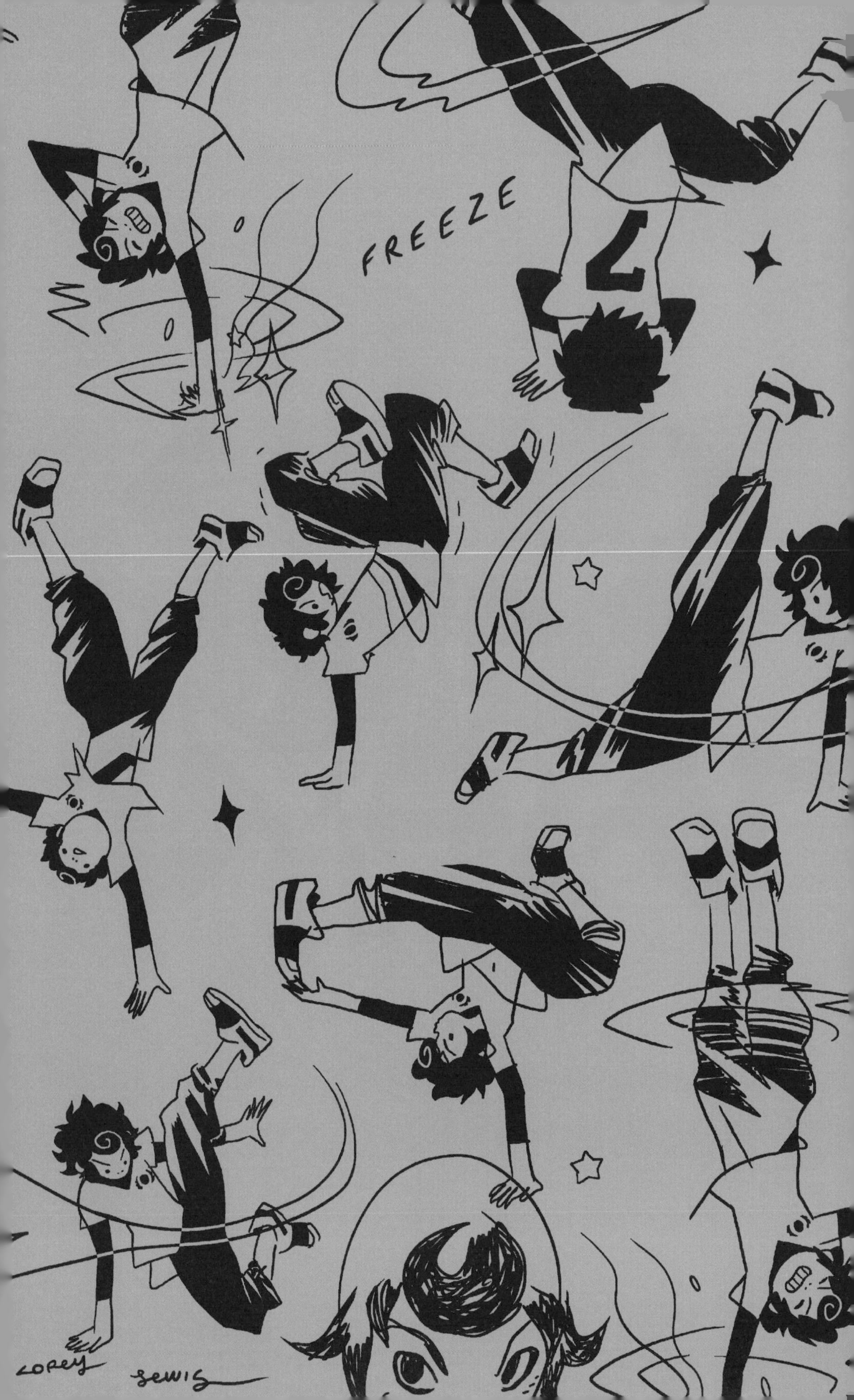
FREEZE
7
Corey Lewis

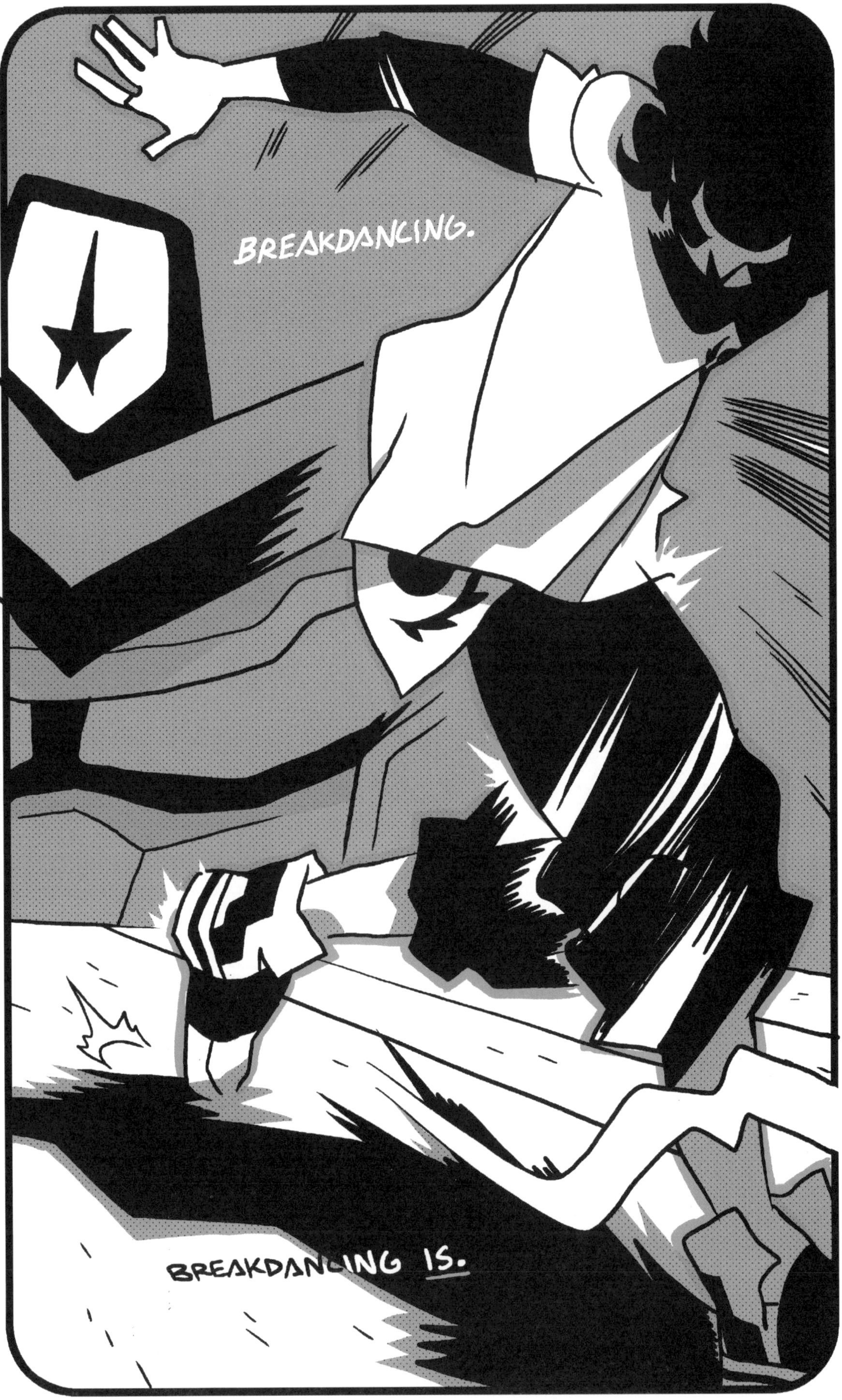
BREAKDANCING.
BREAKDANCING IS.

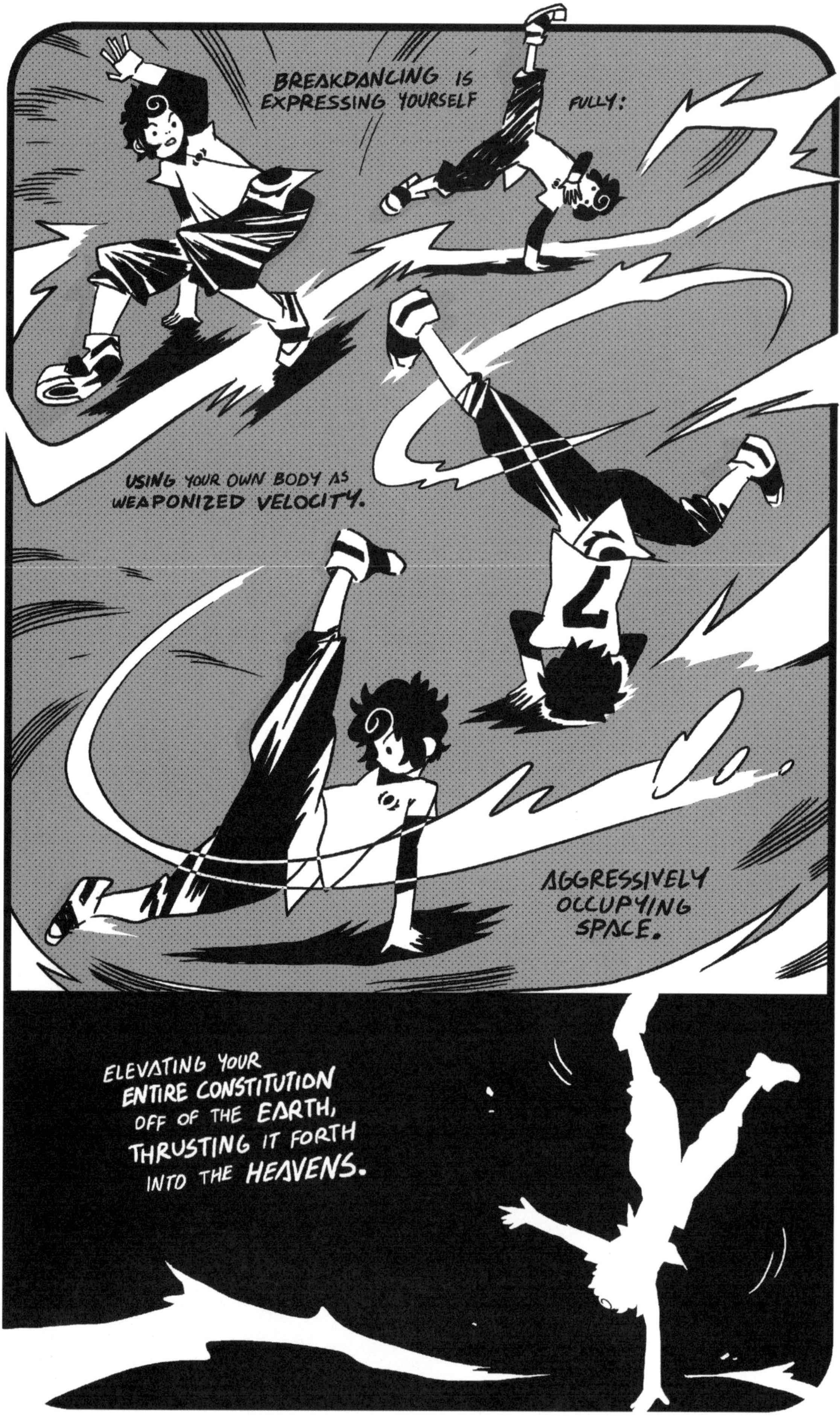
BREAKDANCING IS EXPRESSING YOURSELF FULLY:
USING YOUR OWN BODY AS WEAPONIZED VELOCITY.
AGGRESSIVELY OCCUPYING SPACE.
ELEVATING YOUR ENTIRE CONSTITUTION OFF OF THE EARTH, THRUSTING IT FORTH INTO THE HEAVENS.

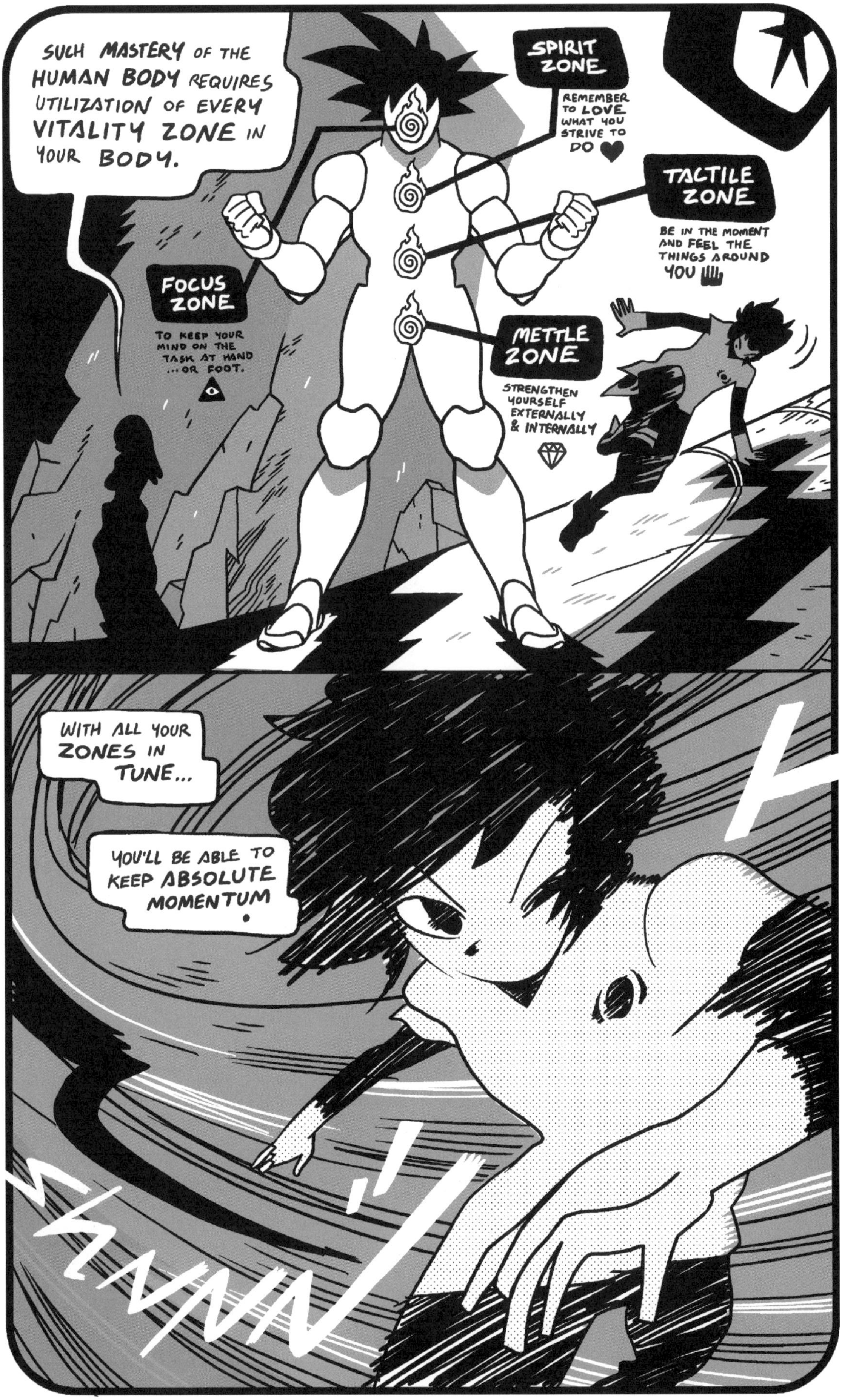
SUCH MASTERY OF THE HUMAN BODY REQUIRES UTILIZATION OF EVERY VITALITY ZONE IN YOUR BODY.
SPIRIT ZONE
REMEMBER TO LOVE WHAT YOU STRIVE TO DO
TACTILE ZONE
BE IN THE MOMENT AND FEEL THE THINGS AROUND YOU
FOCUS ZONE
TO KEEP YOUR MIND ON THE TASK AT HAND ...OR FOOT.
METTLE ZONE
STRENGTHEN YOURSELF EXTERNALLY & INTERNALLY
WITH ALL YOUR ZONES IN TUNE...
YOU'LL BE ABLE TO KEEP ABSOLUTE MOMENTUM.

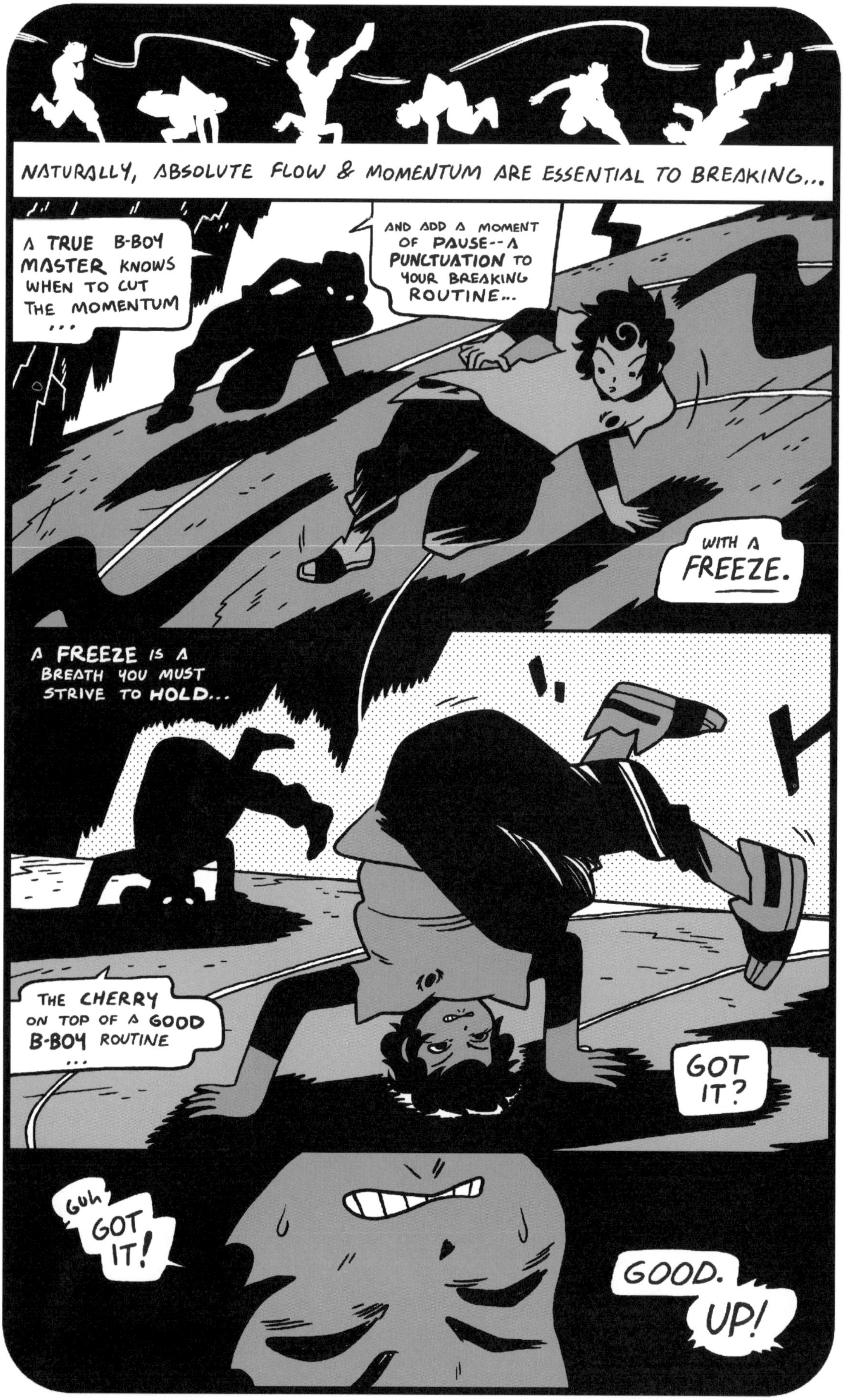
NATURALLY, ABSOLUTE FLOW & MOMENTUM ARE ESSENTIAL TO BREAKING...
A TRUE B-BOY MASTER KNOWS WHEN TO CUT THE MOMENTUM...
AND ADD A MOMENT OF PAUSE--A PUNCTUATION TO YOUR BREAKING ROUTINE...
WITH A FREEZE.
A FREEZE IS A BREATH YOU MUST STRIVE TO HOLD...
THE CHERRY ON TOP OF A GOOD B-BOY ROUTINE...
GOT IT?
GUH GOT IT!
GOOD.
UP!

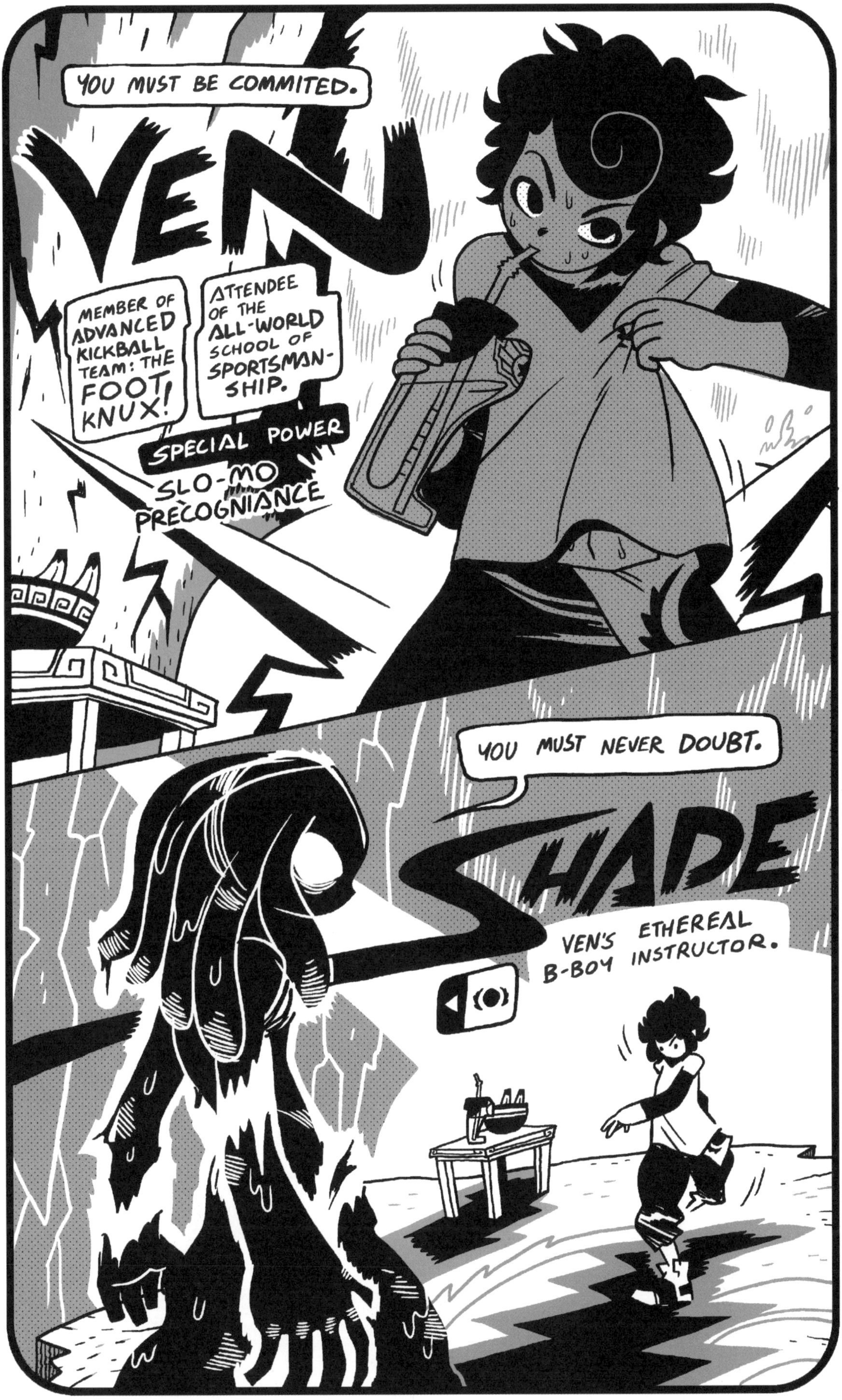
YOU MUST BE COMMITED.
VEN
MEMBER OF ADVANCED KICKBALL TEAM: THE FOOT KNUX!
ATTENDEE OF THE ALL-WORLD SCHOOL OF SPORTSMAN-SHIP.
SPECIAL POWER
SLO-MO PRECOGNIANCE
YOU MUST NEVER DOUBT.
SHADE
VEN'S ETHEREAL B-BOY INSTRUCTOR.

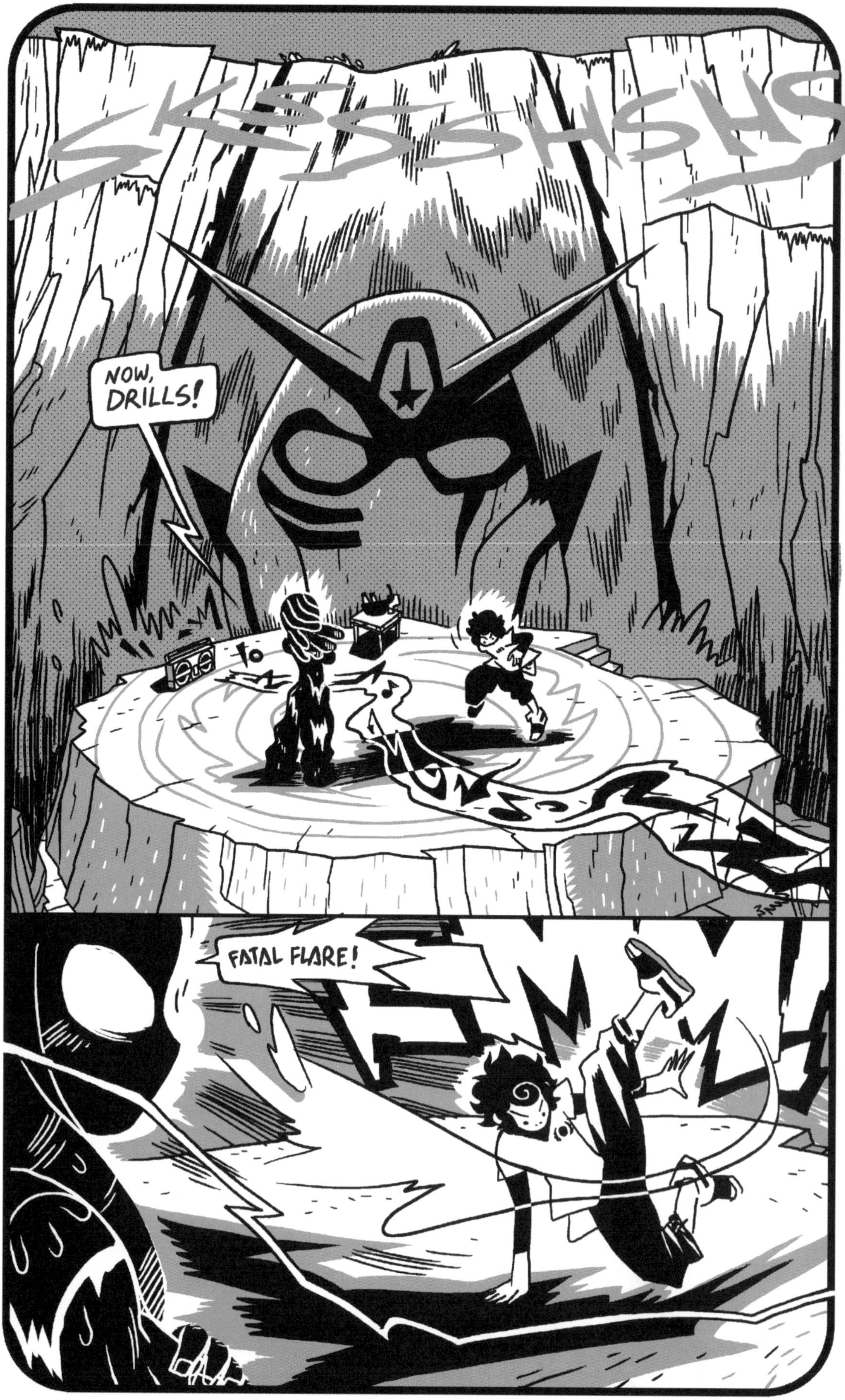
SKSSSHSHS
NOW, DRILLS!
FATAL FLARE!

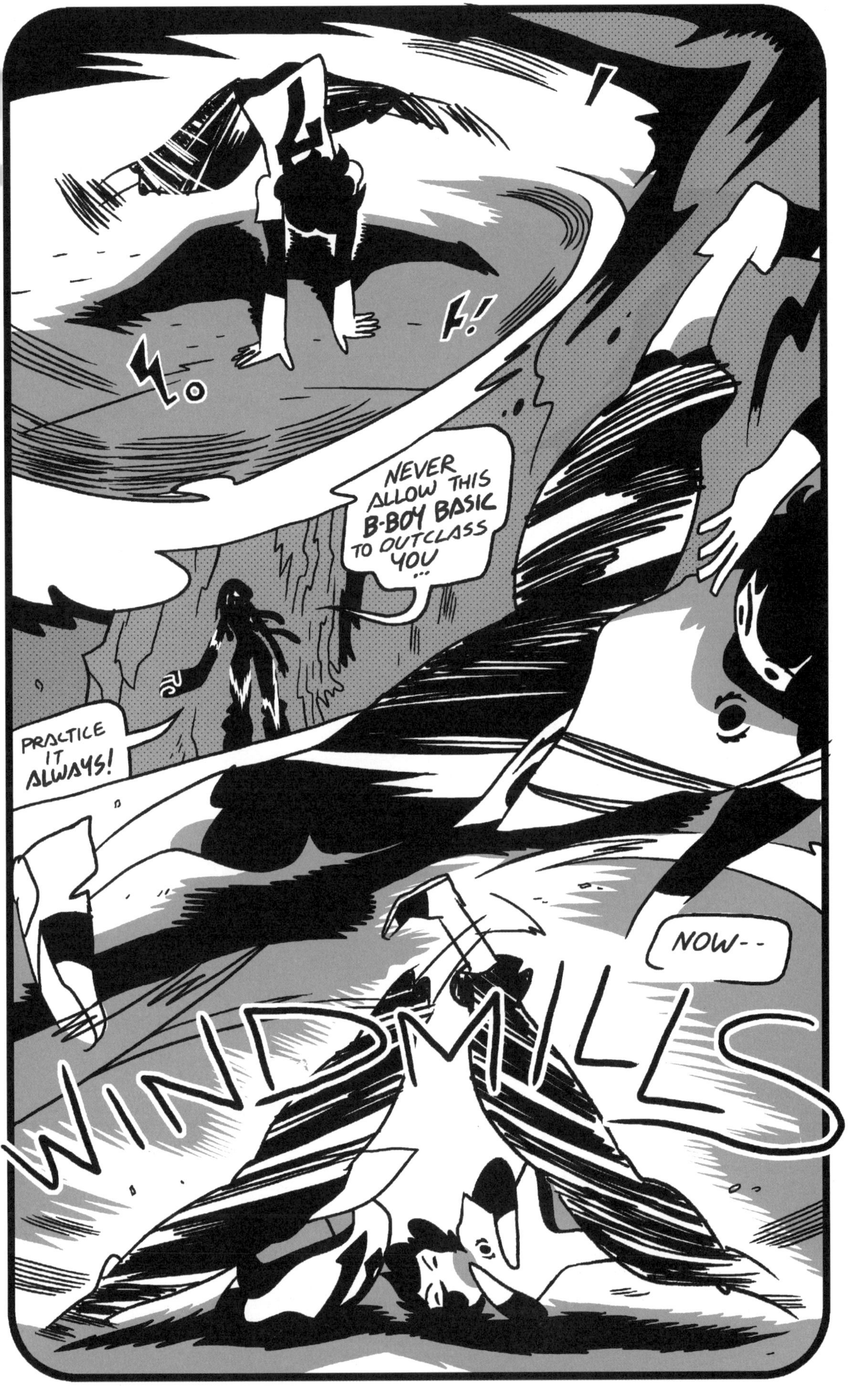

NEVER ALLOW THIS B-BOY BASIC TO OUTCLASS YOU...
PRACTICE IT ALWAYS!
NOW--
WINDMILLS

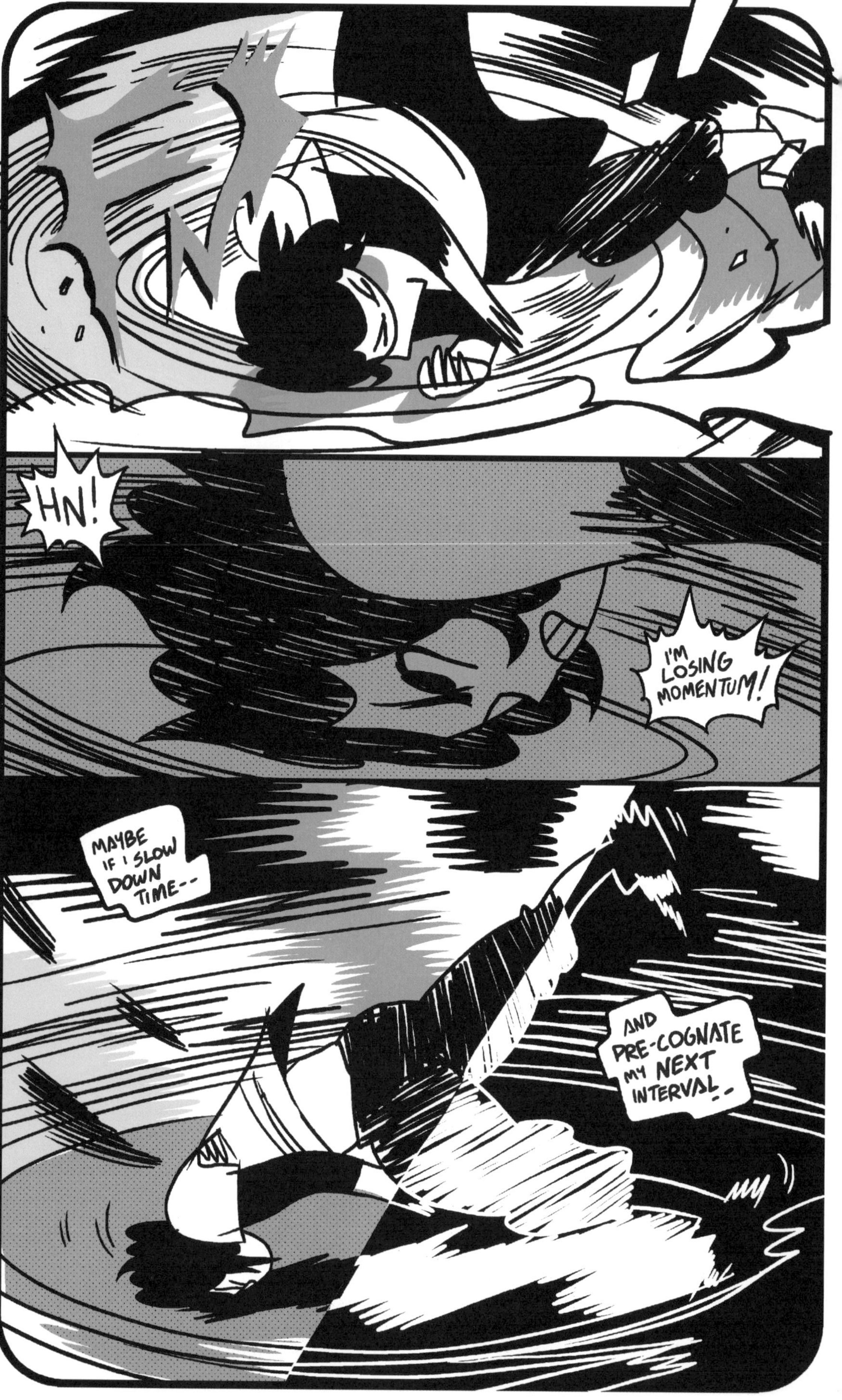
FN
HN!
I'M LOSING MOMENTUM!
MAYBE IF I SLOW DOWN TIME--
AND PRE-COGNATE MY NEXT INTERVAL--

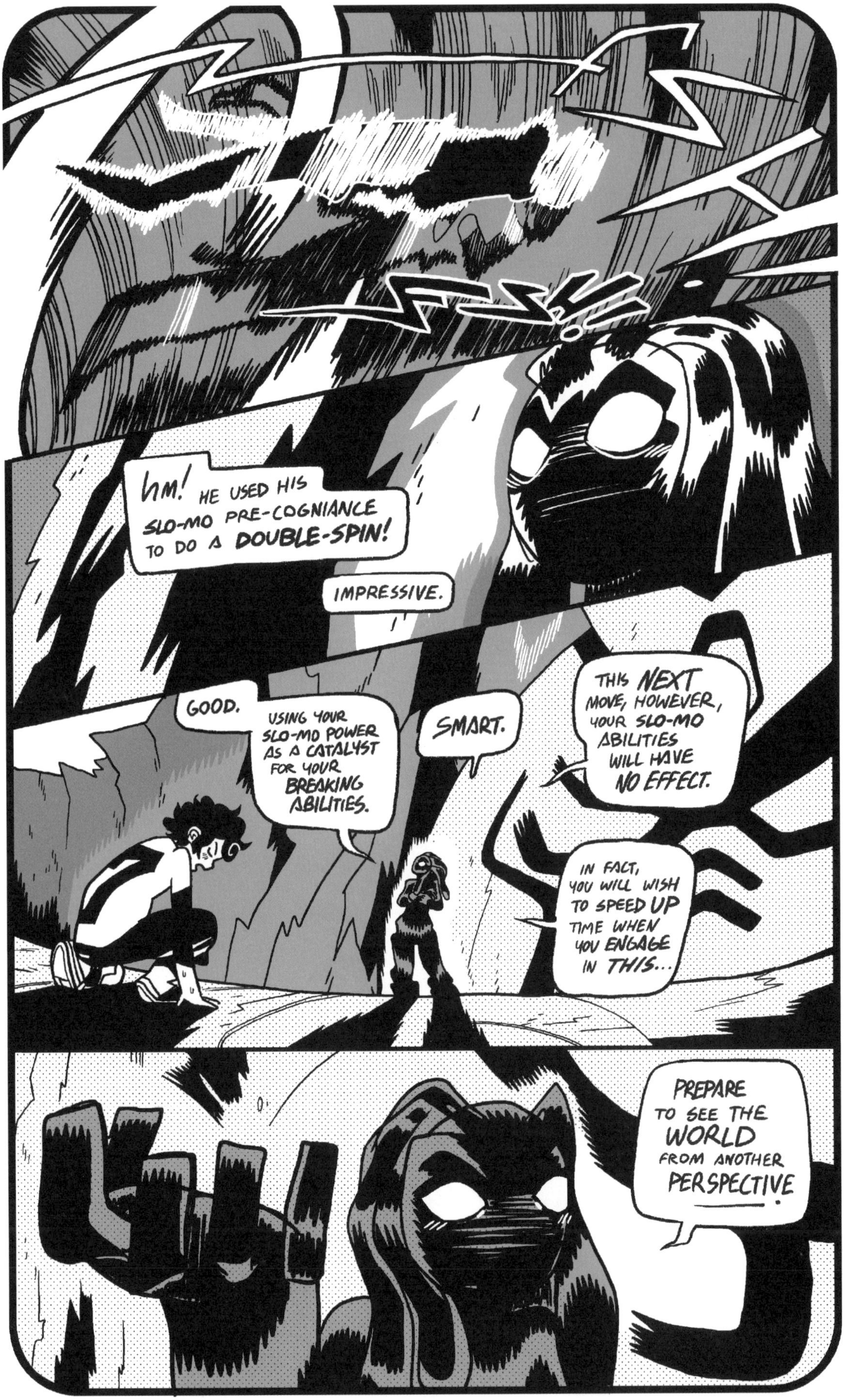
HM! HE USED HIS SLO-MO PRE-COGNIANCE TO DO A DOUBLE-SPIN!
IMPRESSIVE.
GOOD.
USING YOUR SLO-MO POWER AS A CATALYST FOR YOUR BREAKING ABILITIES.
SMART.
THIS NEXT MOVE, HOWEVER, YOUR SLO-MO ABILITIES WILL HAVE NO EFFECT.
IN FACT, YOU WILL WISH TO SPEED UP TIME WHEN YOU ENGAGE IN THIS...
PREPARE TO SEE THE WORLD FROM ANOTHER PERSPECTIVE.

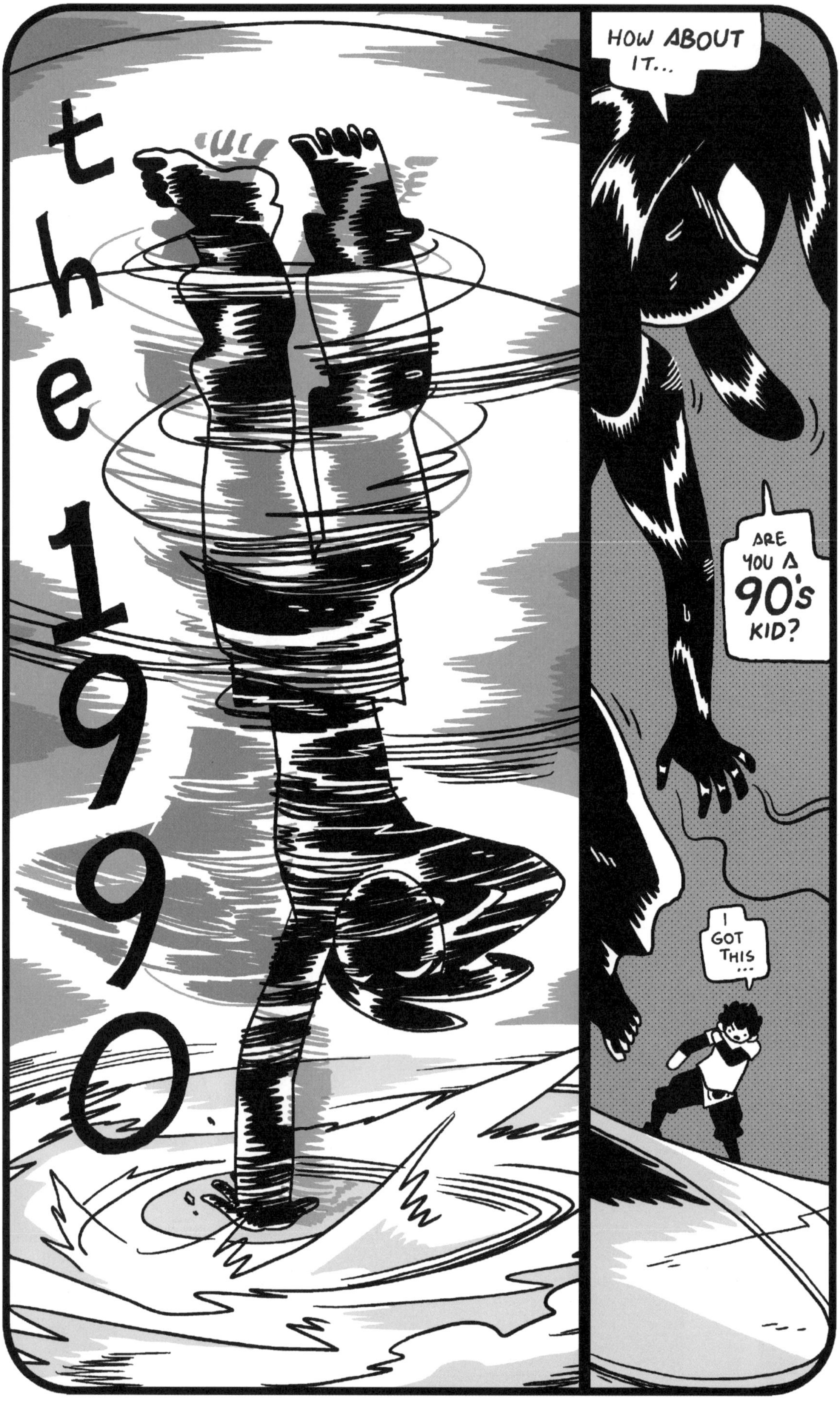
the 1990
HOW ABOUT IT...
ARE YOU A 90's KID?
I GOT THIS...

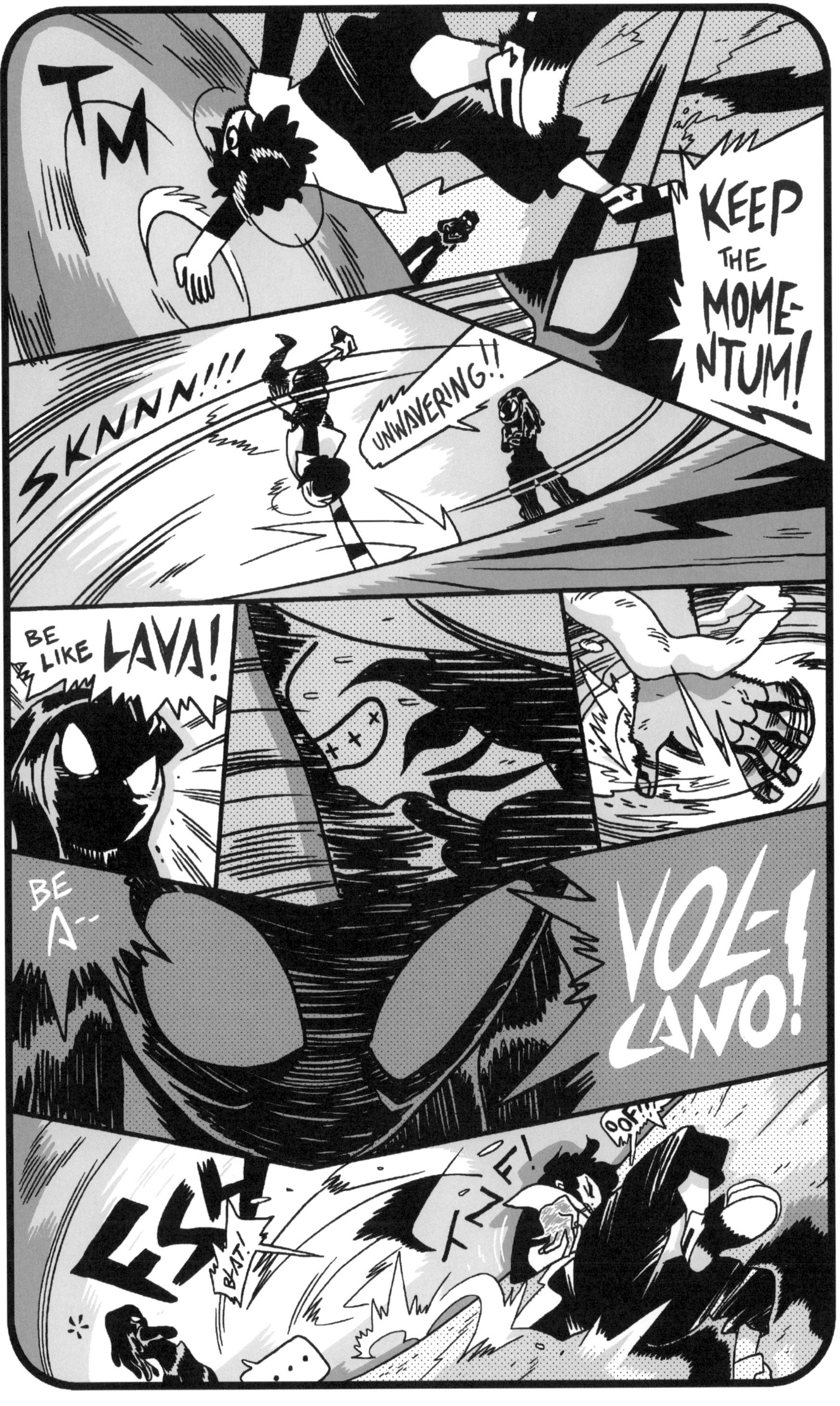
TM
KEEP THE MOME-NTUM!
SKNNN!!!
UNWAVERING!!
BE LIKE LAVA!
BE A--
VOL-CANO!
FSH
BLAT!
TZF!
OOF!

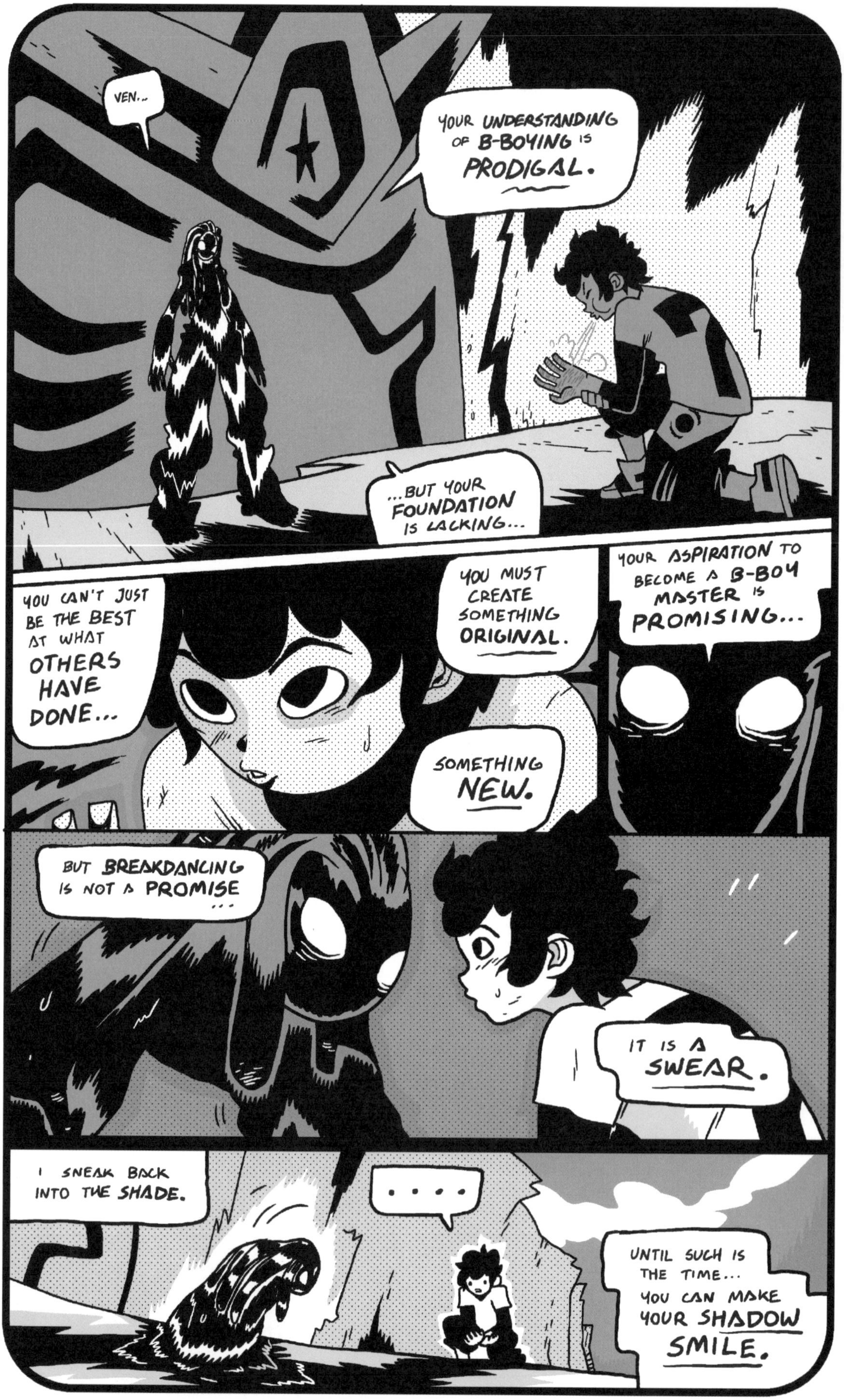
VEN..
YOUR UNDERSTANDING OF B-BOYING IS PRODIGAL.
...BUT YOUR FOUNDATION IS LACKING...
YOU CAN'T JUST BE THE BEST AT WHAT OTHERS HAVE DONE...
YOU MUST CREATE SOMETHING ORIGINAL.
SOMETHING NEW.
YOUR ASPIRATION TO BECOME A B-BOY MASTER IS PROMISING...
BUT BREAKDANCING IS NOT A PROMISE...
IT IS A SWEAR.
I SNEAK BACK INTO THE SHADE.
....
UNTIL SUCH IS THE TIME... YOU CAN MAKE YOUR SHADOW SMILE.

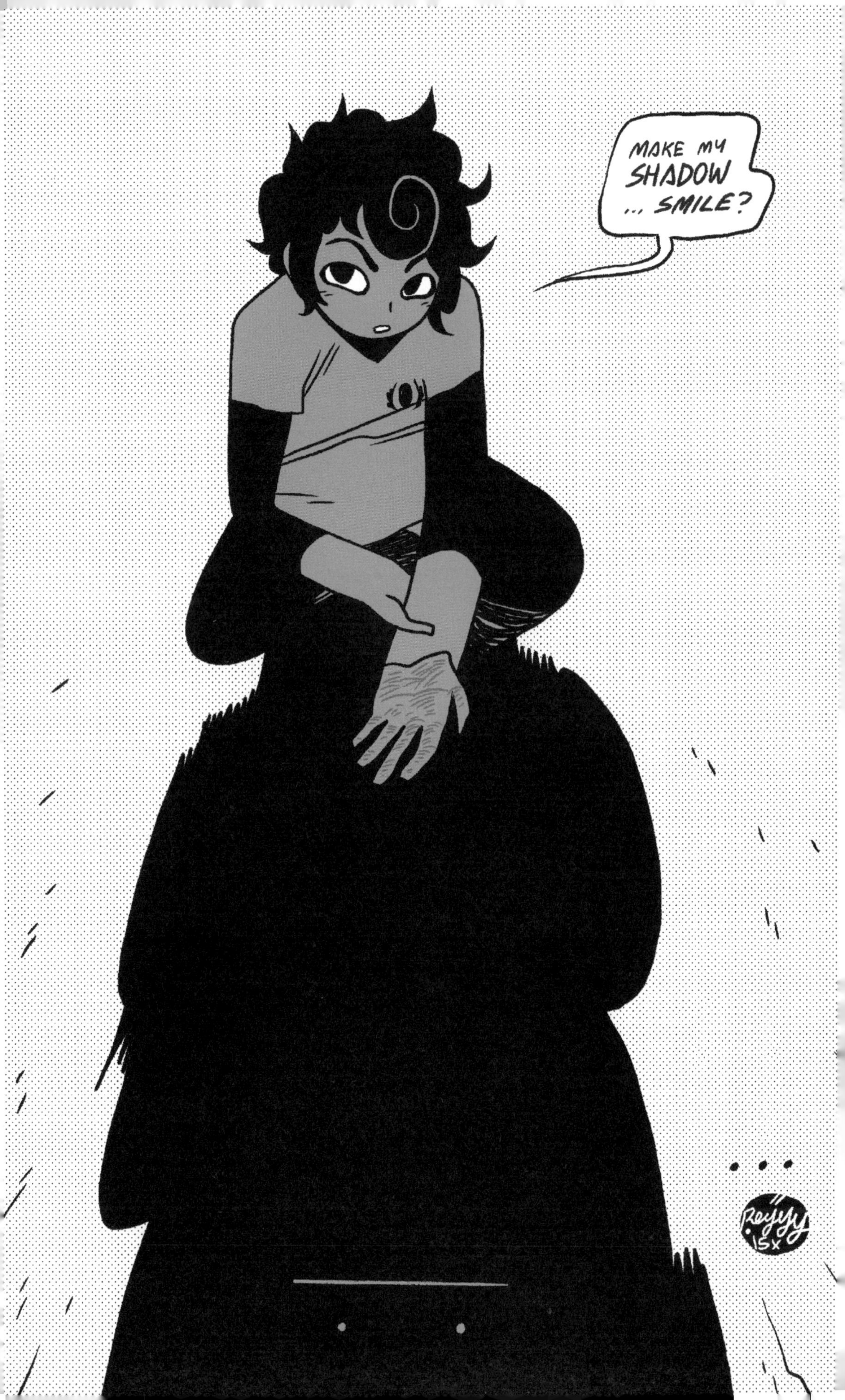
MAKE MY SHADOW ... SMILE?

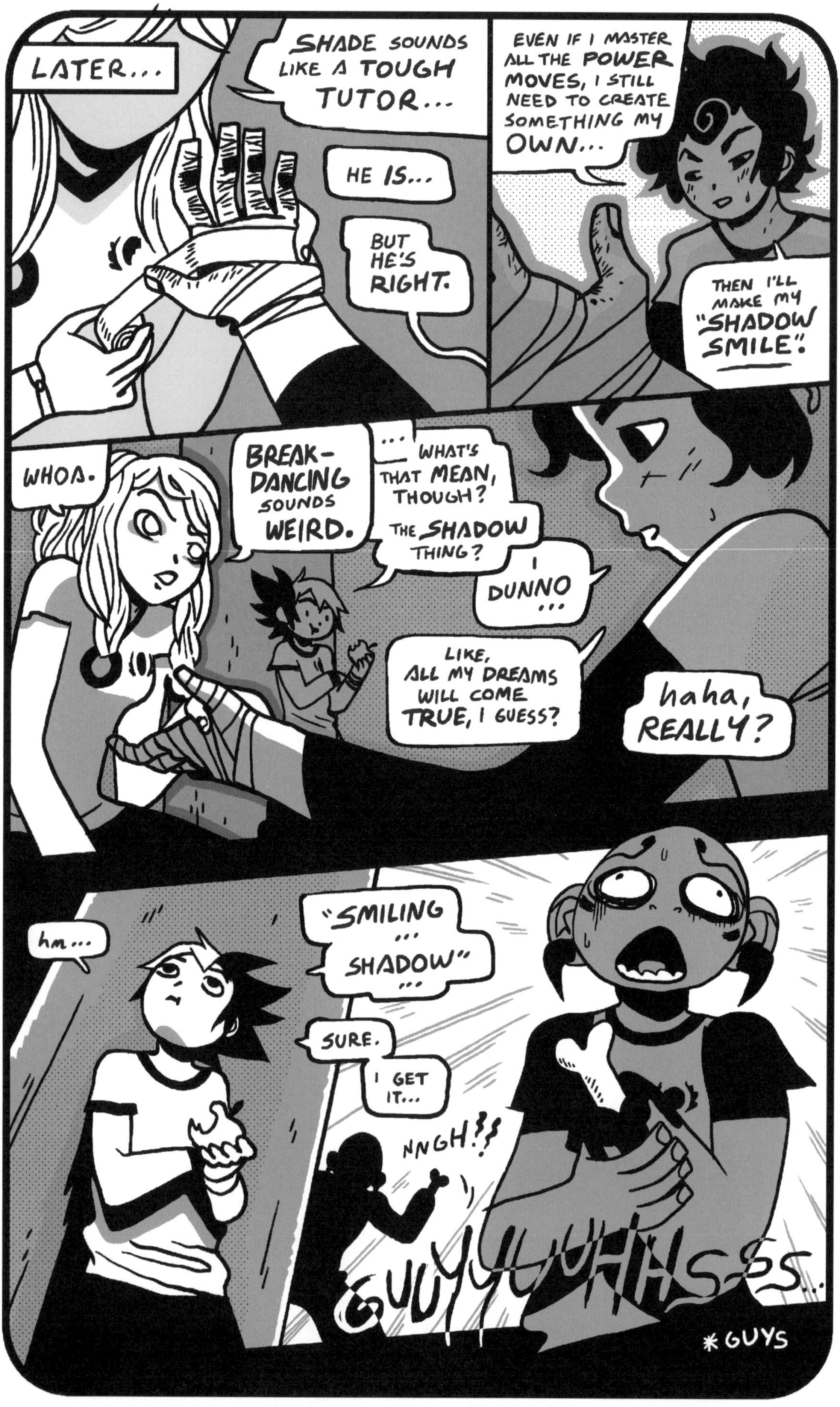
LATER...
SHADE SOUNDS LIKE A TOUGH TUTOR...
HE IS...
BUT HE'S RIGHT.
EVEN IF I MASTER ALL THE POWER MOVES, I STILL NEED TO CREATE SOMETHING MY OWN...
THEN I'LL MAKE MY "SHADOW SMILE".
WHOA.
BREAK-DANCING SOUNDS WEIRD.
... WHAT'S THAT MEAN, THOUGH?
THE SHADOW THING?
I DUNNO ...
LIKE, ALL MY DREAMS WILL COME TRUE, I GUESS?
haha, REALLY?
hm...
"SMILING ... SHADOW" ...
SURE.
I GET IT...
NNGH!?!
GUUYYUUHHSSSS...
* GUYS

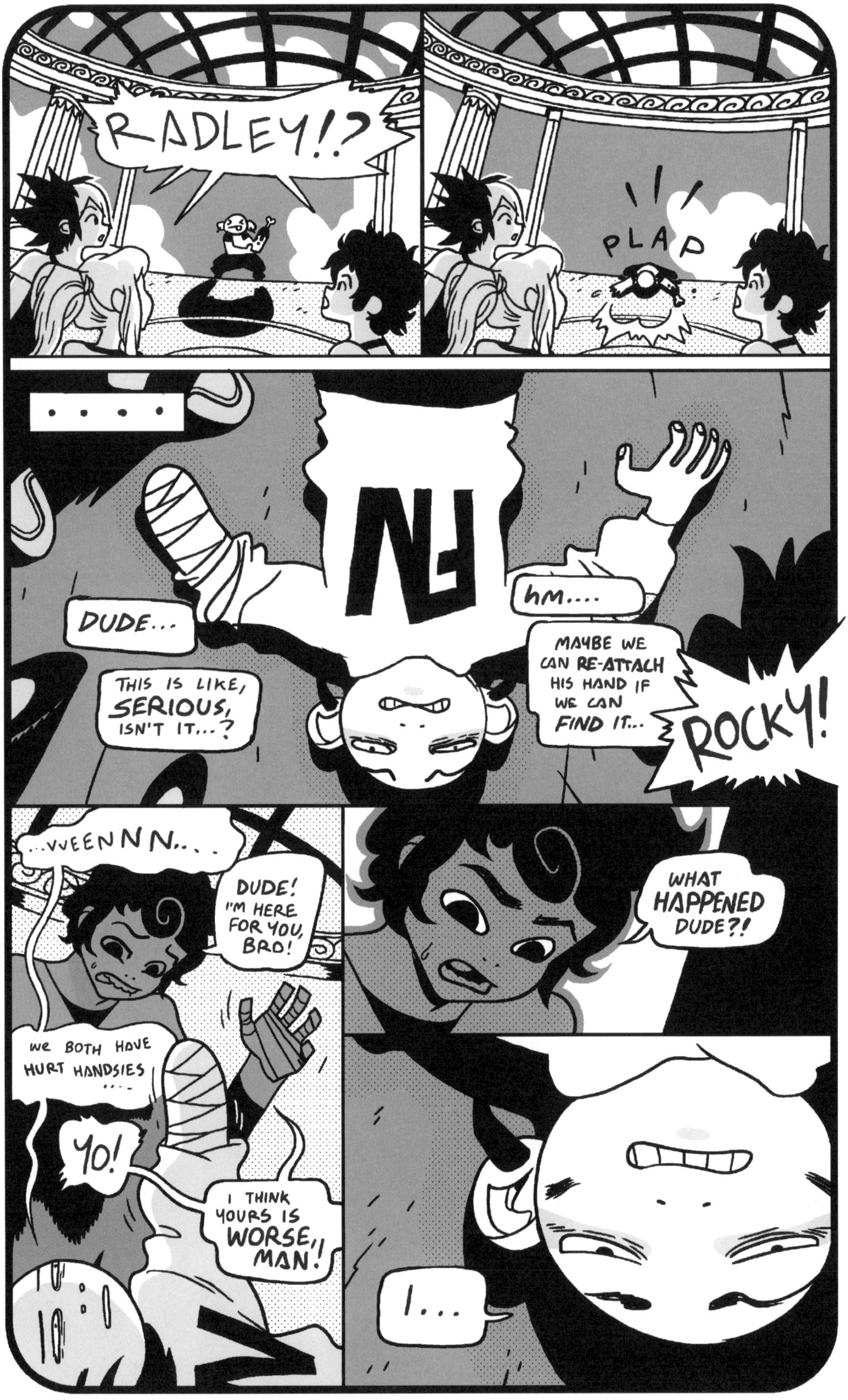
RADLEY!?
PLAP
. . . .
DUDE...
THIS IS LIKE, SERIOUS, ISN'T IT...?
hm....
MAYBE WE CAN RE-ATTACH HIS HAND IF WE CAN FIND IT...
ROCKY!
...VVEENNN...
DUDE! I'M HERE FOR YOU, BRO!
WE BOTH HAVE HURT HANDSIES ...
YO!
I THINK YOURS IS WORSE, MAN!
WHAT HAPPENED DUDE?!
I...

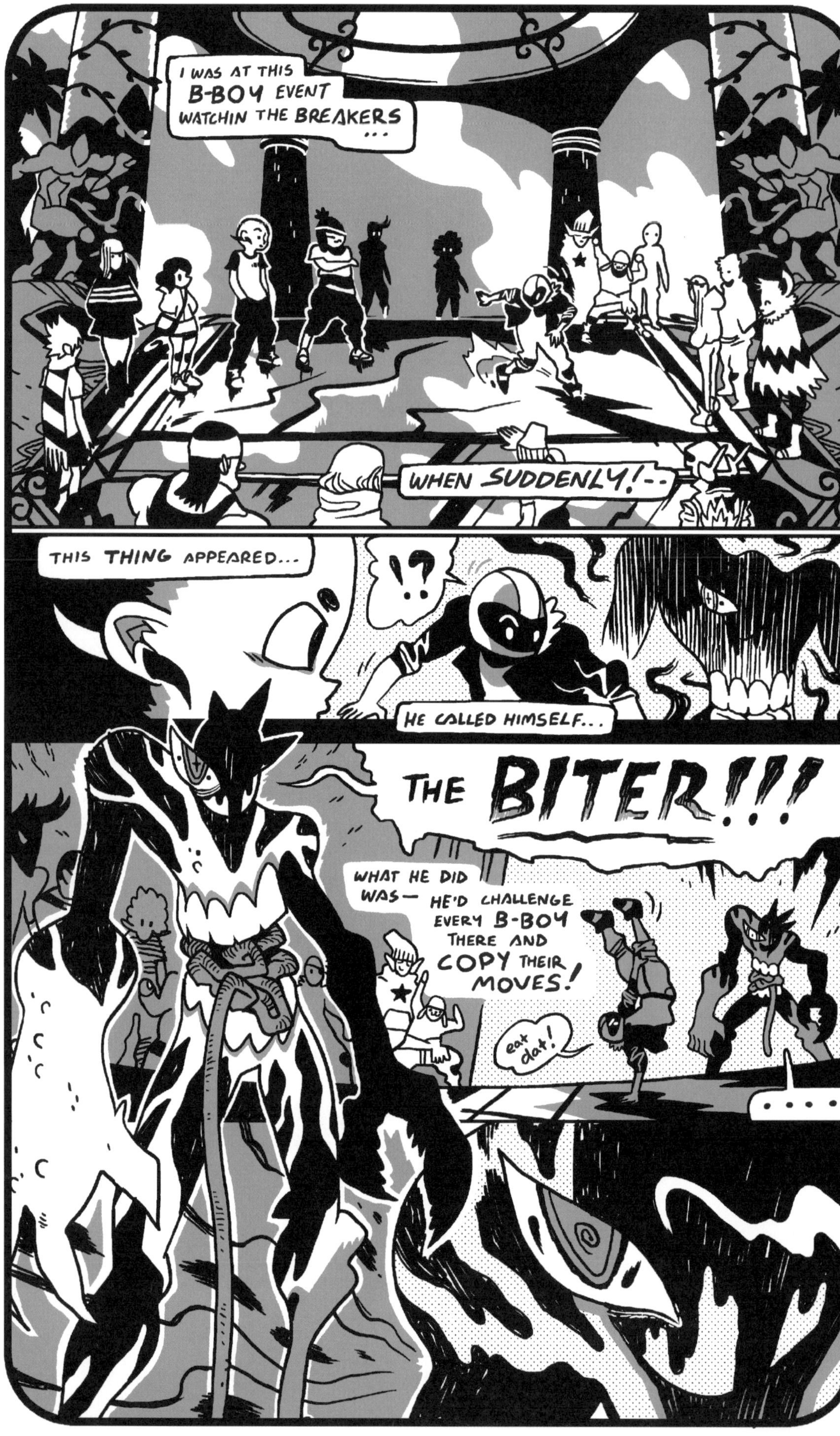
I WAS AT THIS B-BOY EVENT WATCHIN THE BREAKERS ...
WHEN SUDDENLY!--
THIS THING APPEARED...
!?
HE CALLED HIMSELF...
THE BITER!!!
WHAT HE DID WAS— HE'D CHALLENGE EVERY B-BOY THERE AND COPY THEIR MOVES!
eat dat!
...

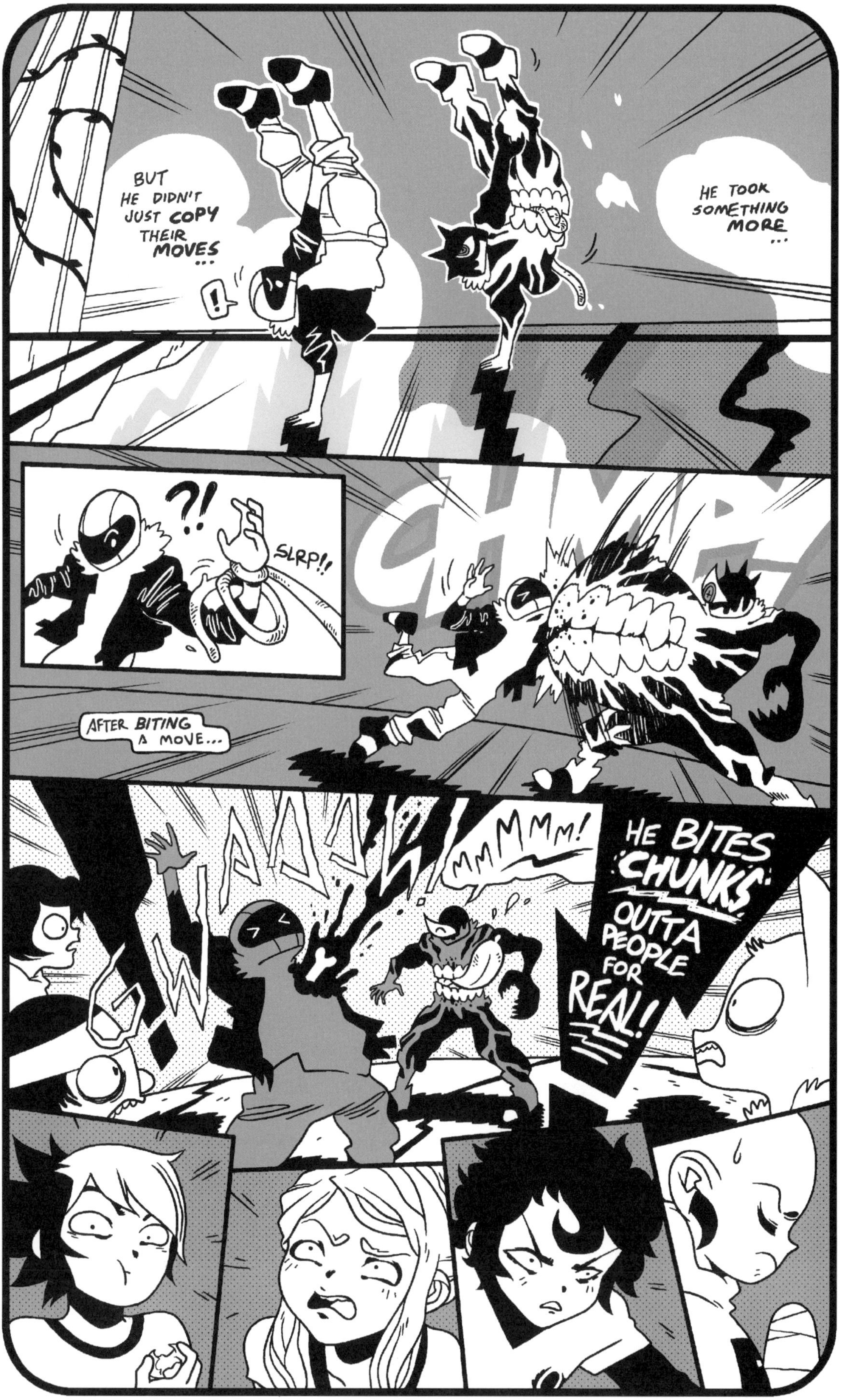
BUT HE DIDN'T JUST COPY THEIR MOVES ...
!
HE TOOK SOMETHING MORE ...
?!
SLRP!!
CHMP!
AFTER BITING A MOVE...
MMMMM!
HE BITES CHUNKS OUTTA PEOPLE FOR REAL!

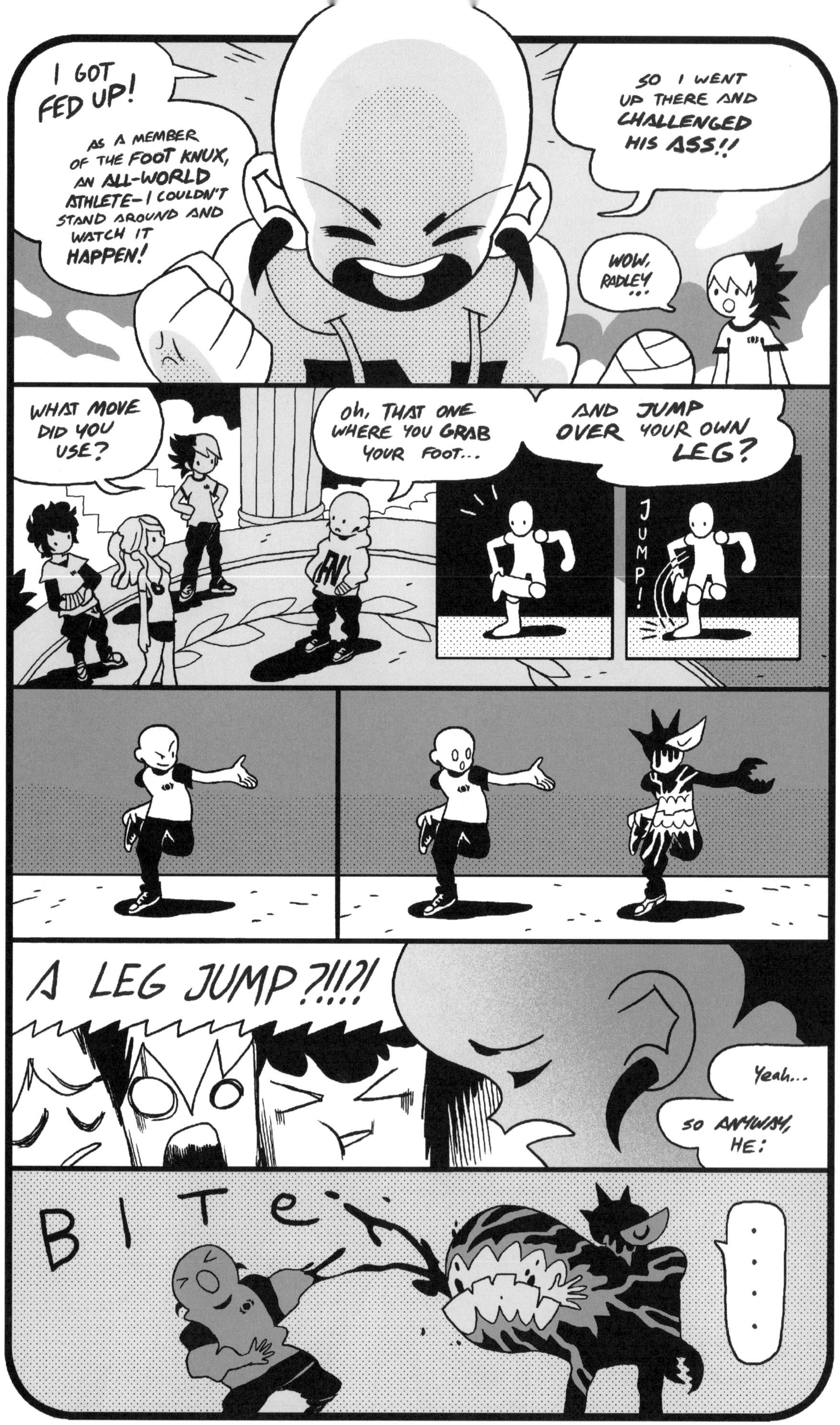
I GOT FED UP!
AS A MEMBER OF THE FOOT KNUX, AN ALL-WORLD ATHLETE—I COULDN'T STAND AROUND AND WATCH IT HAPPEN!
SO I WENT UP THERE AND CHALLENGED HIS ASS!!
WOW, RADLEY...
WHAT MOVE DID YOU USE?
Oh, THAT ONE WHERE YOU GRAB YOUR FOOT...
AND JUMP OVER YOUR OWN LEG?
JUMP!
A LEG JUMP?!!?!
Yeah...
SO ANYWAY, HE:
BITe
. . . .

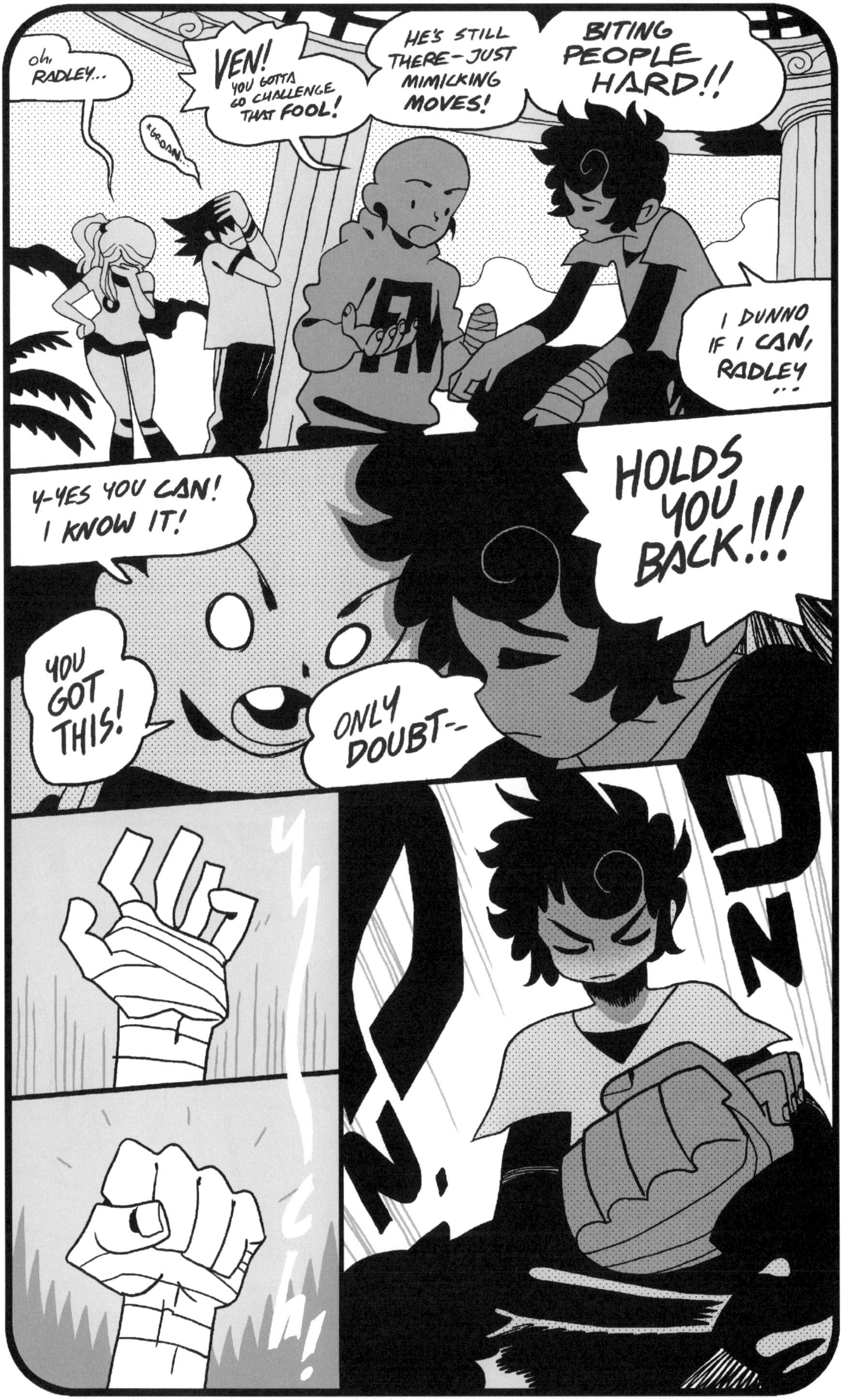
oh, RADLEY...
GROAN...
VEN! YOU GOTTA GO CHALLENGE THAT FOOL!
HE'S STILL THERE--JUST MIMICKING MOVES!
BITING PEOPLE HARD!!
I DUNNO IF I CAN, RADLEY ...
Y-YES YOU CAN! I KNOW IT!
YOU GOT THIS!
ONLY DOUBT--
HOLDS YOU BACK!!!
DUNN...
YYYYC...h!

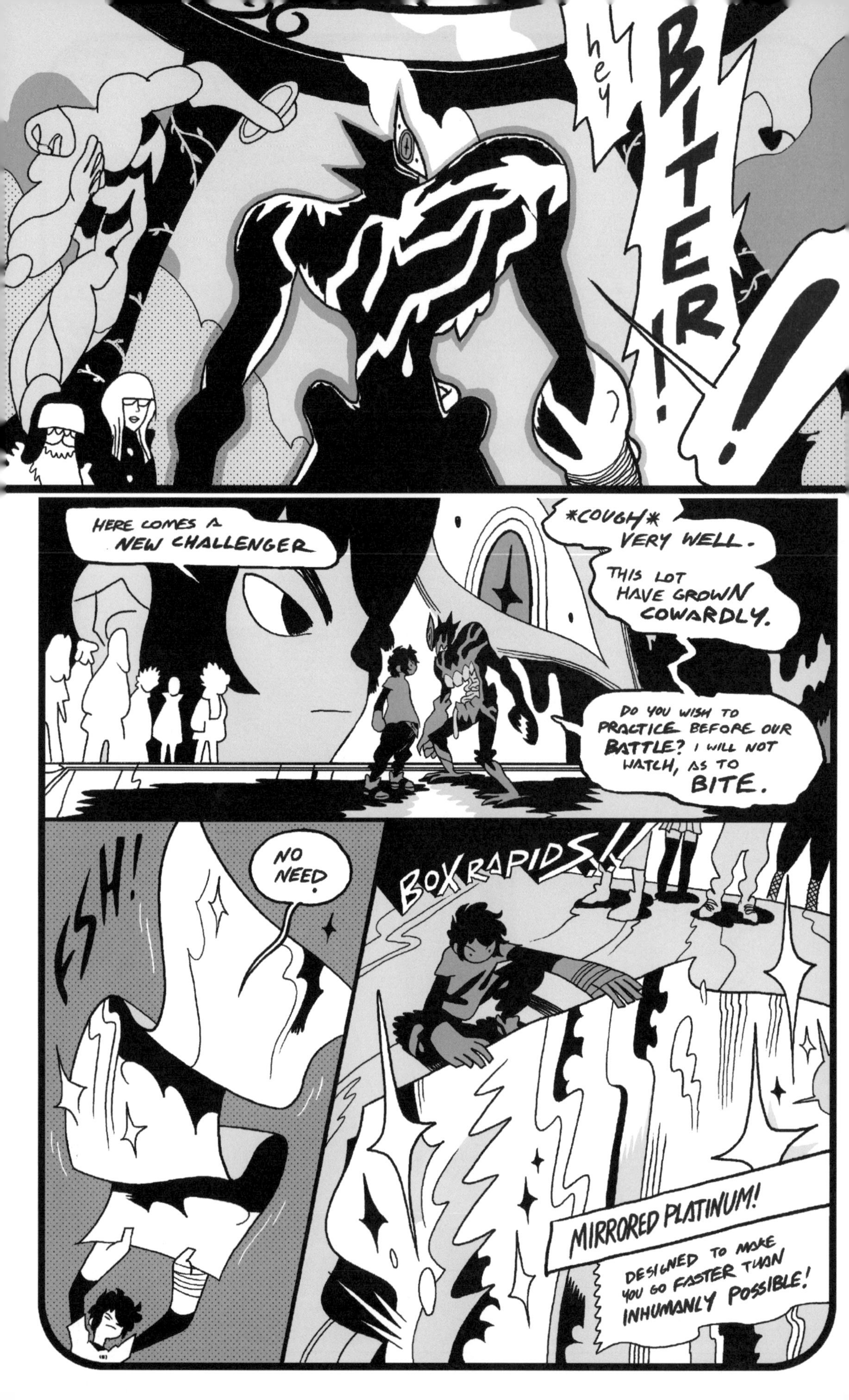
hey
BITER!!
HERE COMES A NEW CHALLENGER
COUGH VERY WELL.
THIS LOT HAVE GROWN COWARDLY.
DO YOU WISH TO PRACTICE BEFORE OUR BATTLE? I WILL NOT WATCH, AS TO BITE.
FSH!
NO NEED.
BOX RAPIDS!!
MIRRORED PLATINUM!
DESIGNED TO MAKE YOU GO FASTER THAN INHUMANLY POSSIBLE!

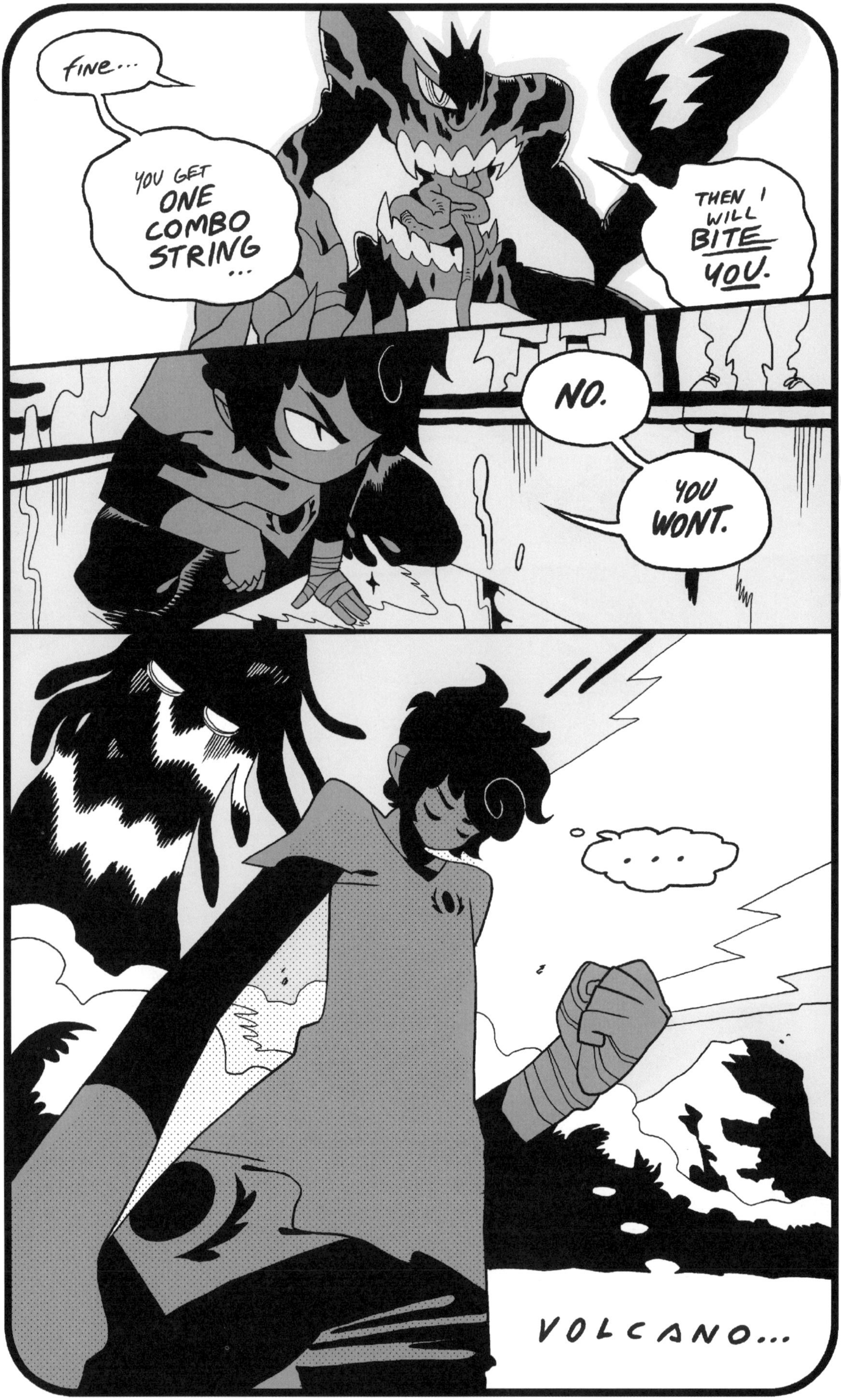
fine...
YOU GET ONE COMBO STRING ...
THEN I WILL BITE YOU.
NO.
YOU WONT.
...
VOLCANO...

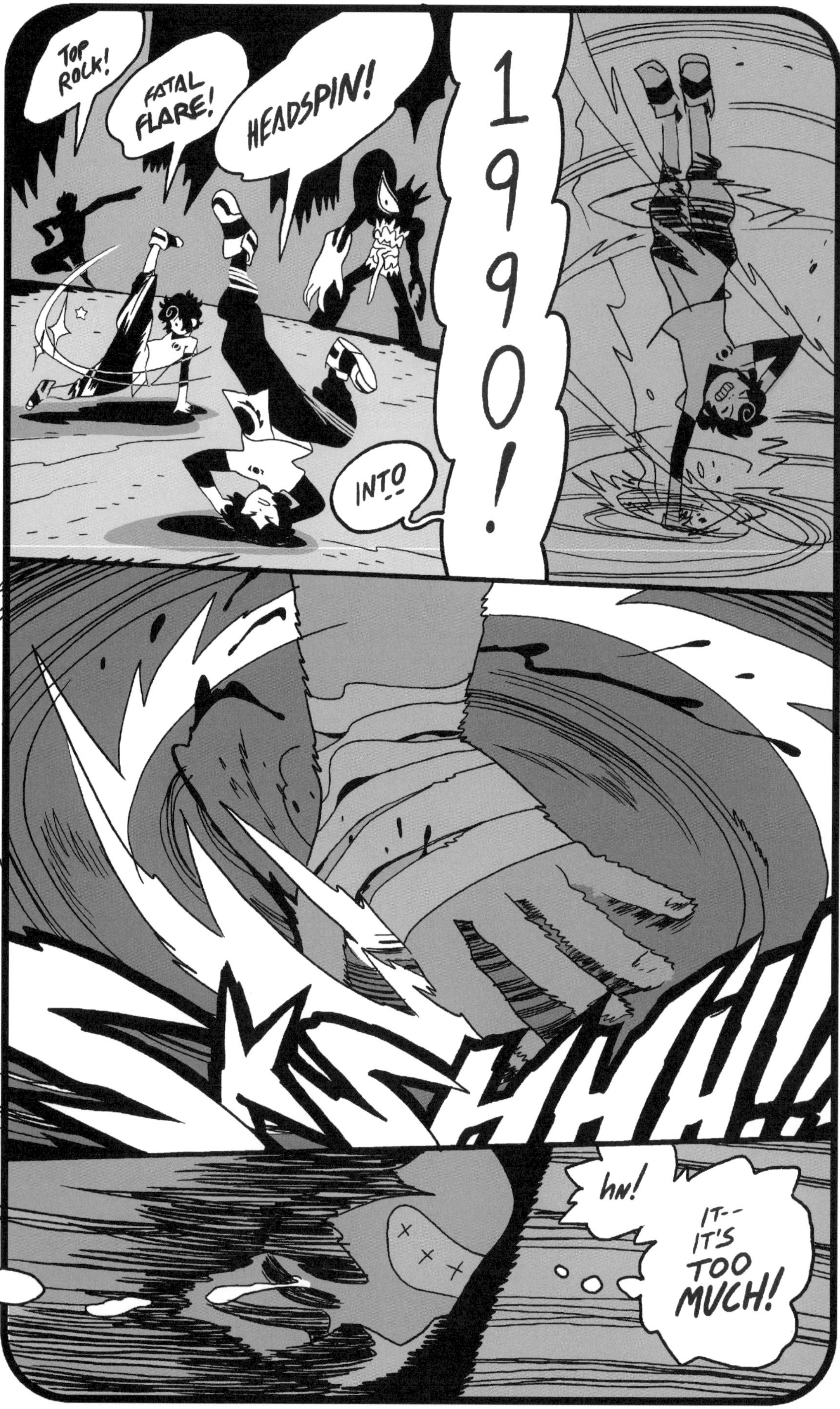
TOP ROCK!
FATAL FLARE!
HEADSPIN!
INTO
1990!
hn!
IT-- IT'S TOO MUCH!

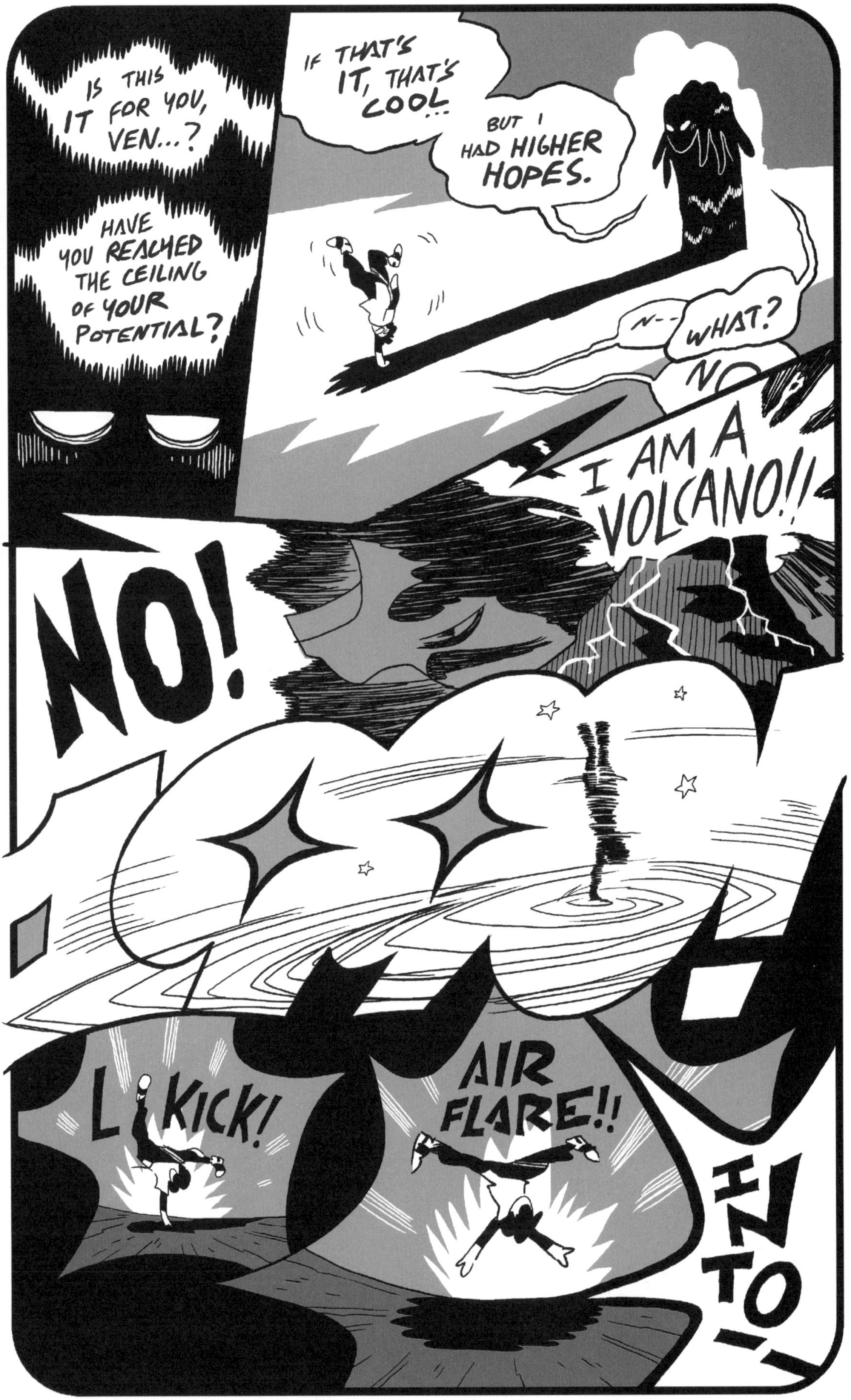
IS THIS IT FOR YOU, VEN...?
HAVE YOU REACHED THE CEILING OF YOUR POTENTIAL?
IF THAT'S IT, THAT'S COOL...
BUT I HAD HIGHER HOPES.
N--
WHAT?
NO
I AM A VOLCANO!!
NO!
L KICK!
AIR FLARE!!
INTO--

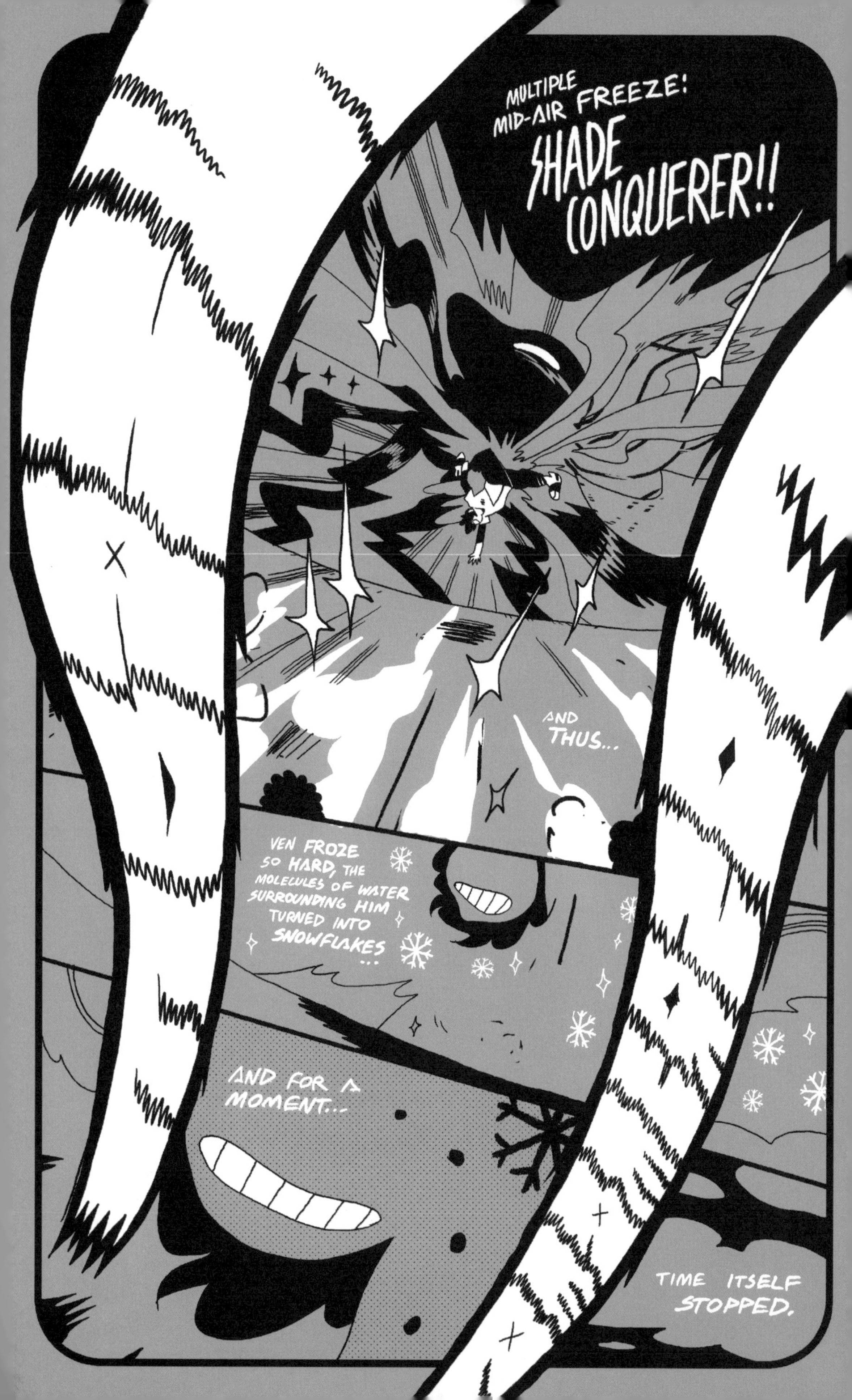
MULTIPLE MID-AIR FREEZE:
SHADE CONQUERER!!
AND THUS...
VEN FROZE SO HARD, THE MOLECULES OF WATER SURROUNDING HIM TURNED INTO SNOWFLAKES...
AND FOR A MOMENT...
TIME ITSELF STOPPED.

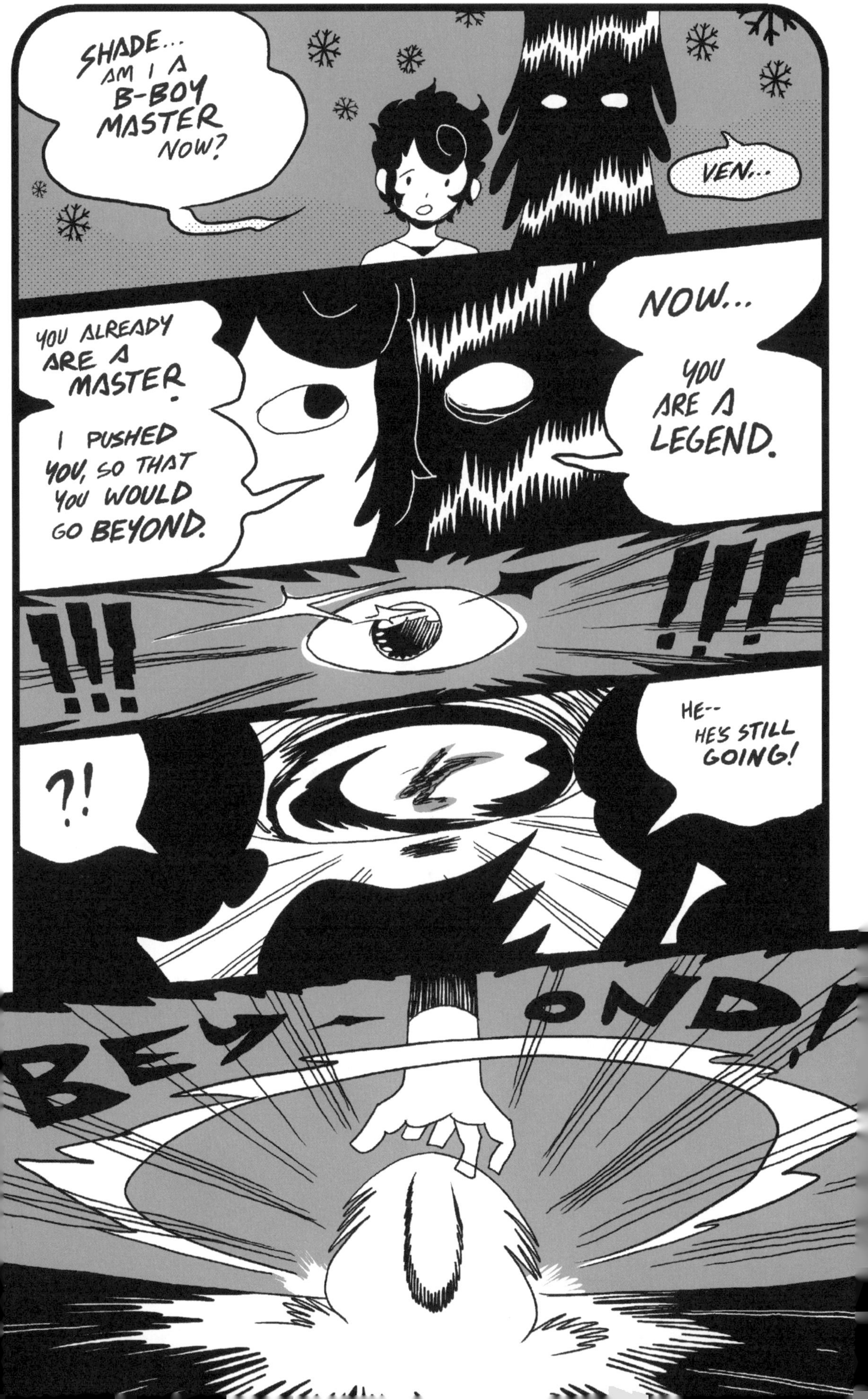
SHADE... AM I A B-BOY MASTER NOW?
VEN...
YOU ALREADY ARE A MASTER.
I PUSHED YOU, SO THAT YOU WOULD GO BEYOND.
NOW...
YOU ARE A LEGEND.
!!!
!!!
?!
HE-- HE'S STILL GOING!
BEY- OND!!

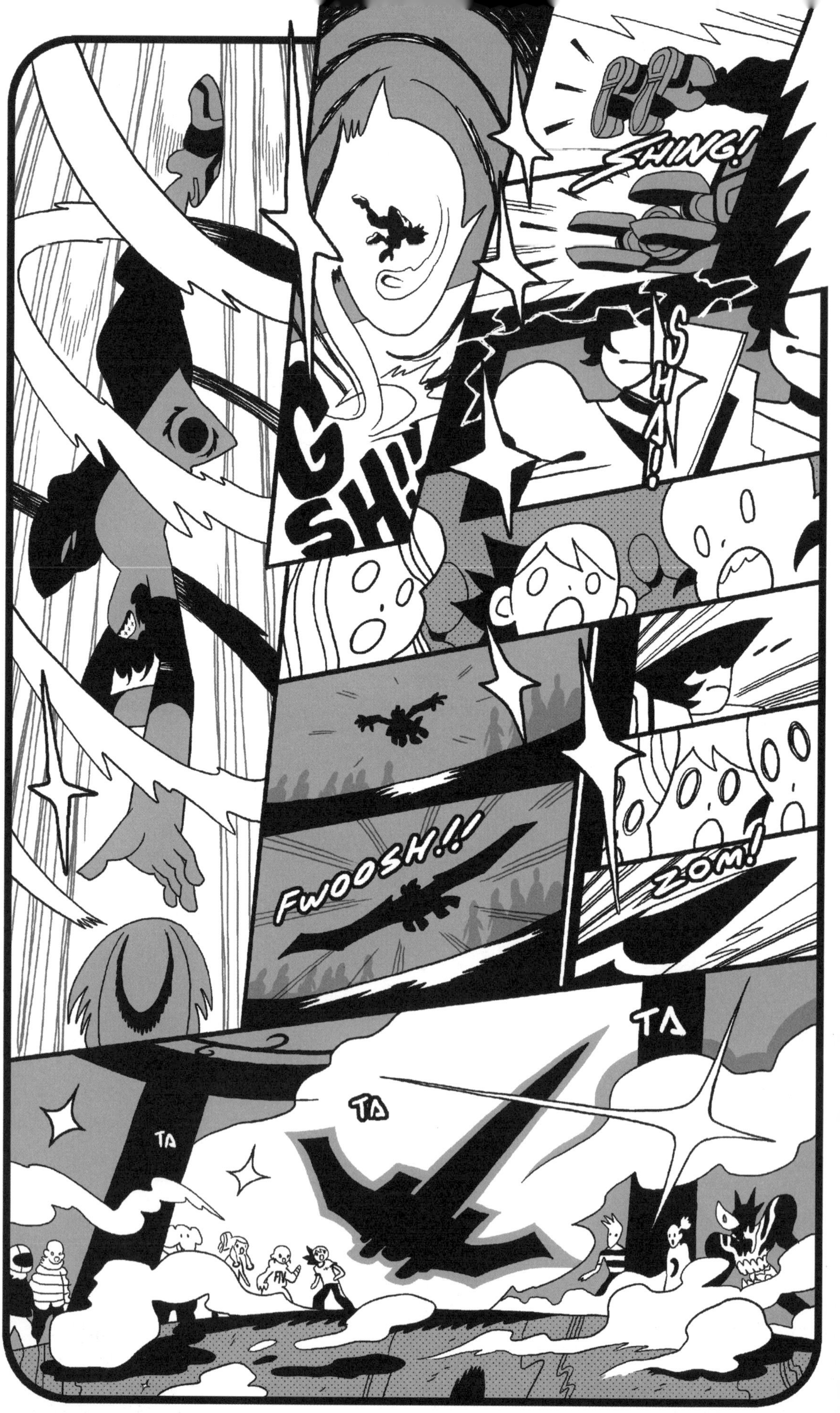
SHING!
SUSHA!
GSH!!
FWOOSH!!
ZOM!
TA
TA
TA

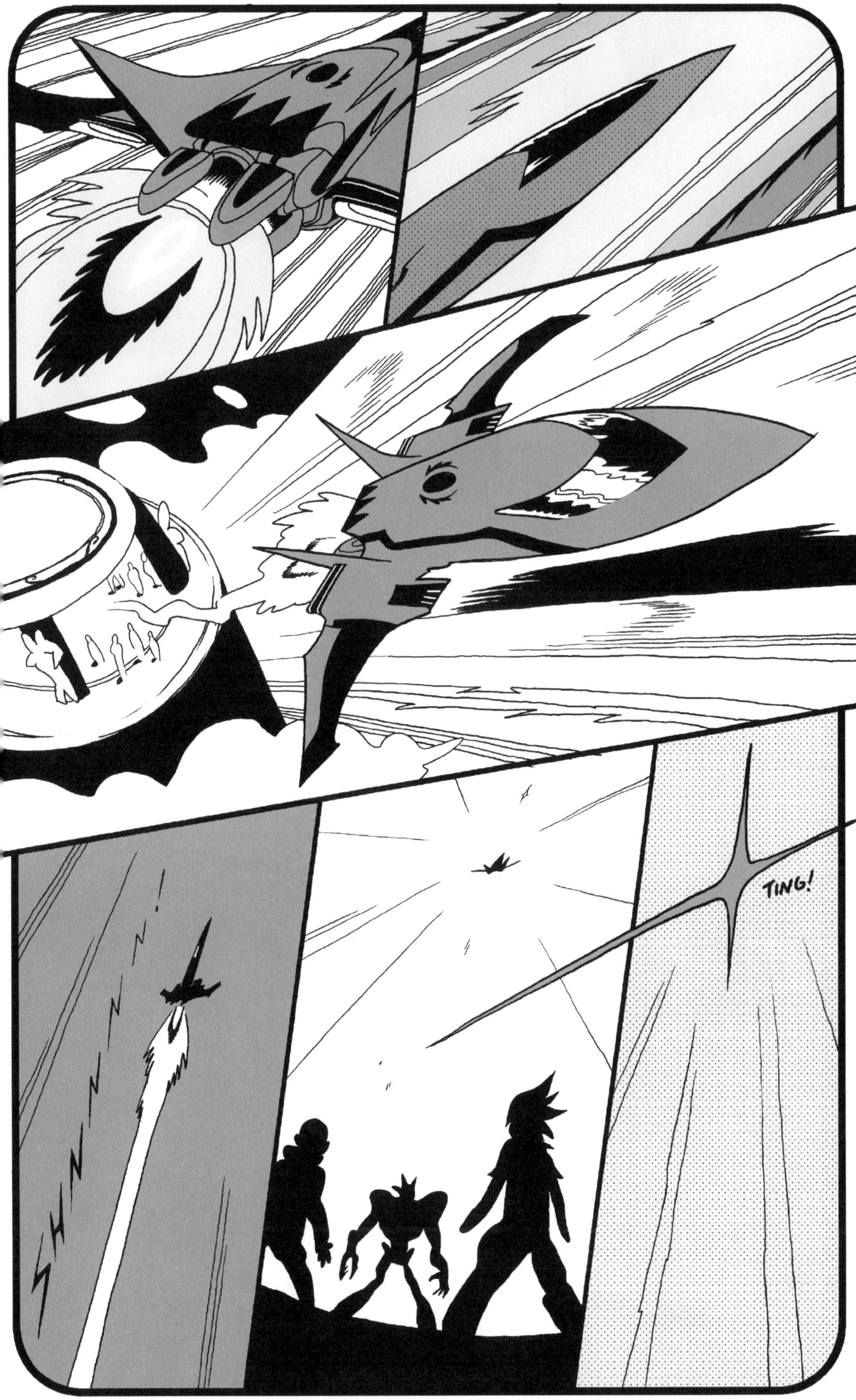
SHNNNN!
TING!

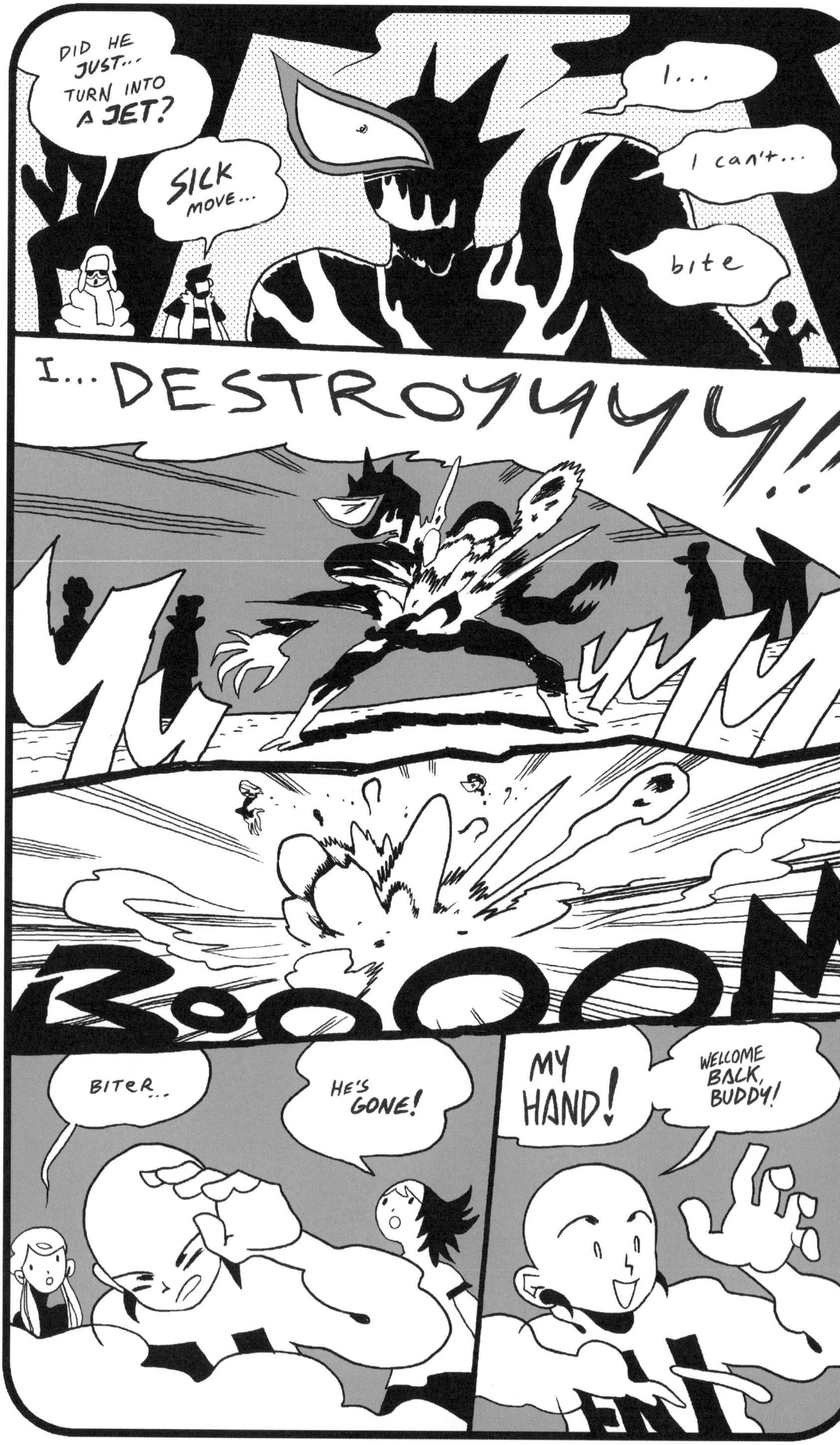
DID HE JUST... TURN INTO A JET?
SICK MOVE...
I...
I can't...
bite
I... DESTROYYYYY!!
YUYYYYM
BOOOOOM
BITER...
HE'S GONE!
MY HAND!
WELLCOME BACK, BUDDY!

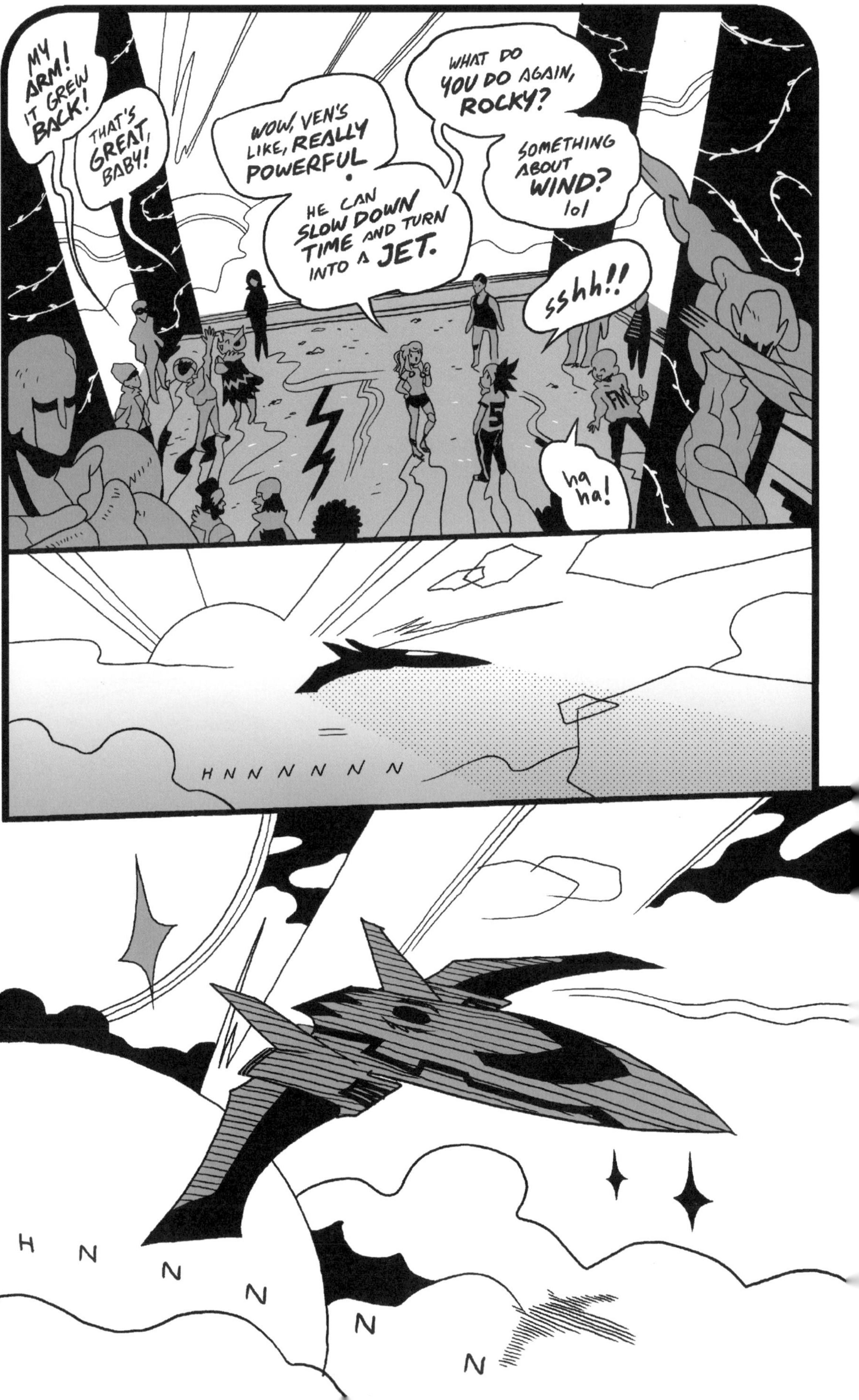
MY ARM! IT GREW BACK!
THAT'S GREAT, BABY!
WOW, VEN'S LIKE, REALLY POWERFUL.
HE CAN SLOW DOWN TIME AND TURN INTO A JET.
WHAT DO YOU DO AGAIN, ROCKY?
SOMETHING ABOUT WIND? lol
sshh!!
ha ha!
FN
5
HNNNNNN
HNNNNN

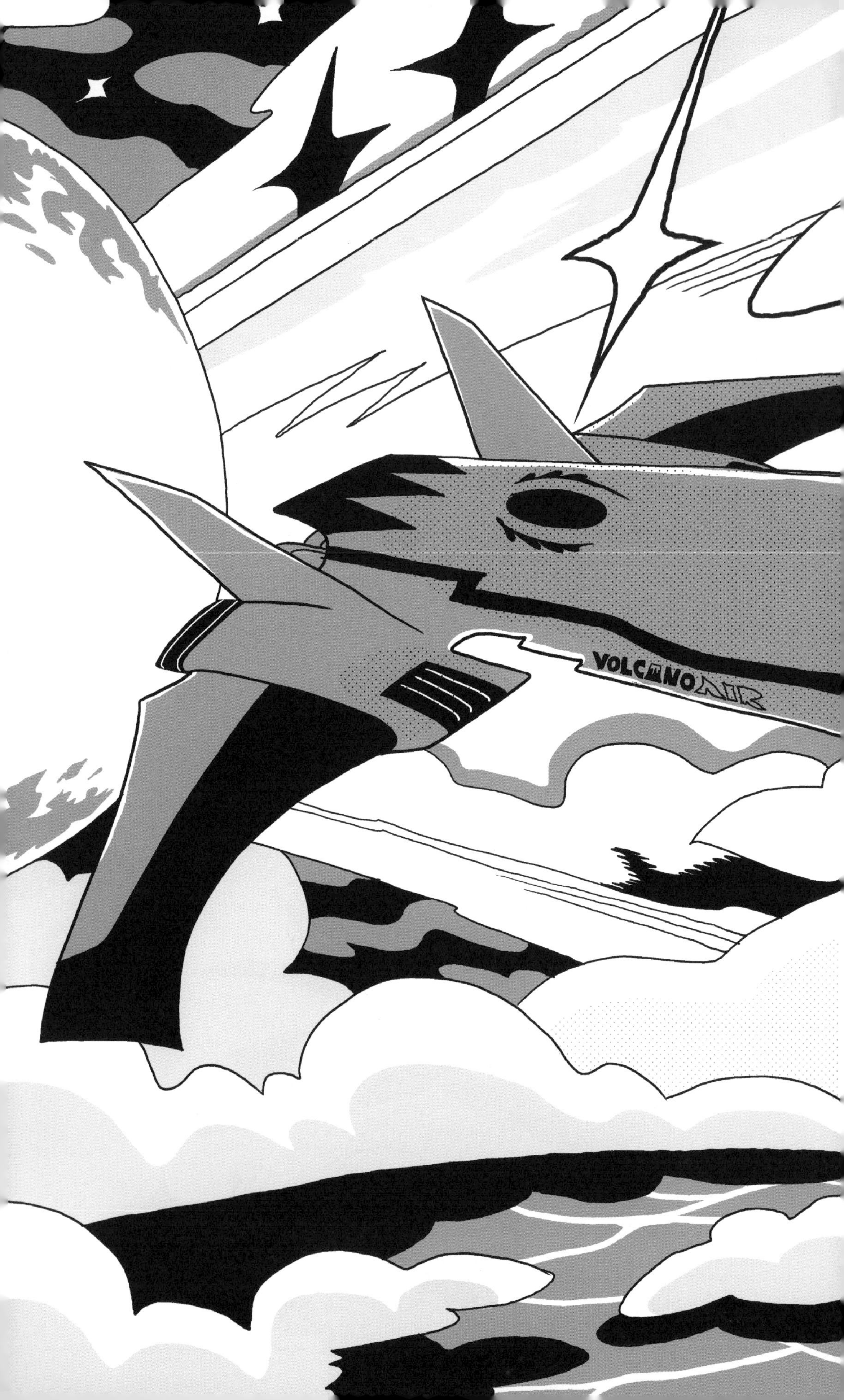
VOLCANO AIR

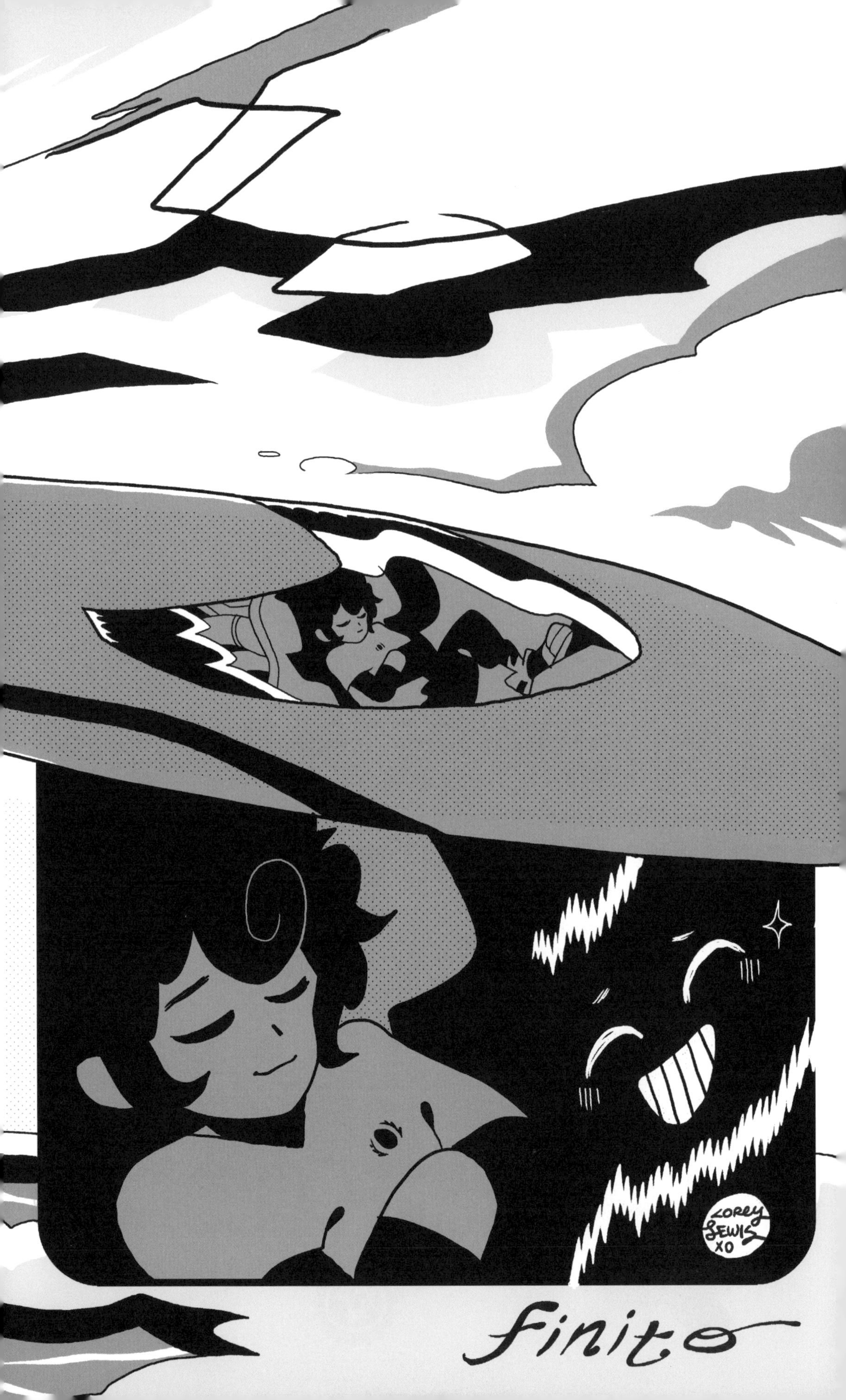
COREY LEWIS XO
finito

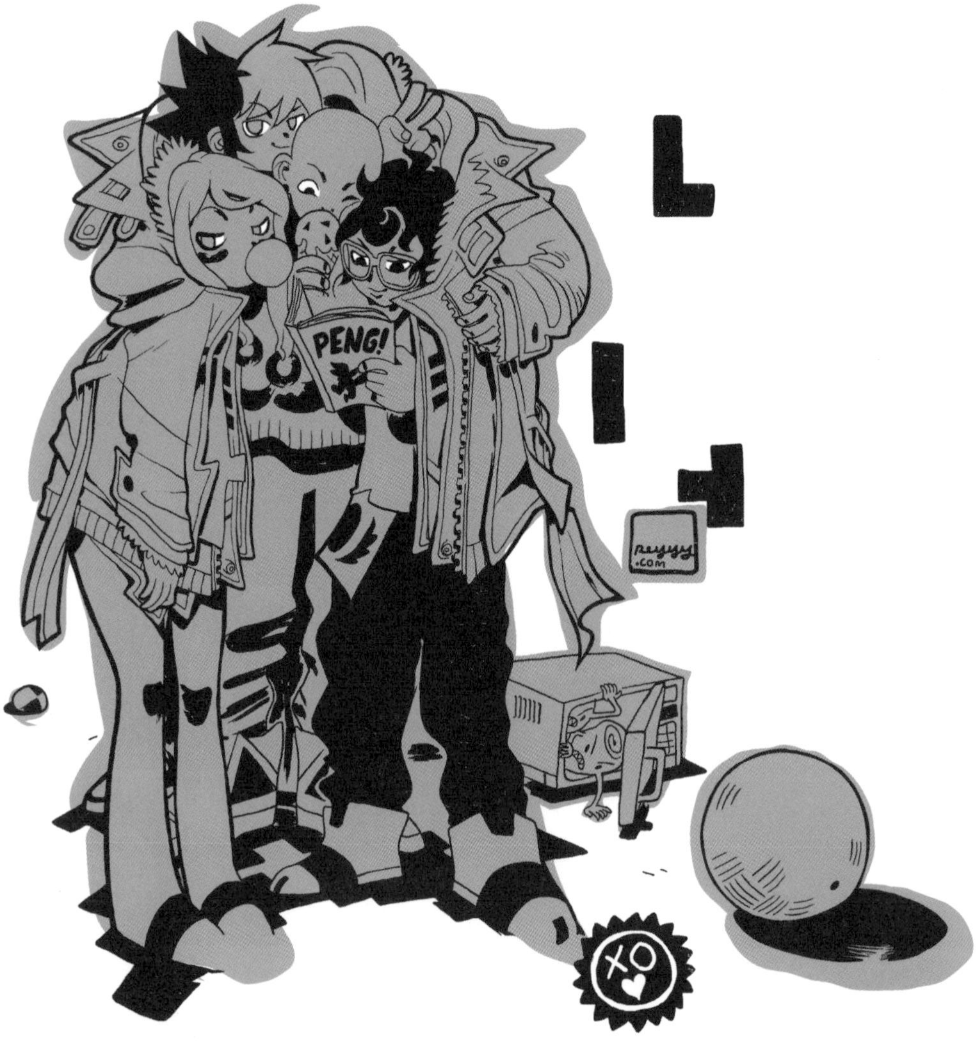
PENG!
XO

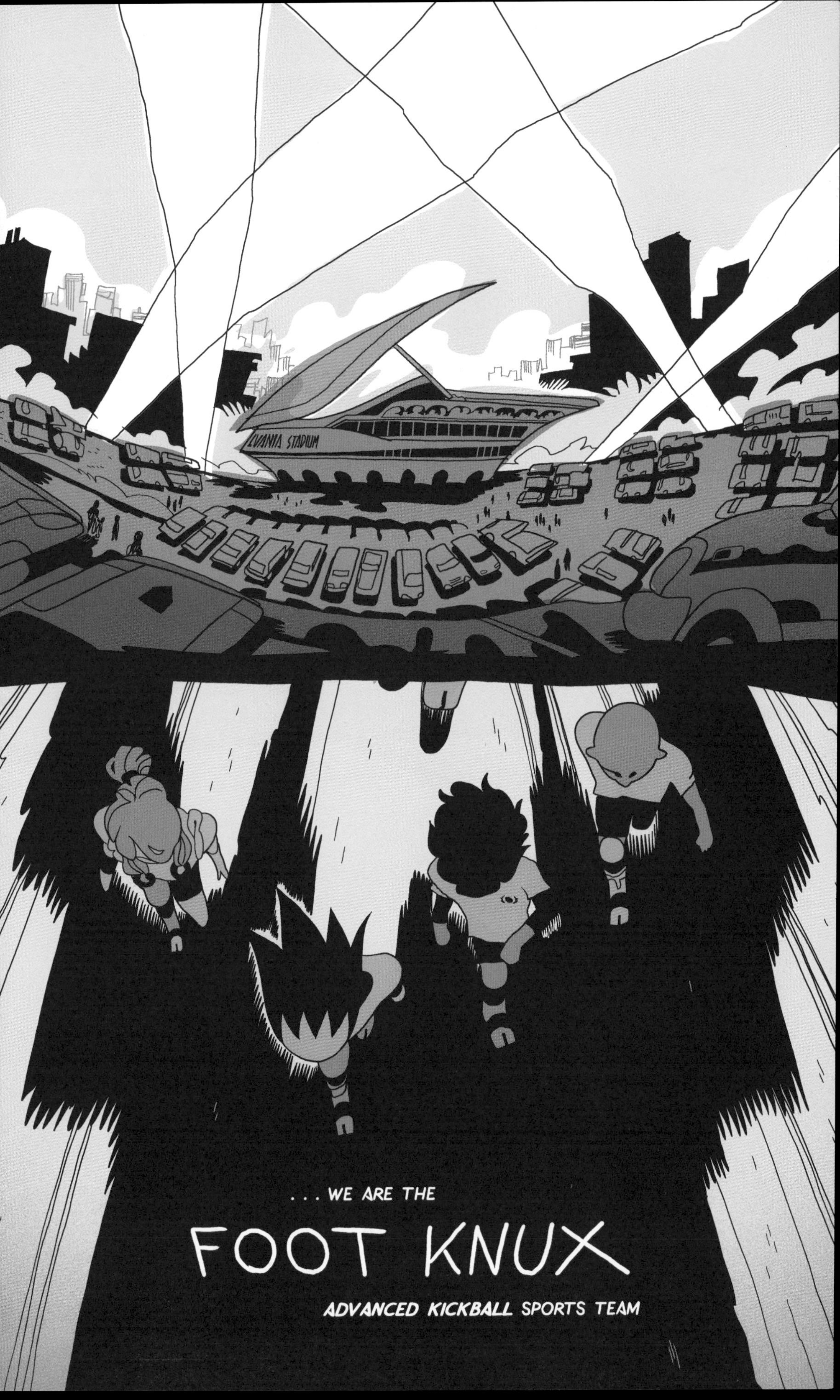

LVANIA STADIUM
. . . WE ARE THE
FOOT KNUX
ADVANCED KICKBALL SPORTS TEAM

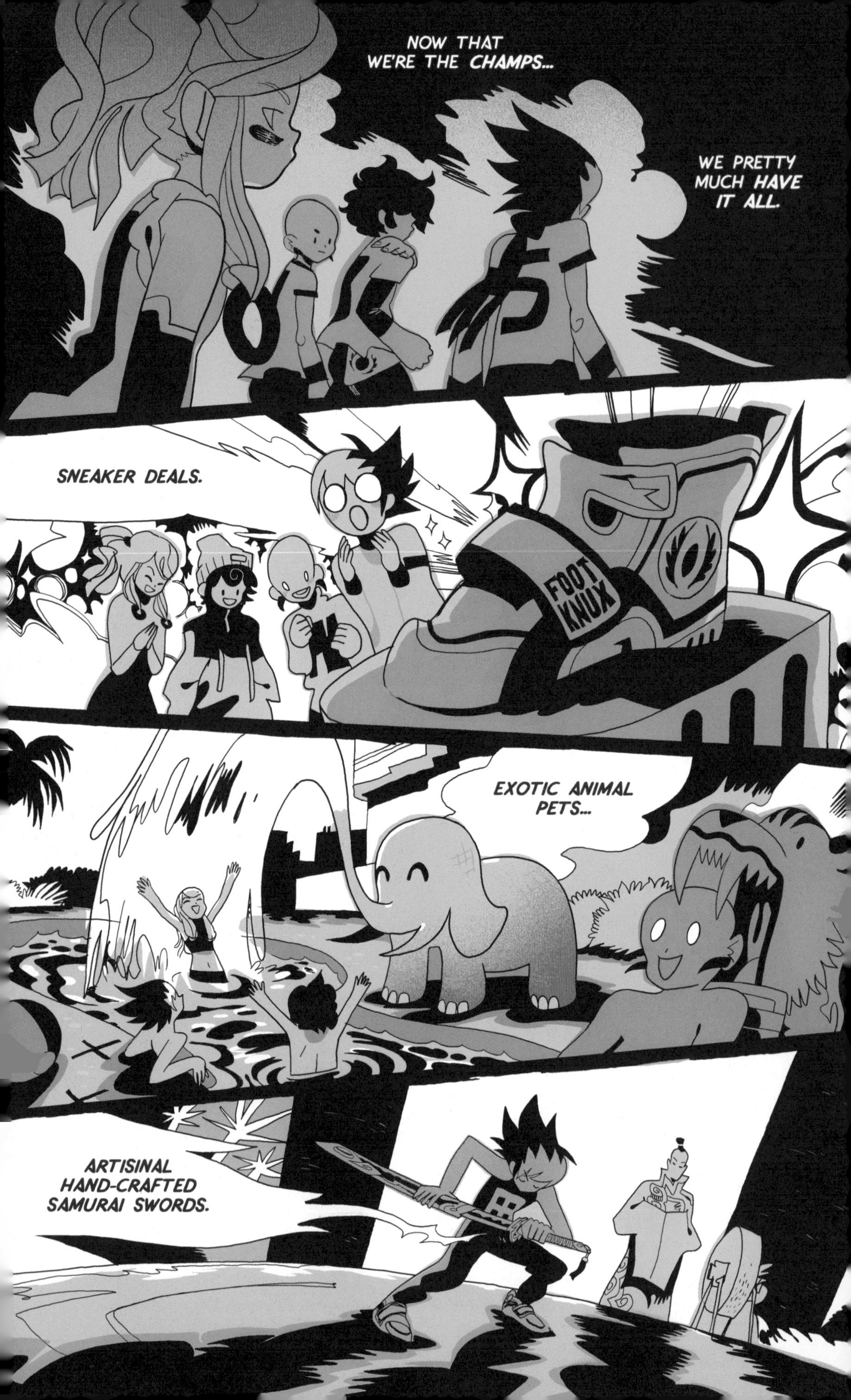
NOW THAT WE'RE THE CHAMPS...
WE PRETTY MUCH HAVE IT ALL.
SNEAKER DEALS.
FOOT KNUX
EXOTIC ANIMAL PETS...
ARTISINAL HAND-CRAFTED SAMURAI SWORDS.

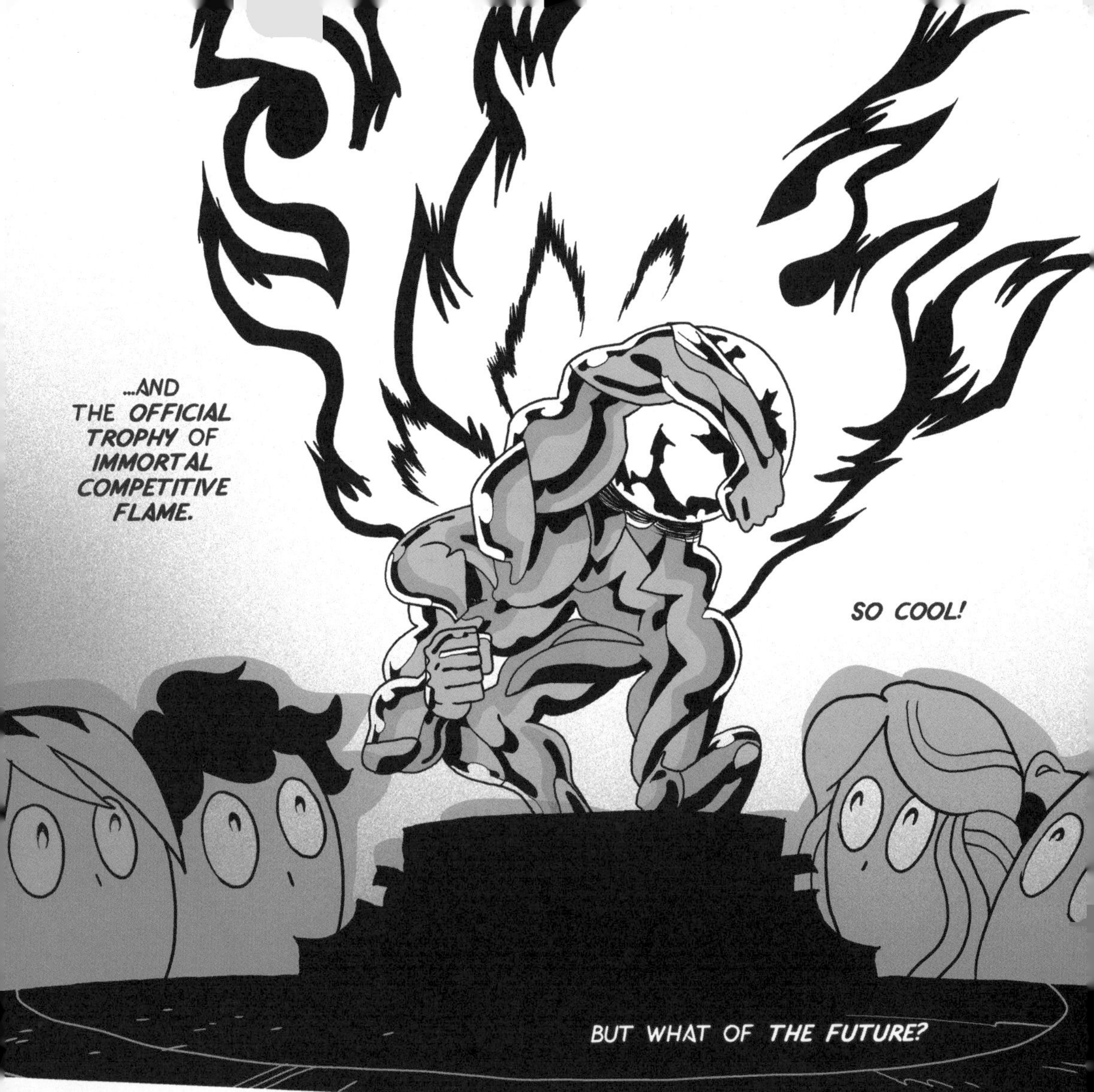
...AND THE OFFICIAL TROPHY OF IMMORTAL COMPETITIVE FLAME.
SO COOL!
BUT WHAT OF THE FUTURE?

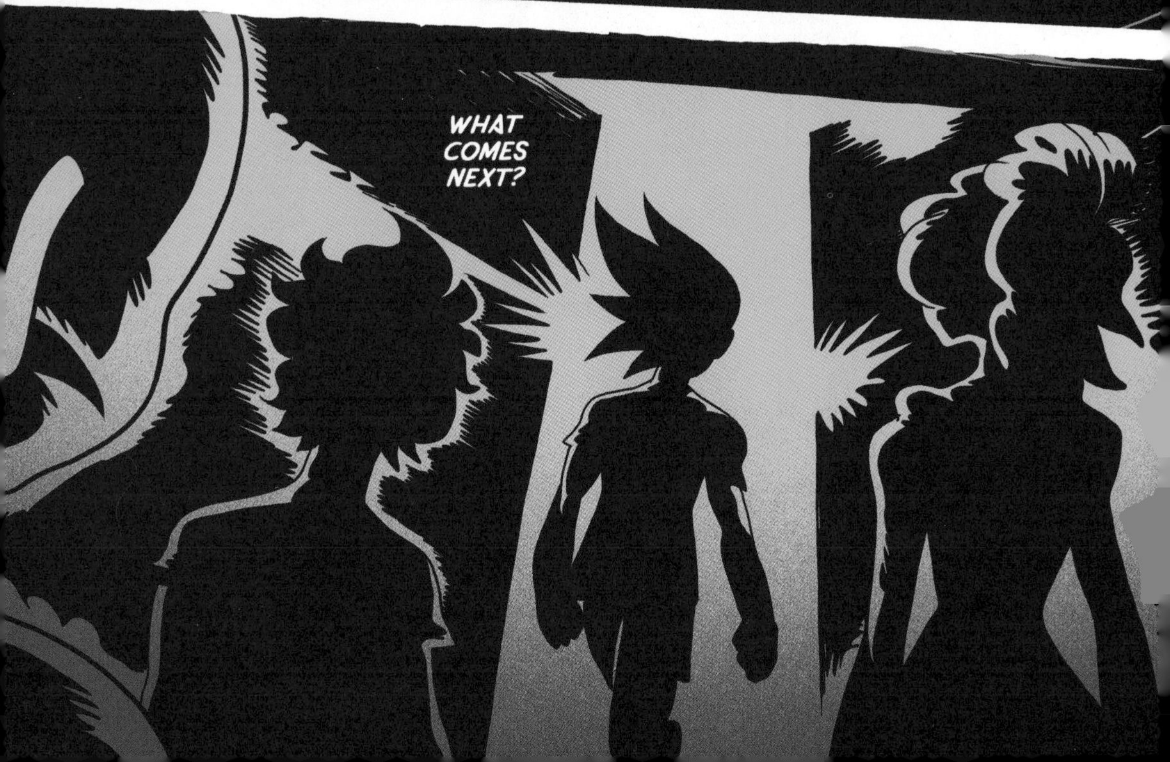
WHAT COMES NEXT?

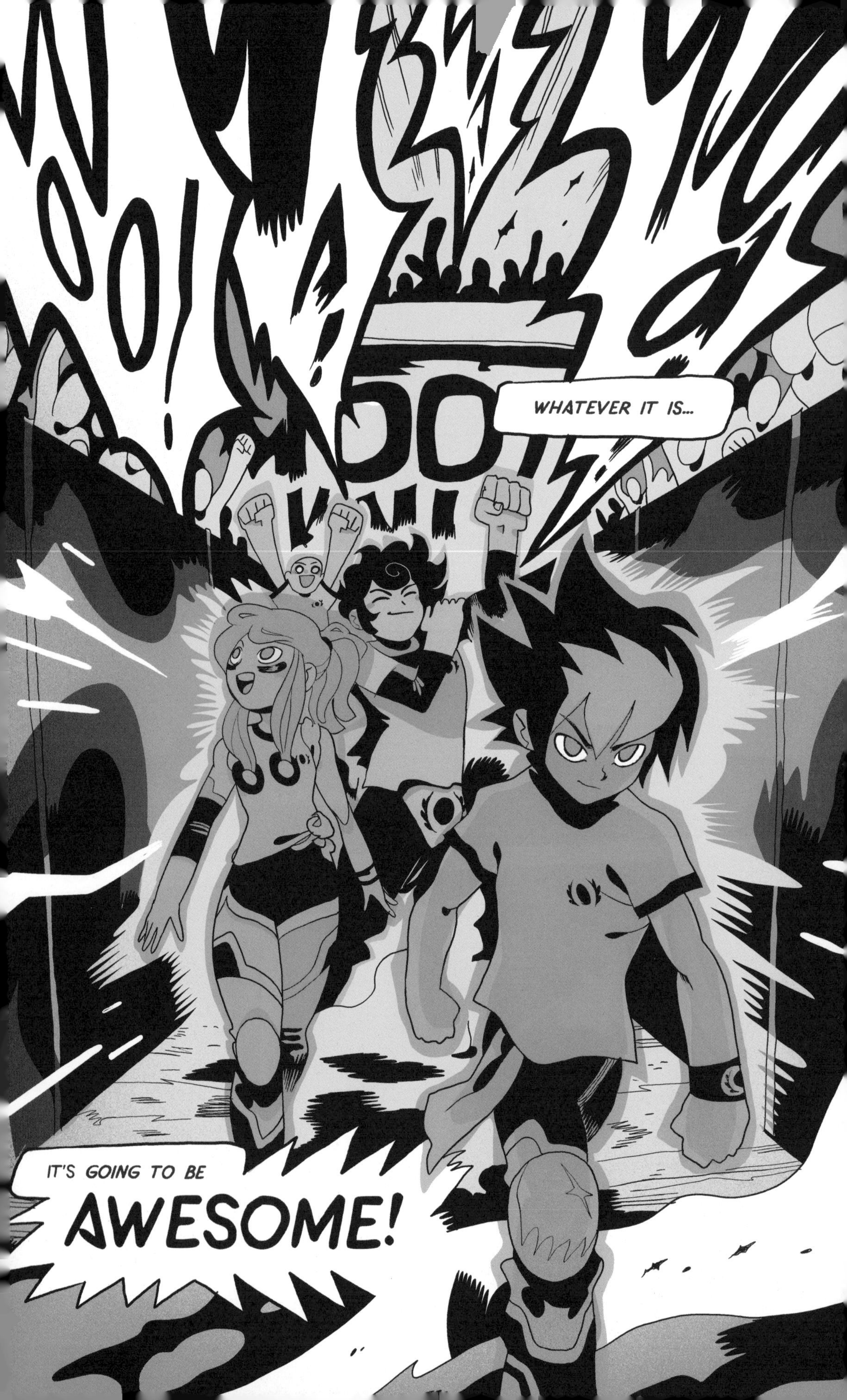
WHATEVER IT IS...
IT'S GOING TO BE
AWESOME!

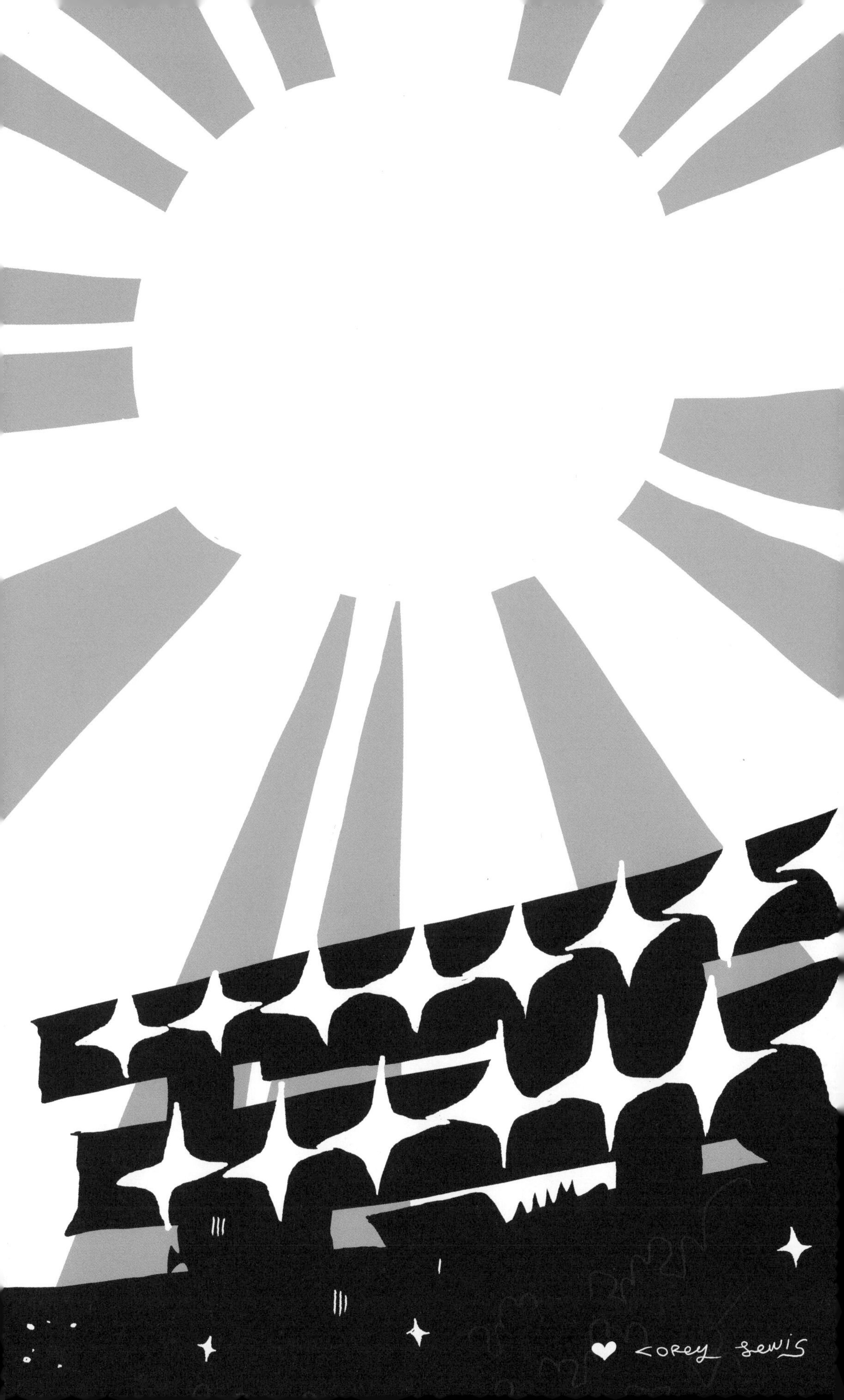
Corey Lewis

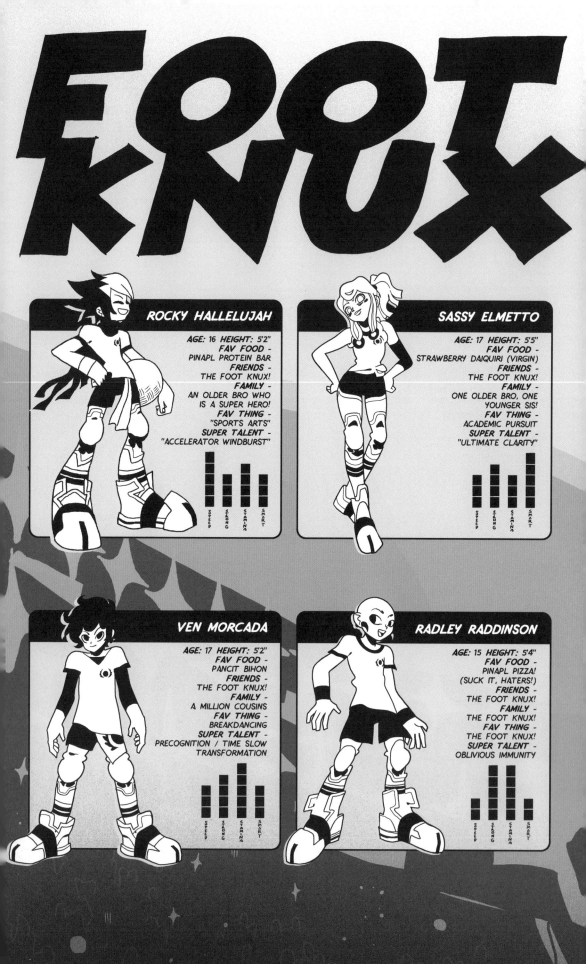

FOOT KNUX

ROCKY HALLELUJAH

AGE: 16 HEIGHT: 5'2"
FAV FOOD -
PINAPL PROTEIN BAR
FRIENDS -
THE FOOT KNUX!
FAMILY -
AN OLDER BRO WHO
IS A SUPER HERO!
FAV THING -
"SPORTS ARTS"
SUPER TALENT -
"ACCELERATOR WINDBURST"

SPEED STRONG STAMINA SMART

SASSY ELMETTO

AGE: 17 HEIGHT: 5'5"
FAV FOOD -
STRAWBERRY DAIQUIRI (VIRGIN)
FRIENDS -
THE FOOT KNUX!
FAMILY -
ONE OLDER BRO, ONE
YOUNGER SIS!
FAV THING -
ACADEMIC PURSUIT
SUPER TALENT -
"ULTIMATE CLARITY"

SPEED STRONG STAMINA SMART

VEN MORCADA

AGE: 17 HEIGHT: 5'2"
FAV FOOD -
PANCIT BIHON
FRIENDS -
THE FOOT KNUX!
FAMILY -
A MILLION COUSINS
FAV THING -
BREAKDANCING
SUPER TALENT -
PRECOGNITION / TIME SLOW
TRANSFORMATION

SPEED STRONG STAMINA SMART

RADLEY RADDINSON

AGE: 15 HEIGHT: 5'4"
FAV FOOD -
PINAPL PIZZA!
(SUCK IT, HATERS!)
FRIENDS -
THE FOOT KNUX!
FAMILY -
THE FOOT KNUX!
FAV THING -
THE FOOT KNUX!
SUPER TALENT -
OBLIVIOUS IMMUNITY

SPEED STRONG STAMINA SMART

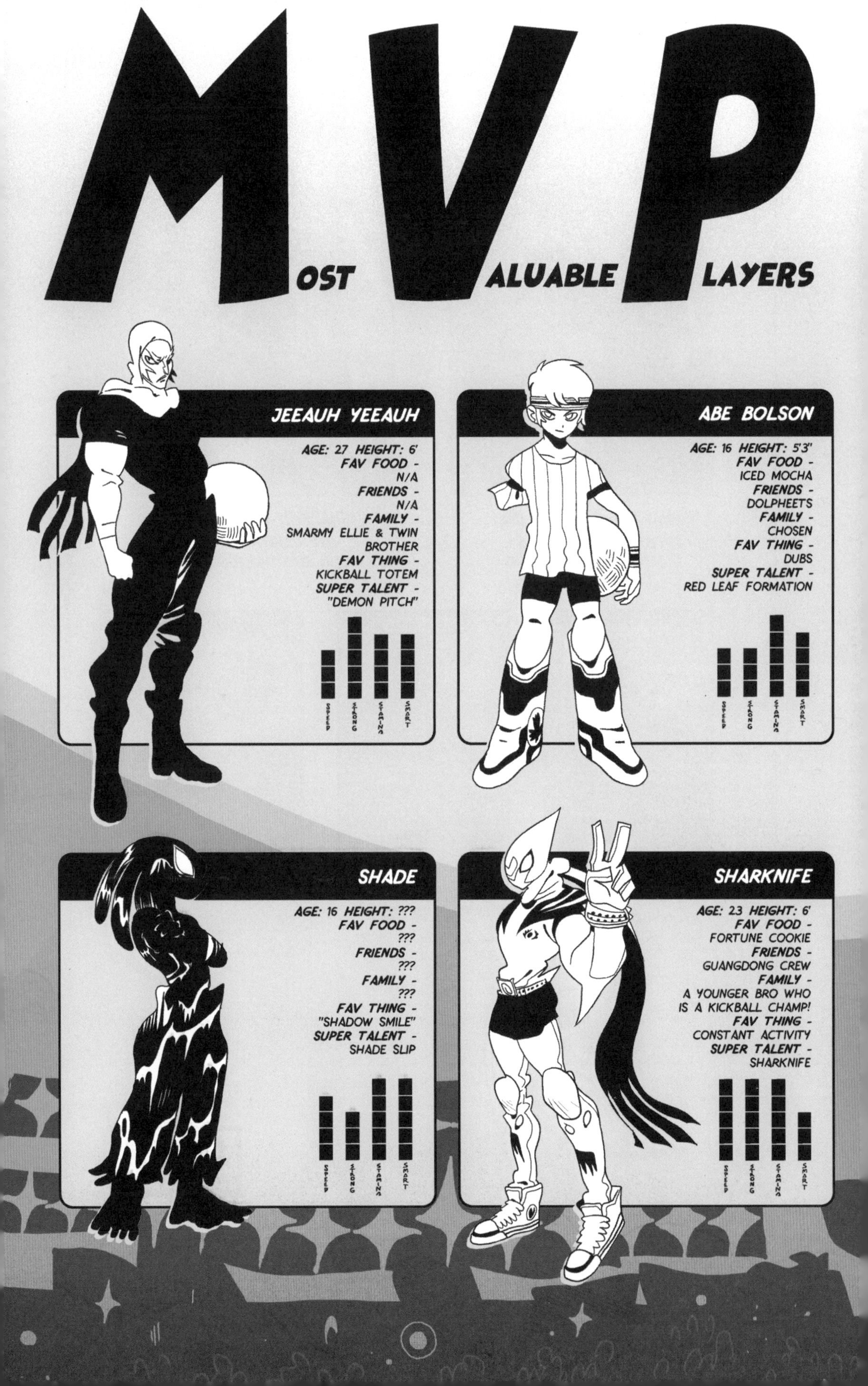
MVP
MOST VALUABLE PLAYERS
JEEAUH YEEAUH
AGE: 27 HEIGHT: 6'
FAV FOOD -
N/A
FRIENDS -
N/A
FAMILY -
SMARMY ELLIE & TWIN BROTHER
FAV THING -
KICKBALL TOTEM
SUPER TALENT -
"DEMON PITCH"
SPEED
STRONG
STAMINA
SMART
ABE BOLSON
AGE: 16 HEIGHT: 5'3"
FAV FOOD -
ICED MOCHA
FRIENDS -
DOLPHEETS
FAMILY -
CHOSEN
FAV THING -
DUBS
SUPER TALENT -
RED LEAF FORMATION
SPEED
STRONG
STAMINA
SMART
SHADE
AGE: 16 HEIGHT: ???
FAV FOOD -
???
FRIENDS -
???
FAMILY -
???
FAV THING -
"SHADOW SMILE"
SUPER TALENT -
SHADE SLIP
SPEED
STRONG
STAMINA
SMART
SHARKNIFE
AGE: 23 HEIGHT: 6'
FAV FOOD -
FORTUNE COOKIE
FRIENDS -
GUANGDONG CREW
FAMILY -
A YOUNGER BRO WHO IS A KICKBALL CHAMP!
FAV THING -
CONSTANT ACTIVITY
SUPER TALENT -
SHARKNIFE
SPEED
STRONG
STAMINA
SMART

MORE TITLES FROM ONI PRESS

COREY LEWIS'
FIRST

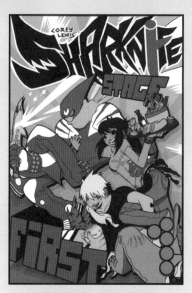

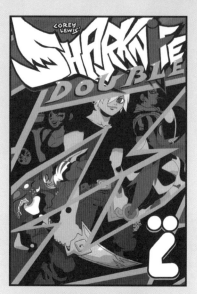

SHARKNIFE: STAGE FIRST
BY COREY LEWIS
ISBN 978-1-93496-464-4

COREY LEWIS'
DOUBLE

SHARKNIFE2: DOUBLE Z
BY COREY LEWIS
ISBN 978-1-93266-427-0

SCI-FU
Book 1
KICK IT OFF
YEHUDI MERCADO

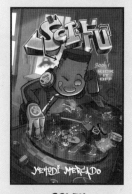

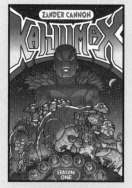

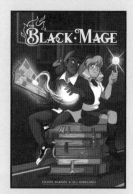

SCI-FU
BY YEHUDI MERCADO
ISBN 978-1-62010-472-9

ZANDER CANNON
KAIJUMAX
SEASON ONE

KAIJUMAX SEASON ONE
BY ZANDER CANNON
ISBN 978-1-62010-270-1

THE BLACK·MAGE
DANIEL BARNES • D.J. KIRKLAND

BLACK MAGE
BY DANIEL BARNES & DJ KIRKLAND
ISBN 978-1-62010-652-5

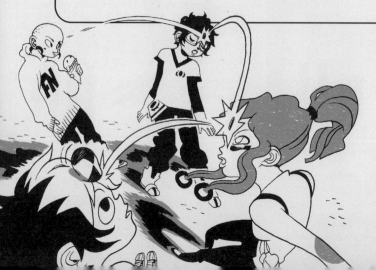

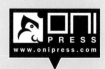

FN

ONI PRESS
www.onipress.com

For more information on these and other fine Oni Press comic books and graphic novels, visit **www.onipress.com.**
To find a comic specialty store in your area, visit **www.comicshops.us.**